Three Hundred Intercessions

~ on ~

Biblical Themes

Susan Sayers

Kevin
Mayhew

First published in 2000 by
KEVIN MAYHEW LTD
Buxhall
Stowmarket
Suffolk IP14 3BW

These intercessions first appeared in
Gathered for Prayer,
Prayers of Intercession Books 1 and 2
Together in Prayer Books 1, 2 and 3

0 1 2 3 4 5 6 7 8 9

ISBN 1 84003 491 2
Catalogue No 1500326

Cover design by Jonathan Stroulger
Edited by Peter Dainty
Typesetting by Louise Selfe

Printed by Colorcraft Hong Kong

CONTENTS

FAITH AND FAITHFULNESS

PRAYER

FOREWORD

A praying church is a living organism, powered by the love of God, and directed by his will. The aim of those leading intercessions in public worship is to provide a suitable climate for prayer, both for the faithful core of praying members, and also for those who drift in as visitors, sometimes willingly and sometimes rather grudgingly.

Since our God is in a far better position to know the needs of each muddle of people who arrive on any particular Sunday, it is obviously sensible to prepare for leading the intercessions by praying for those who will be there, asking our God to lead us with his agenda in mind, rather than taking immediate charge ourselves. Then we have to give him a chance to answer! You may find that a quiet walk enables you to do this, or a time wandering round the empty church, or time spent on some of the mechanical jobs at home while you still your heart and resist the temptation to badger God with good ideas.

The ideas I have provided here may well spark off other thoughts of your own. Do use them however you wish – exactly as they stand, adapted to suit specific needs, or simply as a starting point. They are a resource to help you, not a cage to imprison you.

During the service be alert to what is being said and how God is moving among you, so that you can pick up on these threads, if it seems appropriate, during the intercessions. And if you have young children present, give some thought to how they can also be praying at this time. They might be following a picture prayer trail, singing a quiet worship song, drawing some situation they are praying for, or looking through the pictures provided in suitable children's books.

I have heard it said that since God can hear the prayers, it doesn't really matter if the congregation can't. I don't agree. In public worship it can be very distracting to be straining to hear, or isolating if you can hear only a vague mumble. Do take the trouble to practise speaking clearly and fairly slowly in the church, so that everyone can comfortably take in what you are saying. Bear in mind that nerves usually make us speed up somewhat, so speak extra slowly to allow for this.

Finally, don't recite what you have written, but pray it. Pray it both through the intentions and through the silences. Leading the intercessions carries a great responsibility, but it is also a great privilege.

SUSAN SAYERS

11

God's love and mercy

LOVING FATHER

Let us pray,
with our hearts filled
with thanksgiving,
to the God who loves us
so completely.

We pray that the joy
and wonder of Christ's presence
may infuse our lives,
so that the Good News may be spread
throughout the world.

Silence

Loving Father:
we come to adore.

We pray that all in authority
may be filled with the wisdom
and compassion of God.

Silence

Loving Father:
we come to adore.

We pray that the lonely,
the rejected and the isolated
may have knowledge and confirmation
of God's abiding warmth and love.

Silence

Loving Father:
we come to adore.

We pray that all families may be blessed
with his everlasting joy,
and all homes may be filled
with his peace.

Silence

Loving Father:
we come to adore.

In the silence
of these moments,
we make our particular concerns known to God
our loving Father.

Silence

Father,
accept these prayers:
in wonder and adoration
we offer our lives to you,
with and through
our Lord Jesus Christ.
Amen.

GOD KNOWS US AND LOVES US

Father, we bring to your healing love
our shallowness of faith,
our need for your grace and power
in the Church throughout the world.

Silence

You know us completely:
and love us for ever.

We bring to your healing love
our need for your serenity and wisdom
in the governments of all the nations.

Silence

You know us completely:
and love us for ever.

We bring to your healing love
our need of patience, mutual affection
and forgiveness
in our homes and families.

Silence

You know us completely:
and love us for ever.

We bring to your healing love
the injured and broken-hearted,
the weak and the frightened.

Silence

You know us completely:
and love us for ever.

We bring to your healing love
those whom death has released from pain,
and those in great sorrow at losing loved ones.

Silence

You know us completely:
and love us for ever.

We bring you our thanks and praise
for all that is good and hopeful and positive,
all that is redeemed from suffering.

Silence

Father,
trusting in your great love for us,
we bring you these prayers
in the name of Jesus, your Son.
Amen.

Ever-loving God

In the knowledge of God's
constant presence,
let us pray to our heavenly Father,
the God of mercy and love.

We pray for the world-wide
Christian community,
that unceasing prayer and praise
may be offered as our planet turns
through night and day,
that we may be strengthened and encouraged
to reveal Christ to the world.

Silence

Hear us, ever-loving God:
we trust in you.

We pray for the direction
and guidance of our world;
that in all areas of discussion, negotiation,
policy-making and reform,
Christ may be present,
touching our lives and wills
with his peace.

Silence

Hear us, ever-loving God:
we trust in you.

We pray for all those whose happiness
is less because of war, homelessness,
pain or separation from loved ones;
that in all their troubles they may know
that the humility of Christ's birth,
life and death on this earth
confirms his immense love for us
and his desire to share our suffering.

Silence

Hear us, ever-loving God:
we trust in you.

We pray for our homes and families,
that we may recognise Christ's presence,
living among us,
deepening and extending our love
one for another.

Silence

Hear us, ever-loving God:
we trust in you.

We pray in silence now
for our own particular needs and concerns.

Silence

Father,
with thanks and joy
we offer these prayers
through Jesus our Saviour.
Amen.

THE GLORY OF GOD'S LOVE

Father, wherever your Church has become short-sighted,
inattentive or inflexible,
work in your healing love.

Silence

Lord, awaken us:
to notice your glory.

Father, wherever our nations have lost their way,
their sense of human worth or their integrity,
nourish them with your love.

Silence

Lord, awaken us:
to notice your glory.

Father, wherever our relationships are fragmented,
or shallow or offensive to you,
challenge us with your love.

Silence

Lord, awaken us:
to notice your glory.

Father, wherever people are suffering,
whether physically, mentally or emotionally,
comfort them with your love.

Silence

Lord, awaken us:
to notice your glory.

Father, wherever people are fearful of death,
or anxious for the future,
reassure them with your love.

Silence

Lord, awaken us:
to notice your glory.

Father, wherever your will is being fulfilled,
or hearts are learning to trust your love,
we join you in your joy.

Silence

Open our eyes, Father,
to the light of your glory
in the world you have made,
in the people around us
and in the face of Jesus Christ, our Lord.
Amen.

RESPOND IN LOVE

We pray for all who are fearful
of being themselves;
for those whose lives seem pointless.

Silence

Lord, we trust in you:
we trust you to respond in love.

We pray for those in ordained
and lay ministries;
for a deepening of our own commitment to Christ.

Silence

Lord, we trust in you:
we trust you to respond in love.

We pray for those who are going through
difficult times at the moment;
those whose lives seem full
of pain and darkness.

Silence

Lord, we trust in you:
we trust you to respond in love.

We thank you for all the special blessings
of our own lives;
for all your patience and gentleness with us.

Silence

Lord, we trust in you:
we trust you to respond in love.

Now in a time of silence
let us bring to God
our personal needs and concerns.

Silence

Lord, we trust in you:
**we trust you to respond in love,
filling our days
with the light and peace of your presence,
through Jesus Christ, our Lord.
Amen.**

WISE AND LOVING FATHER

Trusting in the deep love
our heavenly Father has for us,
let us pray.

We pray for the grace and strength
to be obedient, as Christ was,
in whatever God asks us to do,
without thought
for our personal gain or safety.

Silence

Wise and loving Father:
may your will be done.

We pray for greater trust and friendship
between the different nations
on our planet;
for a universal desire for peace,
and the willingness to take
the risks it demands.

Silence

Wise and loving Father:
may your will be done.

We pray for Christ's calming reassurance
to bring peace of mind and spirit
to those worried about the future,
those dreading some difficult event,
and those who are frightened of dying.

Silence

Wise and loving Father:
may your will be done.

We pray for the capacity to be positive
and encouraging

in all our relationships;
for the right words to say
in order to be peacemakers
and witnesses to God's
immeasurable love.

Silence

Wise and loving Father:
may your will be done.

We pray to our heavenly Father,
in silence,
about our own particular concerns.

Silence

Father,
with thankful hearts
we offer these concerns
for the Church and for the world,
though Jesus Christ, our Saviour.
Amen.

SAFE IN GOD'S LOVE

Father, into your care we commit all Christians,
all in ministry and all church leaders.

Silence

O Lord, our God:
it is good to be safe in your love.

Father, into your care we commit our world,
with its needs and failures,
hope and despair.

Silence

O Lord, our God:
it is good to be safe in your love.

Father, into your care we commit those we love,
and those we could love more.

Silence

O Lord, our God:
it is good to be safe in your love.

Father, into your care we commit those of all ages
who are in danger,
and live in fear.

Silence

O Lord, our God:
it is good to be safe in your love.

Father, into your care we commit
those who have recently died
and all who mourn for them.

Silence

O Lord, our God:
it is good to be safe in your love.

Father, we rejoice in the way you look after us,
and thank you for providing for all our needs.

Silence

Heavenly Father,
our help in times of need,
accept these prayers
for the sake of your Son,
Jesus Christ, our Lord.
Amen.

THE LOVE OF GOD AT WORK

Father, work your love in the Church,
her ministers and all her members,
particularly where there is any hardness of heart,
or misunderstanding of your will.

Silence

Lord, we know and believe:
that you will keep us safe.

Father, work your love in our world,
guiding our leaders and redeeming good
from all that is evil.

Silence

Lord, we know and believe:
in the power of love.

Father, work your love in our homes,
making them places of welcome,
understanding and forgiveness.

Silence

Lord, we know and believe:
in the power of love.

Father, work your love in all areas of pain and illness,
anxiety and imprisonment.

Silence

Lord, we know and believe:
in the power of love.

Father, work your love in all areas of sadness
and loneliness,
hopelessness and doubt.

Silence

Lord, we know and believe:
in the power of love.

Father, work your love in all that is beautiful,
all that is growing,
and all that touches our hearts with joy.

Silence

Father, we trust in you,
and ask these prayers
in the name of Jesus Christ, our Lord.
Amen.

WE COMMEND TO YOUR LOVE

My Christian sisters and brothers,
as we rejoice at being called
and chosen by our heavenly Father,
let us speak with him of our needs and concerns.

Father, we commend to your love
all leaders and teachers in the Church;
that in all they do and say they may stay close to you,
alert to your will and constantly prepared
to move forward where you guide.

Silence

Father, hear us:
keep us in your love.

We commend to your love
all talks and negotiations in industry
and in matters of international concern;
that they may be marked by generosity of spirit,
and a desire for reconciliation that comes only from you.

Silence

Father, hear us:
keep us in your love.

We commend to your love
all who are especially precious to us,
and all with whom we find it difficult to relate;
that we may always treat one another
with Christlike love.

Silence

Father, hear us:
keep us in your love.

We commend to your love
all outsiders and outcasts,

all who have been rejected by their family
or their country;
that rifts may be healed, relationships repaired
and new bonds of love forged in Christ.

Silence

Father, hear us:
keep us in your love.

We commend to your love
those who have reached the end
of their journey on earth;
welcome them into your heavenly kingdom
and bring us, too, at death, safely home.

Heavenly Father, with you beside us
our journey is so richly blessed with joy and peace;
how can we ever thank you
for the generosity of your love and ceaseless care!

Silence

Father, with these prayers
we give our lives into your keeping:
through Jesus Christ, our Lord.
Amen.

KEEP US IN YOUR LOVE

My brothers and sisters in Christ,
let us come before God our Father
with our burdens, cares and joys.

Father, bless our Christian family,
both in this church and throughout the world;
may we witness to your love by the kind of lives
we lead and the work we do in your name.

Silence

Father, live among us:
keep us in your love.

Bless and guide the leaders of each country
and each community;
may we not wander as sheep without a shepherd
but rather be led and directed by you
in the path of peace.

Silence

Father, live among us:
keep us in your love.

Father, bless our own homes
and our relationships with our parents,
marriage partners, brothers, sisters and children;
may we learn to see and experience
Christ in one another, and cheerfully love
and serve with generosity of spirit.

Silence

Father, live among us:
keep us in your love.

Bless and protect all families at risk
from evil and danger, either within or without;

all children born with brain damage or deformity
and their families;
all marriages which are strained and difficult;
that wherever much is demanded,
much strength and support may be given.

Silence

Father, live among us:
keep us in your love.

Welcome into your kingdom, Father,
all your children who have died, especially . . .
May we one day share the joy and peace
of coming home to you for ever.

Silence

We thank you for the everyday blessings
and fun of family life;
both in our own and in our spiritual family.

Silence

Father, it is your love
which inspires us to pray.
**May it also inspire us to live
as faithful disciples of Jesus, our Lord.
Amen.**

GOD'S LOVE RESTORES US

Father, we think of the variety of individuals
who make up your Church;
make us quick to encourage one another
and slow to criticise.

Silence

Thank you, Lord:
for restoring us through love.

Father, we think of the responsibility we all have
in looking after our world,
and our desperate need for guidance.

Silence

Thank you, Lord:
for restoring us through love.

Father, we think of the joys and sorrows
among families and friends,
and our need of the grace to forgive one another.

Silence

Thank you, Lord:
for restoring us through love.

Father, we think of the pain
which so many suffer all over the world,
and of their thirst for comfort and encouragement.

Silence

Thank you, Lord:
for restoring us through love.

We pray in silence now
for our own particular needs and concerns.

Silence

Thank you, Lord:
for restoring us through love.

Father, we think of all those who dedicate their lives
to building a better world with you,
and thank you for their faithfulness.

Silence

Father, accept these prayers:
and give us the grace
to walk in your love
all our days,
through Jesus Christ, our Lord.
Amen.

GOD'S LOVE GOES ON AND ON

God of holiness,
cleanse the Church from all that is selfish,
complacent and worldly.

Silence

His love goes on:
his love goes on and on.

God of wisdom and honour,
give our leaders integrity,
and our world the openness to listen,
and the courage to forgive.

Silence

His love goes on:
his love goes on and on.

God of tenderness and understanding,
may our children be brought up
in the knowledge of your love
and every member of every family be valued.

Silence

His love goes on:
his love goes on and on.

God of healing and wholeness,
give to those who are in any pain or suffering
all that they need,
both physically and spiritually.

Silence

His love goes on:
his love goes on and on.

God of eternity,
as you welcome into your kingdom

those who have endured to the end,
we thank you for the example of their lives.

Silence

His love goes on:
his love goes on and on.

God of joy and serenity,
we thank you for your constant help
and loving presence,
and offer you our lives, however things turn out.

Silence

God of patience, accept our prayers
and enlarge our understanding of your will.
Help us to live close to Jesus day by day,
for we come to you in his name.
Amen.

THE POWER OF GOD'S LOVE

My sisters and brothers in Christ,
we have been drawn here today
by the power of God's love;
into that love let us now gather
all those for whom we pray.

Father, we commend to your love
all who serve you as ministers
of your word and sacrament in the Church;
may all they do be an extension of your love.

Silence

Father almighty:
let your will be done.

Father, we commend to your love
all judges and those serving on juries;
those who make laws in our country
and throughout the world;
may our human laws reflect the unchanging law
and love of your goodness and mercy.

Silence

Father almighty:
let your will be done.

We commend to your love our own loved ones;
all who will come to our homes this week;
may the welcome they receive
express your welcoming love.

Silence

Father almighty:
let your will be done.

We commend to your love those whose minds
have been poisoned by exposure to violence;

children who have been abandoned or maltreated;
all who crave affection
but are frightened of getting hurt.

Silence

Father almighty:
let your will be done.

We commend to your love those
who have died in faith;
welcome them into your kingdom
and give them everlasting peace.

Silence

We thank you for the privilege of working with you
to spread the Good News of your saving love;
by your grace may we become
the kind of people you intend us to be.

Silence

Father almighty:
let your will be done,
not only through our prayers
but through our lives,
for the sake of Jesus.
Amen.

LIVE AND WORK IN US ALL

Loving God, we pray for all in your Church
whose journey through life
is hard, dangerous, exhausting or confused.

Silence

Lord of love:
live and work in us all.

We pray for those whose lives are disrupted
by war, famine or political unrest.

Silence

Lord of love:
live and work in us all.

We pray for our families, friends and neighbours,
all who cause us concern,
and all in need of your peace.

Silence

Lord of love:
live and work in us all.

We pray for all whose lives are filled
with pain, resentment or hatred,
all trapped in addiction or despair.

Silence

Lord of love:
live and work in us all.

We pray for those who have died
and those who miss them.

Silence

Lord of love:
live and work in us all.

We give you thanks for the gift of life,
for every moment of every day.

Silence

Heavenly Father, may these prayers
make room for your love
both in our lives
and in the needs of the world around us:
**for the sake of Jesus Christ,
our Saviour and Friend.
Amen.**

MERCIFUL FATHER

Let us pray to God our merciful Father,
with humility and love,
open to his transforming grace.

We pray for all Christians
striving to follow the Lord of Life;
that they may not fall
into the temptation of complacency
or self-righteousness;
that they may joyfully become
the least important
for Christ's sake.

Silence

God, our Father:
be merciful to us sinners.

We pray for all who are involved
in the worldly struggles for power,
all areas of political unrest,
all decision- and policy-makers;
that wisdom, common sense and respect
may encourage just and peaceful government.

Silence

God, our Father:
be merciful to us sinners.

We pray for the physically blind
and their families;
for those who are spiritually blind
and think they can see;
for those whose minds are confused
through accidents, illness or age,
that God's inner sight
may bring enlightenment, order and peace.

Silence

God, our Father:
be merciful to us sinners.

We pray for ourselves and all those
worshipping in this place,
that we may be increasingly open
to the searing light of Christ,
until our darkest corners are lit by his love.

Silence

God, our Father:
be merciful to us sinners.

In silence, now,
we bring our private concerns to God,
who always hears our prayers of faith.

Silence

Lord God,
accept these prayers,
through Christ our Lord.
Amen.

FATHER OF MERCY

Let us pray to our loving and merciful God.

Lord, we thank you for the richness and diversity
of each unique identity.
We pray for the separate members
of this Body of Christ, and our corporate nature,
that we may be filled at every level
with the living breath of your Spirit.

Silence

Father of mercy:
let your purpose be fulfilled.

We thank you for the beauty and variety
of our landscapes and cultures, all over the world;
for starscapes and the wideness of space.
Teach us to cherish and respect
this universe we inhabit
and all those who look or sound different
from ourselves.

Silence

Father of mercy:
let your purpose be fulfilled.

We thank you for the hope
each newborn child brings;
for the gentle gifts of laughter and friendship,
thoughtfulness and sympathy.
We pray that our eyes may see all others
with your affection.

Silence

Father of mercy:
let your purpose be fulfilled.

We thank you for the patient endurance
of so many who suffer so much;
for them all we pray your wholeness
and refreshing,
your upholding and healing.

Silence

Father of mercy:
let your purpose be fulfilled.

We thank you for the promise of mercy
triumphing over judgement,
and commend to your love for ever
our own loved ones who have died.

Silence

Father of mercy:
let your purpose be fulfilled.

We thank you for all our blessings
and pray that we may take none of them
for granted,
but commit ourselves to live out
our thanks each day.

Merciful Father:
**accept these prayers
for the sake of your Son,
our Saviour Jesus Christ.
Amen.**

FATHER, FORGIVE

Let us pray in humility
to our merciful Father.

We pray for the Church, the body of Christ;
for each one of its members who has lapsed
or drifted away;
for those who are struggling
against doubt and temptation.

Silence

Father, forgive:
and lead us safely home.

We pray for the many peoples of this earth;
for the spread of justice,
respect and goodwill;
for a greater capacity to forgive
and restore,
and a weakening
of hardened revenge.

Silence

Father, forgive:
and lead us safely home.

We pray for those who suffer through neglect,
famine, natural disasters or war;
also for those who,
through their own fault,
now suffer.

Silence

Father, forgive:
and lead us safely home.

We pray for each other;
for those we find difficult

to get on with,
those we envy, admire or despise,
that our love may be open and generous,
wide and strong.

Silence

Father, forgive:
and lead us safely home.

Together in silence,
we name those known to us
who especially need our prayer.

Silence

Merciful Father,
accept these prayers,
in the name of our Saviour Jesus Christ.
Amen.

LORD OF MERCY

Let us come before God, our creator and sustainer,
with the needs of the Church and of the world.

We bring to your love, O Lord,
all who have committed their lives to your service;
that they may all be one,
bound together by your Holy Spirit.

Silence

Lord of mercy:
hear us with compassion.

We bring to your love all the areas of the world
in which there are hostility and unrest;
that new routes to negotiation
and reconciliation may emerge.

Silence

Lord of mercy:
hear us with compassion.

We bring to your love
the members of our human families,
especially any we find difficult
to get on with or understand;
that our love for one another
may enter a new dimension
of warm and positive caring, seasoned with laughter.

Silence

Lord of mercy:
hear us with compassion.

We bring to your love
all who have become hard and aggressive
through years of festering hate or jealousy;

that their unresolved conflicts
may be brought to your light and healed.

Silence

Lord of mercy:
hear us with compassion.

We bring to your love all those, dear to us,
who are separated from us by death;
may we come, one day, with them
to share the eternal peace and joy of heaven.

Silence

Lord of mercy:
hear us with compassion.

We thank you for all your blessings and patient loving,
and especially for coming to save us from our sin.

Silence

Lord, we bring to your love
all these our prayers,
trusting to your mercy
our troubles and concerns:
in the name of Jesus, our Saviour.
Amen.

LORD, HAVE MERCY ON ALL WHO SUFFER

We call to mind our brothers and sisters in Christ
who are imprisoned or suffering persecution
simply for believing what we believe.

Silence

Trust in the Lord:
for with the Lord there is mercy.

We call to mind those whose lives
are caught up in war, political unrest,
family feuds or nationalistic grievances.

Silence

Trust in the Lord:
for with the Lord there is mercy.

We call to mind refugees and all who do not know
whether their loved ones are safe or not;
all whose homes are places of violence
and all whose homes are havens of love.

Silence

Trust in the Lord:
for with the Lord there is mercy.

We call to mind those imprisoned by guilt,
addiction or bitterness;
and all those who undergo suffering bravely
and bring joy to those who care for them.

Silence

Trust in the Lord:
for with the Lord there is mercy.

We call to mind those who have recently died
and those who miss them;
those who are nearing death,
and those who support them.

Silence

Trust in the Lord:
for with the Lord there is mercy.

We call to mind the times when God
has carried us through difficulties,
and thank him for his faithful love.

Silence

Lord, we entrust to your love
those we remember in our prayers:
through Jesus Christ, our Lord.
Amen.

GOD'S SUFFICIENT GRACE

As trustful children,
let us confide in our loving Father,
and pour out to him
our fears and concerns.

We pray for all lapsed Christians
and all whose faith is being tested;
all whose spiritual growth is being stunted
by material cares or possessions;
and all who are hesitantly approaching Jesus
for the first time
or after long separation from him.

Silence

Almighty Father:
your grace is sufficient for us.

We pray for the areas in which corruption
has splintered the integrity of government;
for the instances
of double dealing and hypocrisy,
which blunt honour
and breed suspicion and revenge.

Silence

Almighty Father:
your grace is sufficient for us.

We pray for all who are trapped and frustrated
by physical or mental disabilities,
illness or weakness;
for the lonely
and those for whom no one prays.

Silence

Almighty Father:
your grace is sufficient for us.

We pray for enlightenment as to our own areas
of spiritual weakness;
for the courage to desire real,
fundamental changes there,
and for the will to persevere in growing.

Silence

Almighty Father:
your grace is sufficient for us.

In silence now,
we approach our loving Father
with our private prayers.

Silence

Most merciful Father,
who knows us so well,
accept our prayers
in the name of Jesus.
Amen.

HEAVENLY FATHER

In the sure knowledge that God cherishes us,
let us pray to him now.

Heavenly Father, so full of forgiveness and mercy,
fill your Church to the brim with such holiness
that our understanding of your ways
deepens daily,
and all our work and worship glorifies your name.

Silence

Loving God:
we praise your holy name.

Heavenly Father, so wise and perceptive,
take us to the heart of all conflicts,
and give us the grace to share in the healing
between factions and nations,
guided by your Spirit.

Silence

Loving God:
we praise your holy name.

Heavenly Father, so comforting and kind,
help us to notice the needs around us,
in our families, friends and colleagues,
and respond to them in love.

Silence

Loving God:
we praise your holy name.

Heavenly Father, so mindful of our pain,
we bring to you our sisters and brothers
whose joints are stiff
and whose bodies cannot move freely;

thank you for their courage and example;
we pray that you will help their spirits to dance
and fill their hearts with joy.

Silence

Loving God:
we praise your holy name.

Heavenly Father, so welcoming to all,
we commend to your everlasting keeping
those who have recently died,
and those who mourn their going.

Silence

Loving God:
we praise your holy name.

Heavenly Father, so faithful in your promises,
we thank you for the eternal 'Yes' of Christ
which echoes on through lives and generations.

Merciful Father:
**accept these prayers
for the sake of your Son,
our Saviour Jesus Christ.
Amen.**

WE LOOK TO THE CROSS

As followers of Jesus Christ,
let us pray to our loving Father in heaven.

Father, help us all in your Church
to understand what it really means to love and serve you.
At the times of testing, strengthen us,
at unexpected or undeserved suffering, support us,
at the end of our energy, revive us
and teach us through it all the inexplicable peace and joy
that comes from doing your will.

Silence

We look to the cross:
and see your love for us.

Father, have mercy on us for the misdirected use
of time, money and resources in this world.
In the struggle against evil and sin, empower us,
so that justice and righteousness are established,
upheld and celebrated,
as hearts rejoice in the freedom of all that is good.

Silence

We look to the cross:
and see your love for us.

Father, renew our commitment to your loving
in all our relationships, our work and our prayer.
In the hard choices, give us wisdom,
in the painful decisions, affirm us,
and may our words speak your truth,
whether that is to encourage,
to comfort or to challenge.

Silence

We look to the cross:
and see your love for us.

Father, bring healing and wholeness
to those who suffer, in body, mind or spirit.
In the sleepless nights and endless days of pain,
give the grace to persevere with patience,
and turn these dark times
into places of spiritual growth.

Silence

We look to the cross:
and see your love for us.

Father, may those who have died
rest in the eternal peace of your presence,
their burdens laid down and their suffering ended.

Silence

We look to the cross:
and see your love for us.

Father, the full extent of your love for us
is so much greater than we can ever imagine,
and in our love and thankfulness
we offer the praise of our lives.

Merciful Father:
**accept these prayers
for the sake of your Son,
our Saviour Jesus Christ.
Amen.**

FORGIVENESS

In the knowledge of all God has done for us,
let us bring to him our concerns
for the Church and for the world.

Thank you, Father, for the love
which forgives again and again,
and is prepared to trust us
with the care of your people
even after we have let you down many times.
Teach us to minister to one another's needs
with compassion, sensitivity and discipline,
so that all are affirmed and encouraged.

Silence

The Lord is full of compassion:
his love lasts for ever.

Thank you, Father, for the order and variety,
simplicity and complexity of this universe.
Thank you for all that humankind is able to do;
may all these gifts be used wisely and well,
for the good of all, including those as yet unborn.

Silence

The Lord is full of compassion:
his love lasts for ever.

Thank you, Father, for what we have been forgiven
and for the opportunities we have each day
to learn the joy of forgiving others.
Smash through our self-righteousness
and keep us learning in humility at your feet.

Silence

The Lord is full of compassion:
his love lasts for ever.

Thank you, Father, for all those who care for the sick,
the unstable, the ungrateful and the difficult.
We pray for all who are on the receiving end
of hate, deceit, suspicion or abuse,
and for those who cause others pain
and distress of any kind.
We pray for your healing and transforming.

Silence

The Lord is full of compassion:
his love lasts for ever.

Thank you, Father, for those whose living and dying
has taught us much about love.
Freed from their pain and restrictions of age or injury,
may they enjoy for ever the life of heaven.

Silence

The Lord is full of compassion:
his love lasts for ever.

Thank you, Father, for disturbing our complacency
and challenging us to move forward with you,
assured of your company and your love.

Merciful Father:
accept these prayers
for the sake of your Son,
our Saviour Jesus Christ.
Amen.

THE PEACE OF GOD

Let us quieten our hearts
to listen to the Lord of peace,
and to pray to him.

We pray for all Christians
involved in teaching and nursing,
and those who have chosen
to live simple lives;
for the growth and development
of a strong prayer life
in every Christian.

Silence

Unchanging Father:
give us your peace.

We pray for the world of industry
and commerce;
for those whose decisions
affect many lives;
for those who determine the use
of our world's resources.

Silence

Unchanging Father:
give us your peace.

We pray for those who are suffering
from stress and depression;
for psychiatric nursing staff;
for those who cannot cope
with the burdens of their lives.

Silence

Unchanging Father:
give us your peace.

We pray for ourselves and our families;
for a greater simplicity
in the ordering of our lives;
for deeper trust and acceptance.

Silence

Unchanging Father:
give us your peace.

Upheld by God's peace,
we pray now in silence
for any needs known to us personally.

Silence

Heavenly Father,
accept our prayers,
through Jesus Christ our Lord.
Amen.

THE GOODNESS OF GOD

Father, we remember our brothers and sisters in Christ
as they worship in large and small groups
all over the world.

Silence

O give thanks to the Lord:
for he is good.

Father, we think of the world's peacemakers
and all who spend their lives
working constructively for good;
all who uphold Christian values and stand firm
for what is right.

Silence

O give thanks to the Lord:
for he is good.

Father, we remember all who are
bringing their children up carefully and lovingly;
all who care for elderly neighbours and relatives;
all who work to build community where they live.

Silence

O give thanks to the Lord:
for he is good.

Father, we think of the sick and those caring for them;
we think of those who rarely get a break,
but need one;
those who are offering their suffering for you to use.

Silence

O give thanks to the Lord:
for he is good.

Father, we remember those who are dying
and those who have crossed from time into eternity;
we think of the example of their lives
and we remember those who love them.

Silence

O give thanks to the Lord:
for he is good.

Father, we think of the beauty of all you have made
and the daily miracles of life and love.

Silence

O give thanks to the Lord:
for he is good.

Father, in deepest joy
for the love you have shown us:
**we ask you to accept our prayers
through Jesus Christ, our Lord.
Amen.**

THE FAVOUR OF THE LORD

Father, we commend to your love
all Church leaders and those in their care;
all who need encouragement and reassurance.

Silence

May the favour of the Lord:
rest upon us.

Father, we commend to your mercy
all the areas of violence in our world;
the hopes and disillusions,
the potential good and evil.

Silence

May the favour of the Lord:
rest upon us.

Father, we commend to your tenderness
our relatives and friends,
both those who bring joy
and those who cause us great concern.

Silence

May the favour of the Lord:
rest upon us.

Father, we commend to your loving care
all whose lives are caged by guilt or terror;
all who are coming to terms with a disability;
all who suffer through another's cruelty.

Silence

May the favour of the Lord:
rest upon us.

Father, we commend to your welcoming arms
those who have arrived at the point of death,
especially the unnoticed and uncared for.

Silence

May the favour of the Lord:
rest upon us.

Father, we commend to you our thanks and praise
for all that is good and beautiful,
responsive and true.

Silence

Father, with the favour of your blessing upon us
may we go out in confidence
to do your will:
walking with Jesus along the way.
Amen.

THE GIVER OF GOOD

Father, we lay before you our longing
for many to know the joy and freedom of your service,
and we remember the needs of all
who minister your love and teaching.

Silence

The Lord will indeed:
give what is good.

We lay before you our loathing of corruption
and injustice,
and remember the needs of all peacemakers,
negotiators, leaders and advisers.

Silence

The Lord will indeed:
give what is good.

We lay before you our concern for all broken families,
all children being raised in turmoil,
and we remember the needs of all parents.

Silence

The Lord will indeed:
give what is good.

We lay before you our desire to help those
whose lives or bodies are broken through war or abuse,
and we remember the needs of all victims.

Silence

The Lord will indeed:
give what is good.

We lay before you our memories
of those we love who have died,
and entrust them to your everlasting care.

Silence

The Lord will indeed:
give what is good.

We lay before you our thankfulness
for the way you come to search for us
whenever we are lost.

Silence

Father, we lay before you these prayers,
trusting in your goodness,
which we have seen in Jesus.
Amen.

UNCHANGING LORD

As members of the Church of Christ,
let us lay our needs and cares
at the feet of our heavenly Father.

We ask that his love, peace and joy
may fill the Church
in every corner of the earth;
that God's name may be held holy
in unending waves of praise.

Silence

Unchanging Lord:
fix our hearts on your goodness.

We ask that all negotiators
and administrators
may be guided to work with sensitivity,
care and integrity.

Silence

Unchanging Lord:
fix our hearts on your goodness.

We ask that all strained marriages
may be healed and strengthened;
that those whose lives
have been damaged or warped
may be emotionally repaired
and rebuilt.

Silence

Unchanging Lord:
fix our hearts on your goodness.

We ask that our homes may be built
on the solid rock of Christ,

so that when storms come
they may stand firm.

Silence

Unchanging Lord:
fix our hearts on your goodness.

Knowing that God our Father
hears the cry of his children,
we pray in silence
for our needs and cares.

Silence

Father of compassion and mercy,
accept our prayers,
through the person of Jesus Christ.
Amen.

DRAW US TO YOURSELF

While we are still far off
from God our Father,
he comes to welcome us,
and so we pray.

We remember all lapsed Christians,
all who have lost their faith;
that they may return to God
and find him ready
to welcome them home.

Silence

Father of love:
draw us to yourself.

We remember all
who have been made redundant,
all whose work is unhealthy,
or dangerous;
that we may strive to uphold
each person's dignity
and ease each person's burden.

Silence

Father of love:
draw us to yourself.

We remember the rejected and the homeless,
those who have become bitter and twisted
or hard and mean;
that the generous warmth of God's love
will work within them
to thaw what is frozen,
strengthen what is weak,
heal what is hurt
and repair what is damaged.

Silence

Father of love:
draw us to yourself.

We remember our homes,
that they may spread the Good News
of Christ's redeeming love
by the way they reflect his peace,
his understanding and his joy.

Silence

Father of love:
draw us to yourself.

We know that our merciful Father hears us;
let us pray in silence now
for our individual needs.

Silence

Father,
hear our prayers,
through Jesus Christ our Lord.
Amen.

TRUSTING GOD'S GOODNESS

Loving God, we come to plead for the Church
in its weakness and lack of unity;
may we be one as you are one.

Silence

Loving God:
we trust in your goodness.

Loving God, we come to plead for our world
in its confusion and injustices.

Silence

Loving God:
we trust in your goodness.

Loving God, we come to plead for our families and friends
in their needs and difficulties.

Silence

Loving God:
we trust in your goodness.

Loving God, we come to plead for those who suffer
in their pain and weariness.

Silence

Loving God:
we trust in your goodness.

Loving God, we come to plead for the dying
and the bereaved
in their grief and loneliness.

Silence

Loving God:
we trust in your goodness.

Loving God, we come to plead for the coming
of your kingdom
in every place and in every person.

Silence

We thank you, Father,
that your holiness
is full of mercy and compassion.
**Accept these prayers
for the sake of Jesus, our Saviour.
Amen.**

Lord of life

GREAT CREATOR GOD

Let us pray in humility to God
who creates and sustains all things.

We pray for the Church, the body of Christ;
that regardless of rank or position,
its members may be noticeable
by their unselfish humility,
so that through their good work
God may be glorified.

Silence

Great creator God:
let us show your glory.

We bring before God the world's leaders
and their governments,
and all in influential positions;
that they may make good use
of their power,
and aim to serve
the needs of others.

Silence

Great creator God:
let us show your glory.

We remember the disabled,
the mentally and physically disadvantaged,
and those whose bodies or minds
have been damaged
through accidents or violence;
we commit them to the calm and peace of Christ.

Silence

Great creator God:
let us show your glory.

We pray for those we serve in our daily lives,
and all who serve us;
that we may care for each other
with kindness and friendship,
knowing that we are all
brothers and sisters before God.

Silence

Great creator God:
let us show your glory.

In silence, we pray for our own intentions to God,
our loving Father.

Lord God,
Creator of all things,
we ask you to hear these prayers,
through Jesus Christ our Lord.
Amen.

LORD OF CREATION

Humankind has been brought into life by God.
We owe our very existence to him.
Let us pray to him now.

We pray for each living person
inhabiting our world with us,
with all the needs, emotions and experiences we share.
We pray that we may recognise one another
as brothers and sisters
sharing the same heavenly Father.

Silence

Lord of creation:
let your will be done.

We pray for greater reverence for God's creation
in the way we use and manage resources and wildlife.

Silence

Lord of creation:
let your will be done.

We pray for all of us in the ship of the Church,
that whenever storms rock the boat
and appear to threaten us,
we may trust God to bring us safely through.

Silence

Lord of creation:
let your will be done.

We pray for our children
and for all giving birth and being born today.
We long for the world they enter to be welcoming
and full of God's practical love.

Silence

Lord of creation:
let your will be done.

We pray for those who have chronic illness
and have to live in constant pain.
We ask for God's comfort
and reassurance to support them.

Silence

Lord of creation:
let your will be done.

We pray for those who have died,
thanking God for the example of lives well lived,
and for the total healing now received.

Merciful Father:
accept these prayers
for the sake of your Son,
our Saviour Jesus Christ.
Amen.

THE LORD OUR MAKER

Knowing that when we pray in faith
our loving Father will hear us,
let us pray together for the Church,
and for the world he has made.

Bless the work of all who spread
the wonderful news of your love.
May all who profess to be Christians
shine with your light so that others are drawn
to know your glory and experience
the joy of your peace.

Silence

Lord our maker:
hear our prayer.

Sustain and protect Elizabeth our Queen
and guide all world leaders, advisers and politicians
to act with wisdom and integrity.

Silence

Lord our maker:
hear our prayer.

Father, we commend to your loving keeping
all who have died, especially . . .
that they may live for ever
in the glorious peace and joy of your heaven.

Silence

Lord our maker:
hear our prayer.

We offer you thanks and praise
for the rich and beautiful world
you have provided for us,

and for the many blessings in our lives,
and for the gift of life itself.

Silence

Lord our maker:
hear our prayer.

Now let us bring
our personal requests to God
in quietness and trust.

Silence

Lord our maker:
**hear our prayer
which we offer in the name
of Jesus Christ, your Son.
Amen.**

THE GROUND OF OUR BEING

Let us focus our gaze on the great God who made us,
as we pour out to him our prayers.

Lord of all, give your Church such maturity and wisdom
that we may not be swayed from our purpose and calling
by trivialities or worldly pressures,
but know increasingly our dependence
on you in all things and proclaim your Gospel
with steadfastness and joy.

Silence

You, O Lord:
are the ground of our being.

Lord of all, give to all leaders
and heads of state graciousness and integrity,
that all in power and authority
may undertake their duties in a spirit of humility;
that the oppressed may find a voice,
and the nations work together for the good of the world.

Silence

You, O Lord:
are the ground of our being.

Lord of all, give to our homes
and places of work and leisure your harmony and peace;
give us grace to respect one another and ourselves
in the way we talk and think, and in the way we behave.

Silence

You, O Lord:
are the ground of our being.

Lord of all, speak your peace into the hearts
of all who are agitated, anxious or confused.

Lay your hands of healing on all who are ill
and let them know your reassurance and love.

Silence

You, O Lord:
are the ground of our being.

Lord of all, welcome into your kingdom
all who have kept faith
and now can lay their burdens down.
May they rest in your peace for ever.

Silence

You, O Lord:
are the ground of our being.

Lord of all, the order and complexity of creation
sing your praise,
and we give voice to it now
as we offer you our song of lives rededicated
to the work of your kingdom.

Merciful Father:
**accept these prayers
for the sake of your Son,
our Saviour Jesus Christ.
Amen.**

GOD OUR MAKER

Let us pray to the God who made us and sustains us.

Look with mercy on your Church,
with all our faults and failings,
missed opportunities and misunderstandings,
as we learn to be truly your body on earth.

Silence

God our maker:
have mercy on us.

We lay before you the political issues,
the moral dilemmas and the dreams of peace
that concern our world,
and all who share its resources.
Where we can see no clear way forward
give us your vision and enable us
to be good stewards of all you provide.

Silence

God our maker:
have mercy on us.

We ask you to take all our relationships
and drench them in your transforming love,
so that we appreciate one another more,
and value what each has to offer.

Silence

God our maker:
have mercy on us.

Surround with comfort and reassurance
those who feel spiritually dried-up
or emotionally drained;
heal and mend broken bodies and broken hearts,

and provide clear pools of water for those
who are walking the valley of misery and depression.

Silence

God our maker:
have mercy on us.

Gather into your kingdom
those who have run the race
and fought the good fight,
and have mercy on all who are at the point of death.

Silence

God our maker:
have mercy on us.

We give you thanks and praise
for the wideness of your mercy,
and the personal attention
of your provision for us.

Merciful Father:
**accept these prayers
for the sake of your Son,
our Saviour Jesus Christ.
Amen.**

MAKER OF HEAVEN AND EARTH

For all church leaders, bishops, priests and deacons;
for all who are overworked and stressed;
for all who feel they are doing an impossible job;
let us pray.

Silence

Our help is in the name of the Lord:
who has made heaven and earth.

For all world leaders and their advisers;
for judges, and all who work to uphold law and order;
for leaders of oppressive and corrupt regimes;
let us pray.

Silence

Our help is in the name of the Lord:
who has made heaven and earth.

For families coping with difficulties;
for children suffering abuse or neglect;
for those we love, and those we dislike;
let us pray.

Silence

Our help is in the name of the Lord:
who has made heaven and earth.

For all who are dependent on others for everyday care;
for the crippled in body and the confused of mind;
for the victims of violence, carelessness and hatred;
let us pray.

Silence

Our help is in the name of the Lord:
who has made heaven and earth.

For those who are dying, even as we pray;
for those facing death with terror;
for all who have recently gone through
the journey of death;
let us pray.

Silence

Our help is in the name of the Lord:
who has made heaven and earth.

For all that lightens our lives with laughter,
for all that blesses our lives with peace,
let us give God thanks and praise.

Silence

Lord God, creator of all things,
use these our prayers
to bring more love, more joy and more peace
into your world:
through Jesus Christ, our Lord.
Amen.

THE LIVING GOD

Father, renew and deepen the faith of your people;
enable us to spread your good news
by our word and our lives.

Silence

Living God:
we worship you.

Father, breathe your peace into the violence
of our world;
we long for your kingdom to come.

Silence

Living God:
we worship you.

Father, refresh and soothe
all our scratchy and worn relationships;
fill our homes with your love.

Silence

Living God:
we worship you.

Father, comfort and reassure
all those who are suffering;
heal them to wholeness.

Silence

Living God:
we worship you.

Father, have mercy on those who draw close to death;
make us all aware of your abiding presence.

Silence

Living God:
we worship you.

Father, awaken us to see again the wonder
and delight of life;
fill us with thankfulness.

Silence

Living God:
we worship you
and ask you to accept our prayers
for the sake of Jesus Christ, your Son.
Amen.

LORD OF LIFE

As we gather in the company of the living God,
let us pray.

Lord of life, we pray that the Church
may be alive with your risen life,
refreshed and revived by the breath of your Spirit,
purified and refined like gold and silver,
so that we truly offer the possibility
of saving love to the searching world.

Silence

You are the one true God:
and we worship you.

Lord of life, we pray that in all meetings and conferences
where important decisions are taken,
hearts may be turned to honour what is just and true,
compassionate and constructive.
We pray that in all areas
where there is corruption, deceit or distrust,
consciences may be sensitised afresh
to know what is right and strive towards it.

Silence

You are the one true God:
and we worship you.

Lord of life, we pray for the streets
and places of work we represent.
May they be places where the truth of your being
is proclaimed daily by the way we live
and handle the everyday situations, through your leading.
May our words and actions speak of your faithful love,
your graciousness and your purity.

Silence

You are the one true God:
and we worship you.

Lord of life, we lay before you now
those who are struggling with pain and anguish,
or wrestling with tragedy and conflict.
We stand beside them in their suffering
and offer it to your healing love.

Silence

You are the one true God:
and we worship you.

Lord of life, we pray for those who have died
and now see you as you really are.
We ask for mercy and forgiveness,
and commend them to your keeping for ever.

Silence

You are the one true God:
and we worship you.

Lord of life, your love for us is so great
and our love for you so small.
Thank you for accepting what we are able to offer;
and ignite us to a blaze of love.

Merciful Father:
accept these prayers
for the sake of your Son,
our Saviour Jesus Christ.
Amen.

LORD OF HEAVEN AND EARTH

Let us come before God our Maker,
offering our prayers to him,
through Jesus and in the power of the Holy Spirit.

We pray that the Church may be alive
to God's beckoning,
quick to obey his will
and always ready to act in his loving service
for the good of the world.

Silence

Father in heaven:
let your will be done on earth.

We pray that all leaders and heads of state
may take wise advice and act responsibly
for the well-being of all.
We pray for God's guidance
in the way we manage and care for this planet,
its resources, riches and inhabitants.

Silence

Father in heaven:
let your will be done on earth.

We pray for all marriages,
for those seeking marriage partners
and those whose marriages are under strain.
We pray for all in close relationships,
that there may be mutual love and respect.

Silence

Father in heaven:
let your will be done on earth.

We pray for all who are suffering
through illness, accident or deliberate cruelty;

for refugees and all who are abused;
that through the caring of human hands
they may experience the caring hands of God.

Silence

Father in heaven:
let your will be done on earth.

We pray for all who have died violently
or suddenly, or with no one to miss them.
May all who have died in faith
be judged with mercy
and welcomed into eternal life.

Silence

Father in heaven:
let your will be done on earth.

We pour out our thanks and praise
for the gift of life
and the gift of one another.
May we treat each other with renewed reverence.

Merciful Father:
accept these prayers
for the sake of your Son,
our Saviour Jesus Christ.
Amen.

HE DOES ALL THINGS WELL

We think of the Church celebrating in clusters
and crowds all over the world,
and pray for a deepening of love and faith.

Silence

Lord of life:
you do all things well.

We remember the areas of the world
where there is conflict and confusion;
and we pray that all may come to know God's love.

Silence

Lord of life:
you do all things well.

We remember those we have met and talked with
during the week,
and pray for God's blessing on their lives.

Silence

Lord of life:
you do all things well.

We remember those waiting for surgery,
and those in long-term care,
and pray that God's will
may be beautifully accomplished in their lives.

Silence

Lord of life:
you do all things well.

We remember those who have died very young,
and those who are finding this hard to accept,
and we pray for God's grace and reassurance.

Silence

Lord of life:
you do all things well.

We remember the wonder and generosity of God,
his faithfulness and his mercy.

Silence

Lord, hear our prayers
and work them into your loving purposes:
through Jesus Christ, our Saviour and Friend.
Amen.

THANK YOU, GOD, FOR EVERYTHING

Thank you, Father, for the patient love you show
in teaching and guiding us,
challenging and coaxing us.
We ask you to bless each person
on their journey of faith.

Silence

Your ways are holy, Lord:
and your ways are best.

Thank you, Father, for every peace initiative,
each act of goodness, each victory over evil.
Bless and guide the nations of our world.

Silence

Your ways are holy, Lord:
and your ways are best.

Thank you, Father, for the friendships we cherish,
for the members of our families,
and for our neighbours.
Bless each home with your presence.

Silence

Your ways are holy, Lord:
and your ways are best.

Thank you, Father, for all who care for the sick,
the very young and the very old.
Bless all who suffer with the comfort of your love.

Silence

Your ways are holy, Lord:
and your ways are best.

Thank you, Father, for the example of lives well lived
and death honestly and bravely faced.
Welcome into your kingdom all who have died in faith,
and those whose faith is known only to you.

Silence

Your ways are holy, Lord:
and your ways are best.

Thank you, Father, for all the abundance
of life you provide for us.

Silence

Thank you, Father, for hearing our prayers
and guiding us in your ways
of goodness and love,
for the sake of Jesus.
Amen.

LIFE-GIVING LORD

My brothers and sisters in Christ,
knowing the deep love that surrounds us
and reaches out to us in every distress,
let us unload our burdens of care
to the healing power of our heavenly Father.

We bring before you the Church's work
among the homeless, the disillusioned
and the apathetic,
in communities all over the world.

Silence

Life-giving Lord:
hear us and help us, we pray.

We bring before you all areas of the world
where lack of communication
breeds suspicion and fear;
where lack of understanding
breeds insecurity and a spirit of revenge.

Silence

Life-giving Lord:
hear us and help us, we pray.

We bring before you each member of this community,
each individual anxiety and sorrow,
each hope and dream,
each weakness and special need.

Silence

Life-giving Lord:
hear us and help us, we pray.

We bring before you all whose lives are crippled
by unrepented sin or the refusal to forgive;

all whose lives are constantly restless
and devoid of peace.

Silence

Life-giving Lord:
hear us and help us, we pray.

We bring before you those who have died
and those who miss them.

Silence

Life-giving Lord:
hear us and help us, we pray.

We bring before you the joy and happiness
of our daily life,
the blessings that lift our hearts to praise you.

Silence

Lord, in these our prayers
we share our concerns with you.
Give us the faith to know
that you hear and answer,
through Jesus Christ, your Son.
Amen.

You Alone
Can Make Us Whole

Let us approach our heavenly Father in humility,
as we bring to his restoring love
all our concern for the Church and the world.

Lord, we bring to you
the divided Christian community;
lead us tenderly to wholeness and unity.

Silence

Lord God:
you alone can make us whole.

Lord, we bring to you
the divided world,
split between wealth and poverty,
complacency and oppression;
break through all barriers
with your love and reconciliation.

Silence

Lord God:
you alone can make us whole.

Lord, we bring to you
the wounds and hurts of our own lives;
and of our families;
all unresolved tensions and sorrows,
all reunions, joys and healing;
bless and renew our lives with your living presence.

Silence

Lord God:
you alone can make us whole.

Lord, we bring to you
all in pain or distress;
the mentally and physically handicapped
and all whom society prefers to ignore;
may your love nourish and heal, accept and restore.

Silence

Lord God:
you alone can make us whole.

Lord, we commend to your everlasting
love and care, all who have died, especially . . .

Silence

With great joy in our hearts
we offer you thanks and praise
for all the gifts and blessings you lavish on us;
may we proclaim our thankfulness by the lives we lead.

Silence

Father, receive these prayers
which we offer in the name of Jesus Christ, our Lord.
Amen.

LORD, TOUCH OUR LIVES

Wherever Christians are spiritually dry or brittle,
wherever the loving has lost its freshness,
we pray for refreshment.

Silence

Lord, touch our lives:
and make them new.

Wherever the nations scramble for power and revenge,
wherever materialism dulls the spirit,
we pray for realigned priorities and values.

Silence

Lord, touch our lives:
and make them new.

Wherever homes are disturbed by financial problems,
difficult relationships and long-term illness,
we pray for guidance and support.

Silence

Lord, touch our lives:
and make them new.

Wherever slow recovery makes time hang heavily,
wherever hope and joy are fading,
we pray for encouragement and delight.

Silence

Lord, touch our lives:
and make them new.

Wherever people are dying to this world,
wherever lives are cut short by accidents, war or famine,
we pray for your mercy and words of comfort.

Silence

Father, let your loving mercy bring the dead and dying
safely home to heaven,
and give comfort to those who mourn.

Silence

Help us to think with your mind:
and love with your heart.

Father, let your joy fill our lives
as we delight in living according to your ways:
through Jesus Christ, our Lord.
Amen.

YOU CAN
TRANSFORM OUR LIVES

Father, wherever people's faith is stunted or withered,
we plead for your breath of life.

Silence

Lord of power:
you can transform our lives.

Wherever people are trapped by oppression
or weakened by complacency,
we plead for your kingdom to come.

Silence

Lord of power:
you can transform our lives.

Wherever people live out their daily lives
in stress and disappointment,
we plead for your restoring love.

Silence

Lord of power:
you can transform our lives.

Wherever people's lives are restricted
by physical weakness
or hunger or poverty,
we plead for your healing love.

Silence

Lord of power:
you can transform our lives.

Wherever people are dying,
we plead for your mercy and comfort.

Silence

Lord of power:
you can transform our lives.

Wherever there is loveliness and serenity,
integrity and wisdom,
we praise you for your glory.

Silence

Father in heaven,
may your power flow into the world
through the prayers and lives of your people,
filled with the Spirit of Christ.
Amen.

BREATHE ON US, BREATH OF GOD

In the presence of God, the giver of all life,
let us lift our hearts and pray.

We pray for all who are training
for ministry in your Church;
may they grow in wisdom and humility,
and be increasingly filled with the life
you have won for us.

Silence

Lord, breathe into us:
that we may live.

We pray for all areas of bureaucracy
which frustrate and delay the course of useful action;
for areas where anarchy undermines stability;
for areas of political corruption;
that whatever is good may flourish and grow,
so evil is rendered powerless and overthrown.

Silence

Lord, breathe into us:
that we may live.

We pray for all who are engaged or newly married;
for those coping with family problems,
difficult circumstances or bereavement;
may they lean on your loving presence
which dispels all fear, and brings life and peace.

Silence

Lord, breathe into us:
that we may live.

We pray that your calming reassurance
will bring peace of mind and spirit
to those worried about the future,
those dreading some difficult event,
and those who are frightened of dying.

Silence

Lord, breathe into us:
that we may live.

We thank you for the life and example
of all who have lived, worked and died
in the joy of your service;
may we one day share with them
eternal life in your presence.

Silence

Lord, breathe into us:
that we may live.

Father, with thankful hearts we offer ourselves
to be used wherever you need us.
**Accept these prayers
for the sake of Jesus Christ.
Amen.**

THAT WE MAY TRULY LIVE

Let us bring our lives and concerns
to the Father, from whom all life comes,
trusting in his power and love.

We bring to his love all those
who have committed their lives to Christ
in ordained ministries;
that they may grow into spiritual maturity,
and live always
as freed sons and daughters of God.

Silence

O Lord, you have set us free:
that we may truly live.

We bring to his love the world
and its problems, mistakes
and errors of judgement;
that in every society
the Lord's light may shine
and his life and peace be known.

Silence

O Lord, you have set us free:
that we may truly live.

We bring to his love the deaf,
the blind and the partially sighted,
all those who are chronically ill
and all who tend them;
that even in all their hardships
they may know life in all its fullness.

Silence

O Lord, you have set us free:
that we may truly live.

We bring to his love our own parents,
all adoptive and foster parents,
women labouring to bring new life
into the world,
that they may be blessed and strengthened
by him who is life itself.

Silence

O Lord, you have set us free:
that we may truly live.

Meeting our heavenly Father
in the stillness of silence,
let us express to him
our particular burdens of prayer.

Silence

Father,
we bring these prayers
in the name of Jesus Christ,
through whom we have
life in abundance.
Amen.

LORD OF OUR LIVES

As followers of Christ,
let us pray together in his presence
to our merciful Father
who feels with us in our needs.

We bring to his love
all religious communities
and organisations
who offer a constant wave of prayer
as the earth spins;
all who sense that God
might be calling them
to a life of renewal
and deeper commitment,
that his will may be made clear to them.

Silence

Lord of all our lives:
hear us, we pray.

We bring to his love
all who wield power
in each community of our world;
those who persist in challenging
injustice and prejudice;
all who bring to public attention
areas of need and unnoticed hardship
where life is stifled or denied.

Silence

Lord of all our lives:
hear us, we pray.

We bring to his love
all those in hospital,
in wards and on operating tables

throughout the world;
those worn down by constant pain;
those who are struggling
to rebuild broken lives.

Silence

Lord of all our lives:
hear us, we pray.

We bring to his love
our own particular concerns,
hopes, doubts and fears;
our difficulties at work and at home,
our responsibilities.

Silence

Lord of all our lives:
hear us, we pray.

In silence,
we name any we know
who especially need our prayer.

Silence

In great thankfulness
for the gift of life
and for all your blessings to us,
heavenly Father,
we offer you these prayers
through Jesus Christ.
Amen.

THE BREAD OF LIFE

Let us pray to the God who loves us,
knows our needs, and provides for us.

As the travelling people of God,
we pray for a deepening hunger
for the things of God
and a loosening of our grip
on all the wants and expectations
which prevent us from moving forward God's way.

Silence

Feed us, Lord:
with the Bread of Life.

As brothers and sisters with the whole of creation,
we pray for respect and reverence among people
regardless of wealth or status;
for responsible sharing of resources
and consideration for the natural world
of our fragile and beautiful planet.

Silence

Feed us, Lord:
with the Bread of Life.

As we prepare and eat our food each day,
we pray for those who grow and manufacture it,
distribute and sell it, shop for it and cook it,
and for those with whom we share food.
Build us up with your spiritual feeding
which sustains us for ever.

Silence

Feed us, Lord:
with the Bread of Life.

As we ask for daily bread,
we pray for those who are physically starving,
for all who hunger emotionally
or try to survive on spiritual junk food;
for those who mistrust God's feeding.

Silence

Feed us, Lord:
with the Bread of Life.

As we remember with love
those who have journeyed through physical death,
we pray that, nourished by the Bread of Life,
they may travel on eagles' wings
into the brightness of eternal life.

Silence

Feed us, Lord:
with the Bread of Life.

As we grow increasingly aware
of our spiritual hunger,
we give thanks for the wonder of God's feeding,
throughout our days.

Merciful Lord:
**accept these prayers
which we ask in your name.
Amen.**

Bearing Fruit for God

Fellow members of the Body of Christ
full of thankfulness for his abiding love
let us pray to our heavenly Father.

Lord, we ask you to deepen
our personal commitment
so that the life-giving sap of the true vine
can flow through the Church and out into the world.

Silence

Live in us, Father:
that we may bear fruit.

Direct and further all international discussions
so that they lead to peace,
goodwill and mutual understanding.

Silence

Live in us, Father:
that we may bear fruit.

Lord, come and make your home in us,
in our marriages and our families,
our places of work and our local community;
may our characters be forged by your life within us.

Silence

Live in us, Father:
that we may bear fruit.

Bring healing and wholeness
to those who are ill;
peace to the anxious,
courage to the fearful
and rest to the weary.

Silence

Live in us, Father:
that we may bear fruit.

Give everlasting peace
to those who have died in faith;
may they know the joy
of being invited to your heavenly banquet.

Silence

We thank you that we are all invited
to share your life-giving love;
make us worthy of all you have promised.

Silence

Lord, keep us close to yourself
through prayer and service,
that we may live and grow
in fruitful discipleship of Jesus Christ.
Amen.

THE SEED OF GOD'S WORD

Gathered together as the people of God,
and attentive to his will, let us pray.

Heavenly Father, may your words of truth
take root in our hearts and grow to rich maturity.
May we hear your will for us and act upon it;
may we take seriously our responsibility
to encourage and nurture one another in faith
at every age and every stage.

Silence

Lord, sow your seed in our hearts:
your word is life and strength.

Heavenly Father, may every act of selfless giving
and every search for truth be richly blessed and rewarded;
Disturb assumptions and lead
many to ponder more deeply
the spiritual dimension of their lives.
May the word of God reach all who are ready to receive it,
and let us set no boundaries here as to who they might be.

Silence

Lord, sow your seed in our hearts:
your word is life and strength.

Heavenly Father, make our homes
places of love and growth,
welcoming to all who visit them,
and accepting and forgiving to all who are nurtured there.
Help us through the quarrels and heartaches
and remind us to honour one another
as your cherished ones.

Silence

Lord, sow your seed in our hearts:
your word is life and strength.

Heavenly Father, may all whose bodies,
souls or minds are aching
know the comforting and strengthening power
of your companionship, and the healing work of your love.
May we be more ready
to support and befriend one another
through the difficult times,
in the name and love of the God we worship.

Silence

Lord, sow your seed in our hearts:
your word is life and strength.

Heavenly Father, we pray for all
who are making the journey through physical death,
as they put down earthly things
and wake to your presence.
Bring us all to share with them
your life in all its fullness.

Silence

Lord, sow your seed in our hearts:
your word is life and strength.

Heavenly Father, the rain and sunshine,
the growing and harvesting,
sing to us of your faithful love,
and we offer you our thankful praise
for all your gifts to us.

Merciful Father:
**accept these prayers
for the sake of your Son,
our Saviour Jesus Christ.
Amen.**

OUR LIFE IN GOD'S HANDS

As we share a common faith and hope,
let us pray trustingly together
to the God who made us
and sustains us.

Let us pray for all
who profess themselves Christians;
that in fastening our eyes on Christ
we may be led to unity.

Silence

Father almighty:
our life is in your hands.

Let us pray for the political, industrial
and commercial administrations
throughout our planet;
that our material and economic organisation
may reveal good stewardship
of the gifts God has provided.

Silence

Father almighty:
our life is in your hands.

Let us pray for all convicted prisoners,
and for the victims of their crimes;
for all who are eaten up
with hatred or jealousy;
for all who are finding it impossible
to forgive their enemies.

Silence

Father almighty:
our life is in your hands.

Let us pray for the homes and families
represented here;
for our loved ones
from whom we are separated
by distance or death;
for a deepening love towards each other
in all our relationships.

Silence

Father almighty:
our life is in your hands.

In the silence of our hearts,
we pray for any needs
known to us personally.

Silence

Father,
with grateful thanks for the gift of life,
we offer you these prayers
together with ourselves
for your service;
in Jesus' name we pray.
Amen.

HEAL THIS WORLD

Let us pray for spiritual growth
in the Church and the world.

We pray that the good news of God's salvation
may never be taken for granted
but accepted and shared
with thankfulness and joy.

Silence

Life-giving God:
heal this world.

We pray that all nations may have courage
to fight against what is evil
and to nurture what is good
in an atmosphere of respect
and consideration for others.

Silence

Life-giving God:
heal this world.

We pray for those whose lives
have been twisted and spoilt by sin;
that the lost and weary
may turn to the God of love
for guidance and peace.

Silence

Life-giving God:
heal this world.

We pray for all those living in this district;
that we may use our gifts
in serving one another

and spreading the love of Jesus
throughout the world.

Silence

Life-giving God:
heal this world.

God our Father loves us;
in silence we bring
our personal prayers to him now.

Silence

Father, we ask all these things
through Jesus Christ our Lord.
Amen.

God of light

GOD'S GRACE AND GLORY

Father, we pray for the Church on earth;
wherever your vision is disturbing our assumptions,
wherever your promptings are nudging us to action,
we ask you to keep us attentive and obedient.

Silence

Give us your grace:
and let your glory shine.

Father, we pray for our world;
wherever self-interest is blinding us to needs,
wherever past evils are preventing peace,
we ask you to renew us in love.

Silence

Give us your grace:
and let your glory shine.

Father, we pray for our homes and our neighbourhood,
wherever there is a breakdown in communication,
wherever patience wears thin, or interests clash,
we ask for your guidance and protection.

Silence

Give us your grace:
and let your glory shine.

Father, we pray for those who are suffering,
wherever pain or terror is overwhelming,
wherever lives are damaged and wounded,
we ask you to bind up and make whole again.

Silence

Give us your grace:
and let your glory shine.

Father, we pray for the dead and dying,
and those who mourn;
wherever souls are approaching your eternal kingdom,
wherever loved ones grieve,
we ask for your mercy and comfort.

Silence

Give us your grace:
and let your glory shine.

Father, we pray for our hearts to be filled
with thankfulness.
Wherever we see beauty and loveliness,
wherever we experience compassion and forgiveness,
we ask you to lift our hearts to give you glory.

Silence

Father, let the light of Jesus Christ
shine into your world,
for his name's sake.
Amen.

THE LORD IS OUR LIGHT

Our heavenly Father
guides us faithfully
and enlightens our lives.
Let us pray to him now,
for the Church
and for the world.

We pray that we may be ready
to follow Christ wherever he leads us,
even if the direction is unexpected
or demanding.

Silence

Lord of light:
enlighten our lives.

We pray that all nations may rejoice
in the light of goodness
and reject the darkness of evil.

Silence

Lord of light:
enlighten our lives.

We pray that in the brightness of love,
Christ may be revealed
turning the doubtful to faith,
the despairing to hope,
and the revengeful to forgiveness.

Silence

Lord of light:
enlighten our lives.

We pray that no opportunity may be lost
in sharing the joy and peace of Christ

with those we meet
in our daily lives.

Silence

Lord of light:
enlighten our lives.

We pray to the Lord in silence,
for our own needs and cares

Silence

Father,
we commend our lives
to your loving care,
through Jesus Christ our Lord.
Amen.

THE LIGHT OF GOD'S GLORY

Let us pray to God,
whose glory is all around us,
with thankful and adoring hearts.

We bring to the Lord
all those involved
with teaching the Christian faith;
our schools and children's ministry,
and missionaries – especially…
[Any missionary work
connected with or supported by
the particular church.]

Silence

Father of Light:
shine in the darkness.

We bring to the Lord
all peoples of our earth
with their different cultures,
philosophies and traditions;
multi-racial communities,
especially those experiencing problems
with mutual understanding and harmony.

Silence

Father of Light:
shine in the darkness.

We bring to the Lord all new-born babies,
especially those who are unwanted
or abandoned;
all people who are elderly
and approaching death,
especially those who are frightened.

Silence

Father of Light:
shine in the darkness.

We bring to the Lord our own local church,
our programme for education and outreach,
our availability to those who do not yet know
the richness of God's love;
its areas of stagnation
and its potential for growth.

Silence

Father of Light:
shine in the darkness.

In silence,
as God the Father listens with love,
we name our own particular cares and concerns.

Silence

Heavenly Father,
we ask you to accept these prayers,
through Christ our Saviour.
Amen.

OPEN OUR EYES

In the knowledge that God is here present with us,
let us pray.

Father, we thank you for the gifts of sight and insight,
and ask you to be there in all our looking.
Help us always to see with eyes of faith, love and honesty.

Silence

Lord of light, open our eyes:
to see things your way.

We pray for our church leaders
in their demanding ministry of love,
that they may be given all the support,
grace and anointing they need.

Silence

Lord of light, open our eyes:
to see things your way.

We pray for the gifts of discernment and integrity
among all those who govern, advise and lead.
Clear away all self-centred ambition
to free our leaders to serve.

Silence

Lord of light, open our eyes:
to see things your way.

Whenever we have eye contact with family, friends,
neighbours or colleagues,
be there in that communication,
and remind us of our calling to love one another.

Silence

Lord of light, open our eyes:
to see things your way.

We call to mind those whose eyes are wet with tears
or tense with pain.
Help them to sense your reassuring love
which can bring us through the darkest of valleys.

Silence

Lord of light, open our eyes:
to see things your way.

Jesus is the firstfruit
of the new and eternal life we are promised in you.
We commend to your love
those who have recently walked through death
into that promise, and thank you for the privilege
of knowing them here on earth.

Silence

Lord of light, open our eyes:
to see things your way.

Father we thank you for loving us
right through death into new life,
and we rejoice in your victory over evil.

Merciful Father:
**accept these prayers
for the sake of your Son,
our Saviour Jesus Christ.
Amen.**

SHINE THROUGH OUR LIVES

My friends in Christ,
let us pray to our heavenly Father
trusting in his generous mercy.

We pray for the Church
as it witnesses to Christ in the world;
may its members be always aware
that they are called to be servants,
ready and happy to minister
to the spiritual, emotional and physical needs
of all people.

Silence

Lord of light:
shine through our lives.

We pray for the leaders of every community and nation;
may governments reflect the values
of responsible caring, compassion and integrity,
so that no individual or minority group
is abused or left in need.

Silence

Lord of light:
shine through our lives.

We pray for a breaking down of any complacency
or blindness in us
until we are able to see the needs around us,
and can work in your strength,
giving our whole lives away
in loving those whom you love.

Silence

Lord of light:
shine through our lives.

We pray for the rejected, neglected,
shunned or despised;
for the unwanted and the disturbed;
for the ill and the injured;
may they be healed, restored and comforted.

Silence

Lord of light:
shine through our lives.

We pray for those who have passed
through the gateway of death into eternity;
may they know the joy of your presence for ever.

Silence

We offer you our thanks
for every opportunity we are given
to witness to your unfailing love;
may our words and our lives proclaim your glory:
through Jesus Christ, our Lord.
Amen.

LIGHTEN OUR DARKNESS

In humility and love
let us draw near to our God
and pray to him now.

Lord God, we pray that our lives
may be upright and holy;
that our church communities may shine
with goodness and love, humility and truth;
we pray for all leaning lives to be straightened up
through your merciful forgiveness.

Silence

Holy God, scatter all darkness:
and bathe our world in your light.

Lord God, we pray that many
may be empowered to recognise evil
and fight against it;
to discern your warnings and speak them out;
to notice the sparks of love and goodness
and celebrate them.

Silence

Holy God, scatter all darkness:
and bathe our world in your light.

Lord God, we pray that our households
and neighbourhoods,
our places of work and leisure,
may be arenas of praise and thankfulness,
not only in the comfort zones
but particularly through the disturbed
and difficult times.

Silence

Holy God, scatter all darkness:
and bathe our world in your light.

Lord God, we pray for those in prison;
for those leading cruel and violent lives;
for all victims of oppression or abuse;
for all who suffer mental anguish or physical pain.

Silence

Holy God, scatter all darkness:
and bathe our world in your light.

Lord God, we pray for those who have died,
that they, and we in our turn, may be given
merciful judgement through Jesus our Saviour,
and brought into the unquenchable light of heaven.

Silence

Holy God, scatter all darkness:
and bathe our world in your light.

Lord God, we pray for more thankful hearts
to bless you, because the gifts we receive from you
are so much more than we deserve.

Merciful Father:
accept these prayers
for the sake of your Son,
our Saviour Jesus Christ.
Amen.

SHINING WITH THE LIGHT OF GOD

Companions in Christ, in confidence
let us pray to our heavenly Father.

We pray that all baptised Christians
may pray without ceasing
and work enthusiastically
to serve the world with love and sensitivity.

Silence

Almighty Father:
may we shine with your light.

We pray that all disputes and misunderstandings
may be brought to a settled peace,
based on mutual respect, honour,
and a concern for each other's grievances.

Silence

Almighty Father:
may we shine with your light.

We pray that every home in this community
may be enfolded in your love,
brightened by your joy
and calmed by your unbroken peace.

Silence

Almighty Father:
may we shine with your light.

We pray that any who are in great pain
may be granted relief and comfort;
that all who live in constant fear or distress

may be granted a real assurance
of your undergirding and full protection.

Silence

Almighty Father:
may we shine with your light.

We pray that all who have died may,
through your mercy,
rest in your peace.

Silence

We thank you for all your blessings
and especially for the example of Jesus,
in whose strength we offer ourselves for your service.

Silence

Almighty Father:
may we shine with your light,
as we learn to love and pray,
in the name of Jesus, our Lord.
Amen.

CANCELLING DARKNESS

We remember the bickering and petty-mindedness
that goes on in all areas of church life,
and ask for your healing love.

Silence

Show up our darkness:
and cancel it with your light.

We remember the bitterness and greed
which tears our world apart,
and ask for your peace.

Silence

Show up our darkness:
and cancel it with your light.

We remember our families, and the homes in this community,
with their laughter and crying, anger and frustration,
and ask for your caring love.

Silence

Show up our darkness:
and cancel it with your light.

We remember those who suffer
and find life hard to cope with,
and ask for your comfort and encouragement.

Silence

Show up our darkness:
and cancel it with your light.

We remember those who are moving
from this life into eternity,
and those heartbroken at their going.
We ask for greater trust in you.

Silence

Show up our darkness:
and cancel it with your light.

We thank you and give you glory
for all you are doing in our lives,
and all you have in mind for the future.

Silence

Lord of light,
shine into our darkness with your love,
that we may walk with confidence
in the Way:
through Jesus Christ, our Lord.
Amen.

FROM DARKNESS TO LIGHT

Let us lay at the feet
of God our Father
our needs and our cares,
as we pray together
in the Spirit of Jesus.

We lay at his feet
the need for ministry and leadership,
for a firm witness by all Christians
in the face of materialism and oppression;
for zeal and dedication among all members
of the body of Christ.

Silence

Lord, we trust you:
lead us from darkness to light.

We lay at his feet
the needs of our divided, fractious world;
its systems and schemes,
fashions and disasters;
that God's kingdom of love
may be established on earth,
as it is in heaven.

Silence

Lord, we trust you:
lead us from darkness to light.

We lay at his feet
the needs of all who suffer
in earthquakes, floods, droughts,
famine and epidemics;
all who try to supply relief
and medical aid;
that in Christ we may labour
for the good of the world.

Silence

Lord, we trust you:
lead us from darkness to light.

We lay at his feet
the needs of this community;
the local problems and injustices;
our Christian usefulness
in this corner of God's world.

Silence

Lord, we trust you:
lead us from darkness to light.

In silence, now,
we bring our private prayers to God
who knows what is in our hearts.

Silence

God our Father,
trusting in your constant care and protection,
we bring you these prayers
in the name of Jesus.
Amen.

TEACH US TO
WALK IN YOUR LIGHT

Father, we call to mind the world Church;
we acknowledge our divisions and mistakes
and thank you for transforming them
even as we pray.

Silence

Teach us, Lord,
to walk in your light.

Father, we call to mind the wounds of our world
born of collective greed and terrible blunders
throughout history;
and we praise you as you work to bring wholeness.

Silence

Teach us, Lord:
to walk in your light.

Father, we call to mind the nurturing of children
and the responsibility of parenthood and community;
we need your guidance and grace,
your protection and courage.

Silence

Teach us, Lord:
to walk in your light.

Father, we call to mind those trapped in addictions,
imprisoned by guilt,
and drained through grief;
on their behalf, we plead for rescue.

Silence

Teach us, Lord:
to walk in your light.

Father, we call to mind those who have died,
and those who are dying now,
unnoticed and unloved.

Silence

Teach us, Lord:
to walk in your light.

Father, we call to mind
the way you have dealt with us
so lovingly in the past,
and we commit our future into your keeping.
Teach us, Lord:
to walk in your light,
and lead us on right paths
to your perfect kingdom,
through Jesus Christ, our Saviour.
Amen.

GODLY WISDOM

Our God made us and our universe,
and delights in us.
Prompted by the Spirit of God in us,
let us pray.

We pray for the godly wisdom
that is touched by the beauty of creation,
delights in the diversity of people,
and warms to the possibilities
of co-operative prayer and work
for the coming of the kingdom.

Silence

Wise and holy God:
we are your children.

We pray for the godly wisdom
that, in observing symptoms, discerns causes
and responds to the real needs;
that strives not to control but enable,
not to manipulate but empower.

Silence

Wise and holy God:
we are your children.

We pray for the godly wisdom
that gives others both space and support,
that encourages and guides,
that knows when to speak
and when to be silent.

Silence

Wise and holy God:
we are your children.

We pray for the godly wisdom
that recognises the poverty of the rich
and the wealth among the poor;
that questions assumptions of worth
and cherishes those whom the world discards.

Silence

Wise and holy God:
we are your children.

We pray for the godly wisdom
that sees time in the context of eternity,
and death as the gateway to heaven.

Silence

Wise and holy God:
we are your children.

We pray for the godly wisdom
that lives simply and thankfully,
rejoicing in all that God is and does.

Merciful Father:
accept these prayers
for the sake of your Son,
our Saviour Jesus Christ.
Amen.

God's help
and strength

GOD OUR ROCK

When the pressures of the day
fragment our peace,
keep us watchful and alert,
both for ourselves and for the world.

Silence

For who is God but the Lord:
who is our rock but our God?

When false values are paraded
among the true,
keep us watchful and alert,
both for ourselves and for our young.

Silence

For who is God but the Lord:
who is our rock but our God?

When our tight schedules
leave no time for being merely available,
keep us watchful and alert,
both for ourselves and for those who need a listener.

Silence

For who is God but the Lord:
who is our rock but our God?

When the injustice of the world
laughs at our insignificance,
keep us watchful and alert,
both for ourselves and for all who rely
on our solidarity with them.

Silence

For who is God but the Lord:
who is our rock but our God?

When we begin to take the wonder of
your creation for granted,
keep us watchful and alert,
both for ourselves and for every person
you cherish.

Silence

For who is God but the Lord:
who is our rock but our God?

Now let us spend time in silence
as we bring our personal requests
before God in prayer.

Silence

We thank you, Lord,
that you always watch over our needs.
Help us also to be alert to the needs of others,
for the sake of Jesus Christ.
Amen.

OUR STRONG ROCK
AND OUR SHELTER

As living stones,
let us pray for the building up of God's Church,
and for the world God loves.

Living God, our life is in your hands,
and we offer you all that we are,
all that our past has made us, and all that we may become.
Build us up by the power of your Spirit
into a spiritual temple
where you are glorified day after day,
in all our praise and worship,
and in our love for one another.

Silence

You are our strong rock:
our strong rock and our shelter.

Living God, our planet,
with its frenzied life on its fragile skin,
is unnervingly small and vulnerable to evil.
Sharpen our consciences to sense your direction
and protect us from all that draws us away from you.
Guide our leaders in the way of truth
and realign us all to the values which are built on you.

Silence

You are our strong rock:
our strong rock and our shelter.

Living God, may the Way which Jesus shows us
be the Way we live out our daily lives
around the table, in the daylight and the dark,
in the misunderstandings, the tensions and the rush,
in the eye contact, the conversations and the growing.

Silence

You are our strong rock:
our strong rock and our shelter.

Living God,
we pray for all who feel out of their depth,
who are drowning in their pain, sorrow and guilt.
Save them, Lord,
and help them to a place of safety.
Fix their feet on the solid rock of your love.

Silence

You are our strong rock:
our strong rock and our shelter.

Living God, we remember those who have died
and pray for them now.
Lead them out of their pain
into the light of eternity,
and keep us all in the Way that leads us
to share that everlasting life with you.

Silence

You are our strong rock:
our strong rock and our shelter.

Living God, we thank you
for showing us the Way,
in human terms that we find easier to understand.

Merciful Father:
accept these prayers
for the sake of your Son,
our Saviour Jesus Christ.
Amen.

SUFFICIENT FOR OUR NEEDS

Let us pray to our heavenly Father,
who holds all creation in his care.

We pray for the Christian Church;
that it may truly serve the world,
and proclaim God's love
not only by word
but also through action.

Silence

Yours, Lord, is the power:
sufficient for our needs.

We pray for the world
with its areas of luxury
and deprivation;
that as we become more aware
of the problems,
we may be guided and inspired
to solve them,
and as technology brings us closer,
we may grow in mutual respect
and understanding.

Silence

Yours, Lord, is the power:
sufficient for our needs.

We ask for an outpouring of God's love
on the unnoticed, the unloved
and those for whom no one cares;
those whose lives
are plagued with poverty and disease;
the homeless and the refugees.

Silence

Yours, Lord, is the power:
sufficient for our needs.

We remember the families represented here,
and all families of every nationality;
that children may be nurtured
in love and security,
and homes may be places
of peace and joy.

Silence

Yours, Lord, is the power:
sufficient for our needs.

In silence let us commend
our own particular needs and thankfulness
to the God of power and mercy.

Heavenly Father,
hear these prayers,
through your Son Jesus Christ.
Amen.

THE LORD IS OUR STRENGTH

Let us pray to God, who has promised to hear us
and is always true to his word.

We pray for the world-wide Christian family;
that it may offer hope
to the despairing,
peace to the distressed,
fulfilment to those who seek,
and refreshment to the weary.

Silence

Lord, you are our strength:
we believe and trust in you.

We pray for a shrinking world
and those whose authority can affect it
for good or ill;
that we may all learn
to trust one another
and forgive each other
more readily.

Silence

Lord, you are our strength:
we believe and trust in you.

We bring before their Creator
those who are chronically ill
and in constant pain;
those who are frightened by their illness
and those who are approaching death;
that they may receive the sustaining
peace of Christ,
who knows them personally,
and whose love for them extends
even through death itself.

Silence

Lord, you are our strength:
we believe and trust in you.

We ask God's blessing upon
members of our own families
with their particular needs and difficulties;
on our own lives and spiritual growth;
that we may learn to trust more in God
than in ourselves,
and be alert to his guidance each day.

Silence

Lord, you are our strength:
we believe and trust in you.

We pray in silence to God
who created us and knows our needs.

God our Father,
accept our prayers;
as we learn to trust more in your love,
may we grow to be more like Christ
and reflect the radiance of his love;
through the same Jesus Christ our Lord.
Amen.

STRENGTH IN OUR WEAKNESS

Fellow members of Christ,
let us approach our heavenly Father,
acknowledging the wonder of his involvement with us,
and asking him to help us.

We pray for all who labour to spread the good news,
especially those who face threatening behaviour,
imprisonment or persecution;
for those who are tempted to remain silent
in order to avoid danger to themselves or their families;
that they may be given your courage and your peace.

Silence

Lord, in our weakness:
we ask for your help.

We pray for all the injustice, cruelty
and oppression of our world;
its confusion of priorities,
its lost opportunities and misdirected zeal;
that we may be guided unceasingly
by the level-headed, compassionate leadership
of your Holy Spirit.

Silence

Lord, in our weakness:
we ask for your help.

We pray for our families, friends and neighbours;
for the very young and the very old in our care;
for wisdom to see opportunities of Christ's love,
and for enough energy and time
to do what you need us to.

Silence

Lord, in our weakness:
we ask for your help.

We pray for all who are wounded and injured –
those in hospital and all in pain;
that they may find Christ among them
in their suffering.
We pray for those who inflict pain on others;
for terrorists, murderers
and all who are fired with hatred;
that their lives may be transformed
by encountering Christ.

Silence

Lord, in our weakness:
we ask for your help.

We pray for those on the verge of death
and those who have passed into eternity;
may they rest in your peace for ever.
We give you thanks for all your care and healing love.

Silence

Lord, you are our strength in times of weakness:
accept these prayers
for the sake of Jesus Christ, our Saviour.
Amen.

UPHELD AND BLESSED

As brothers and sisters in Christ,
let us pray
with confidence and faith
to the true and living God.

We pray for the newly baptised
and the recently ordained;
for those who have rejected
their former faith,
and those who are besieged by doubt.

Silence

Father of heaven:
uphold and bless them all.

We pray for those under pressure,
who are tempted
to compromise God's values
of truth and love;
for all who make
far-reaching decisions.

Silence

Father of heaven:
uphold and bless them all.

We pray for all the victims of power struggles,
suffering poverty, neglect,
disease and malnutrition;
for all whose health has been wrecked
by insanitary living and working conditions.

Silence

Father of heaven:
uphold and bless them all.

We pray for ourselves,
for our neighbours and our friends,
for any we have hurt or offended;
for any who have hurt or offended us.

Silence

Father of heaven:
uphold and bless them all.

Together in silence now,
we offer our own private prayers.

Silence

Most loving and merciful Father,
we ask you to take over our lives
and live through them,
and accept these our prayers
in the name of Jesus.
Amen.

LOOKING FOR GOD'S HELP

Companions in Christ, as we remember with gratitude
all that God has done for us,
let us bring to his love the needs and concerns
of the Church and of the world.

We bring to your love, Lord,
the daily work of each member of Christ's body;
that in constant prayer we may learn your will
and your way of doing things,
until we work exclusively for your glory.

Silence

In you we trust:
we look to you for help.

We bring to your love, Lord,
the mistakes, short-sightedness
and arrogance of our world;
that in Christ we may learn to respect one another
and the treasures of the planet we inhabit.

Silence

In you we trust:
we look to you for help.

We bring to your love, Lord,
the wounded and the afraid,
the despairing and the rejected;
that they may find Christ suffering alongside them
and allow him to restore them to wholeness.

Silence

In you we trust:
we look to you for help.

We bring to your love, Lord,
our busy concern with unimportant things;
that in spending more time in Christ's company
we may learn to act and react in all our relationships
with the character and Spirit of Jesus.

Silence

In you we trust:
we look to you for help.

We bring to your love, Lord,
all our dear ones who are separated
from us through death;
that as children of eternity we may always
remember how close they are,
linked by your eternal love.

Silence

In you we trust:
we look to you for help.

Almighty Father, hear the prayers we offer,
and use our bodies, minds and spirits
in establishing your kingdom.

Silence

Lord, give us the faith
to know that you are near
and ready to answer our prayers
for the sake of Jesus, your Son.
Amen.

OUR HELP COMES FROM THE LORD

Lord of glory, we ask you to show us
more of yourself,
to inspire all ministers and teachers of your word,
freshen our faith and cultivate our love.

Silence

Our help comes from the Lord:
who has made heaven and earth.

Lord of glory, we ask your help
in the governing of our planet,
in all national and international decisions
and in the organisation of our resources.

Silence

Our help comes from the Lord:
who has made heaven and earth.

Lord of glory, we ask you to bring
healing and reassurance, comfort and wholeness
to all who suffer.

Silence

Our help comes from the Lord:
who has made heaven and earth.

Lord of glory, we ask you to welcome
into your presence
those who have reached the point of physical death.

Silence

Our help comes from the Lord:
who has made heaven and earth.

Lord of glory, we give you thanks and praise
for all that is good and lovely,
honest and pure.

Silence

Lord of glory:
**may your light shine through our lives
as we try to follow Jesus.
Amen.**

GOD OUR COMPANION

Let us pray to the faithful God who knows us already,
and loves us so much.

We pray that any barriers within the Church,
built up by fear or prejudice, misunderstanding or hurt,
may be broken down in Christ and unity restored.

Silence

As we journey, O Lord:
walk with us on the way.

We pray for our world to be governed wisely and well,
with proper consideration
for the vulnerable and weak,
with co-operation, honesty and respect for all.

Silence

As we journey, O Lord:
walk with us on the way.

We pray for the healing
of hurts and tensions in our families;
and for our friends,
thanking you for the blessings they give;
as friends of Christ, may we be
generous in our friendships.

Silence

As we journey, O Lord:
walk with us on the way.

We pray for those disturbed by mental illness,
and for all who are rejected and despised.
We pray for all in desolate situations at the moment,
and ask for your comfort and healing.

Silence

As we journey, O Lord:
walk with us on the way.

We remember those whose earthly life has ended,
and for those grieving for loved ones.
Enfold them in your love
and let them become aware of you beside them.

Silence

As we journey, O Lord:
walk with us on the way.

We give you thanks, O Lord,
for the loving way you provide for us,
even during the darkest times.

Merciful Father:
accept these prayers
for the sake of your Son,
our Saviour Jesus Christ.
Amen.

GOD KNOWS

Let us pray to the God who has watched our growing
throughout our lives, and loves us.

Lord, there is nothing hidden from you.
All our thoughts and plans and secret fears
are open to you, even when we try to hide them.
Deal with the doubts and misgivings
and fears of your Church,
with the love and mercy which are part of your nature.

Silence

Gracious God:
in you we can trust.

Lord, you feel for the oppressed and the forgotten;
you understand the damage which can lead to violence,
the insecurity which can lead to defensiveness,
and the neglect which can lead to lack of control.
Heal the nations; restore what has been lost;
and turn our hearts to discern your will.

Silence

Gracious God:
in you we can trust.

Lord, you see the point at which
discussions turn to arguments
and preferences to selfishness.
You know the love inside our hearts for one another
that sings and dances and aches and worries.
Work on us now in the depth of our being
and bless our loved ones with a sense of joy.

Silence

Gracious God:
in you we can trust.

Lord, you suffer with those who suffer
and weep with those who weep;
we, too, stand alongside them now
in whatever pain, distress or sorrow
is engulfing them,
longing for them to be comforted.

Silence

Gracious God:
in you we can trust.

Lord, the death and resurrection of Jesus
proclaim the message of hope
amongst the tears of our grieving
for those who have died.
Welcome them into the eternal light of your kingdom.

Silence

Gracious God:
in you we can trust.

Lord, your way may be costly
but to whom else could we go?
For you alone have the words of eternal life,
and we offer you ourselves.

Merciful Father:
**accept these prayers
for the sake of your Son,
our Saviour Jesus Christ.
Amen.**

GOD WILL NEVER LET US DOWN

Father, we remember the church communities
which are thriving
and those which seem to be dying;
we pray for all in both lay and ordained ministry,
and ask you to breathe new life into us all.

Silence

God is with us:
he will never let us down.

Father, we remember the world's leaders
and all in local and national government;
we pray for your wisdom, sensitivity
and integrity.

Silence

God is with us:
he will never let us down.

Father, we remember those we live,
work and relax with;
we pray for your loving to enrich all our relationships
and your spirit of forgiveness
to become second nature to us.

Silence

God is with us:
he will never let us down.

Father, we remember those whose bodies ache,
whose spirits shudder
and whose memories terrify.
We pray for your healing and wholeness.

Silence

God is with us:
he will never let us down.

Father, we remember with thankfulness
the lives and examples of loved ones who have died.
We commend the dead and dying
to your merciful love.

Silence

God is with us:
he will never let us down.

Father, we offer you our thanks and praise
for the many times you have rescued us
and the many blessings you lavish on us each day.

Silence

Father, we give our prayers and our lives
into your hands.
**Use them to fulfil your purpose,
through Jesus Christ, our Lord.
Amen.**

EVER-FAITHFUL GOD

Loving God, because we trust you,
we come to you now with our concerns
for the Church and the world.

We bring all those who find it so hard to believe,
so hard to trust in a faithful loving God;
we bring those who teach the faith;
all who preach and chat the Good News.
Give the right words for each situation and each person,
and enable the seed to take root and grow.

Silence

Ever-faithful God:
in you we put our trust.

We bring those whose authority and decisions
affect the lives of many people and the health of the planet.
We pray for sensitivity and honesty,
and the strength to retain integrity
even in positions of power.

Silence

Ever-faithful God:
in you we put our trust.

We bring the newly born and their parents,
and all whose family circumstances face change;
give us the spiritual flexibility
to adapt to your guiding in all our relationships,
and above all in our relationship with you.

Silence

Ever-faithful God:
in you we put our trust.

We bring all for whom illness or injury
has caused disruption, uncertainty

and the prospect of long-term change;
all who find their lives are spinning
out of their control;
give them working knowledge
of your total loving and unchanging presence,
so that in all the changes and troubles of life
they may be assured of your everlasting protection.

Silence

Ever-faithful God:
in you we put our trust.

We commend to your love and mercy
all those who have made the journey through death,
especially any who have died unprepared,
or violent deaths.
We thank you for your understanding and compassion
and pray that they may know the forgiveness,
peace and joy of heaven.

Silence

Ever-faithful God:
in you we put our trust.

As we call to mind the guidance and help
you give us each moment of every day,
we thank you and praise you, Holy God,
for you alone have the words of eternal life.

Merciful Father:
accept these prayers
for the sake of your Son,
our Saviour Jesus Christ.
Amen.

GOD WORKS IN ALL THINGS FOR OUR GOOD

Father, we pray for the Church
and all Christians in their various callings;
we remember the conflicts and divisions,
and the movement towards unity.

Silence

Lord, we believe:
that in all things you work for our good.

We pray for those who have been given
great responsibility in this world.

Silence

Lord, we believe:
that in all things you work for our good.

We pray for our parents
and all who have influenced our thinking.

Silence

Lord, we believe:
that in all things you work for our good.

We pray for those in great need,
financially, emotionally or physically.

Silence

Lord, we believe:
that in all things you work for our good.

We pray for those whose earthly journey
has come to an end;
and we pray for those who feel empty
without their physical company.

Silence

Lord, we believe:
that in all things you work for our good.

We praise and thank you, Father,
that we can trust you with our lives
both in darkness and in light,
in sorrow and in joy,
in the strength of Jesus Christ,
our Saviour, Companion and Friend.
Amen.

IN THE SHADOW
OF YOUR WINGS

When we are teased or laughed at
for what we believe;
when we find it hard to be faithful,
then we take refuge:
in the shadow of your wings.

Silence

When we are confronted with violence,
homelessness and war,
and stand alongside the victims and outcasts,
then we take refuge:
in the shadow of your wings.

Silence

When we remember our homes,
and those we live near,
and plead for those who do not know
what it is to be loved,
then we take refuge:
in the shadow of your wings.

Silence

When we are ill or in pain,
anxious or fearful,
then we take refuge:
in the shadow of your wings.

Silence

When we approach death;
when we mourn the loss of loved ones,
then we take refuge:
in the shadow of your wings.

Silence

When we delight in the freshness of creation;
when we feel your joy uplifting us,
then we take refuge:
in the shadow of your wings.

Silence

Lord, we find strength and peace
when we come to you in prayer.
**Now send us on our way
equipped to do your will,
through Jesus Christ, our Lord.
Amen.**

SAFE IN THE PALM OF GOD'S HAND

Father, we pray for the Church,
your body on earth, with its richness of variety
and its poverty of splits and schisms.

Silence

You hold our lives:
safe in the palm of your hand.

Father, we pray for the world you have created,
with its struggles for peace
and its cravings for fulfilment.

Silence

You hold our lives:
safe in the palm of your hand.

Father, we pray for this neighbourhood
in which you have placed us,
with its visible activity
and its hidden problems.

Silence

You hold our lives:
safe in the palm of your hand.

Father, we pray for those who are ill
at home or in hospital,
with their longing for health
and their struggle with pain.

Silence

You hold our lives:
safe in the palm of your hand.

We pray for the dead and dying,
with their need for mercy
and their hope of heaven.

Silence

You hold our lives:
safe in the palm of your hand.

We pray with thankfulness and love
for the Spirit transforming our lives.

Silence

Father, help us to know
that through prayer, obedience and love
your kingdom comes:
by the grace of Jesus Christ, our Lord.
Amen.

GOD HEALS AND RESTORES US

Father, we come to you
well aware of our habit of selfishness
which distorts your will
and wastes your opportunities;
and yet in trust we can lean on your love.

Silence

You are our God:
the God who heals and restores us.

Father, we come to you
recognising the human weaknesses
of the Church
and sorrowful at her divisions;
and yet in anticipation we can lean on your love.

Silence

You are our God:
the God who heals and restores us.

Father, we come to you
wearied and angered by the cruelty
and injustice of a self-centred world;
and yet in hope we can lean on your love.

Silence

You are our God:
the God who heals and restores us.

Father, we come to you
sharing the pain of all those who suffer,
sharing the grief of all those who mourn;
and yet in peace we can lean on your love.

Silence

You are our God:
the God who heals and restores us.

Father, we come to you
thrilled by your beauty and wisdom and grace;
and filled with your joy we can lean on your love.

Silence

Father, we come to you in prayer.
**Reach out to us with your healing touch,
through Jesus Christ, our Saviour.
Amen.**

HE RESTORES OUR SOULS

Father, we remember all those who spend
their lives proclaiming your truth and love;
protect them from danger within and without,
and refresh them in times of weariness.

Silence

God of tenderness:
you restore our souls.

Father, we remember all heads of state,
ambassadors and political advisers;
let your will for our world be accomplished
through the decisions they make.

Silence

God of tenderness:
you restore our souls.

Father, we remember all families where
relationships are strained;
let peace and understanding love
find their way into every room.

Silence

God of tenderness:
you restore our souls.

Father, we remember those whose bodies
do not function effectively,
and those whose bodies are abused;
bring some good from their suffering
and healing to their needs.

Silence

God of tenderness:
you restore our souls.

Father, we remember those who have died
and also their families and friends;
let their sadness be comforted.

Silence

God of tenderness:
you restore our souls.

Father, we remember all the ordinary,
everyday delights which make us smile
and lift our hearts.

Silence

God of tenderness:
you restore our souls.
Now may your refreshing Spirit
lift us up
and send us on our way rejoicing
in the company of Christ, our Lord.
Amen.

WE TURN TO YOU FOR HELP

As brothers and sisters in Christ,
let us bring our needs and cares
to the mercy of our heavenly Father.

Let us pray for deepening of prayerfulness
among all Christians,
that firmer faith and greater openness
will lead to a rediscovery
of the love and the purpose of God.

Silence

Father of mercy:
we turn to you for help.

Let us pray for our world,
especially for areas of degradation
and moral decay;
that there may be a turning away
from self-indulgence to self-discipline;
from deception to integrity;
from lawlessness to ordered peace.

Silence

Father of mercy:
we turn to you for help.

Let us pray for those
who have been damaged or injured
through violent abuse, or terrorism;
for all victims of war and rebellion,
and for those who are responsible.

Silence

Father of mercy:
we turn to you for help.

Let us pray for God's strength
in our own lives,
especially in those areas
we know to be weak and open to temptation;
that we may rely more and more on his power
so that we live in him and he in us.

Silence

Father of mercy:
we turn to you for help.

The God of peace is listening:
in this silence
we name our particular concerns.

Silence

Father, hear the prayers of your people,
for the sake of Jesus Christ.
Amen.

WE COME TO
YOU FOR STRENGTH

United in the love of Christ,
let us unburden our needs and cares
to our heavenly Father.

We pray for all lapsed Christians;
all who have known him but rejected him;
all who doubt his love or are hesitant
to trust him with their lives;
that they may all be led back
to his welcoming arms.

Silence

In our weakness, Lord:
we come to you for strength.

We pray for our world
with its blundering mistakes;
its weaknesses for self-indulgence and greed,
its misplaced affections
and well-meant interference;
that lives may be ordered and calmed
by the breath of his Spirit.

Silence

In our weakness, Lord:
we come to you for strength.

We pray for all missing persons
and their families;
all who have lost their way emotionally
or professionally;
all whose minds are blurred or confused;
that all who are lost may be found,
and know the security

of being loved and protected
by their Creator.

Silence

In our weakness, Lord:
we come to you for strength.

We pray for our own lives;
that they may be re-ordered,
calmed and refreshed by his Spirit,
and healed of all that shuts them off
from his love.

Silence

In our weakness, Lord:
we come to you for strength.

God our Father knows our needs;
let us pray to him now
for our own intentions.

Silence

Father,
in thankful love
we ask you to hear our prayers,
for the sake of Jesus Christ.
Amen.

OUR STRENGTH AND JOY

Remembering our dependence
on the power of God for all things,
let us pray to the Lord.

We pray for those whose Christian witness
has brought embarrassment,
rejection or persecution;
that with their sights fixed on Jesus,
Christians may be strengthened and encouraged,
and remain his faithful friends.

Silence

Hear us, Father:
you are our strength and joy.

We pray for all negotiators, diplomats,
envoys and advisers;
that they may seek peace
rather than war,
unity rather than division,
and justice
rather than personal success.

Silence

Hear us, Father:
you are our strength and joy.

We pray that the healing love of God
may work within those
who have been discouraged or hurt;
all who harbour resentment
and the desire for revenge;
the lonely, the timid,
the vulnerable and the abused.

Silence

Hear us, Father:
you are our strength and joy.

We pray for our local community
and all its homes, shops,
schools, surgeries and leisure facilities;
that we, as Christians,
may bring Christ's life and brightness
to this place
so that it is infused with his love.

Silence

Hear us, Father:
you are our strength and joy.

Trustingly, we pray in silence
to God our Father,
who considers each one of us special.

Silence

Loving Father,
hear our prayers,
through Jesus Christ our Lord.
Amen.

LEANING ON GOD

Father, we lean on your love as we pray
for your Church – collectively,
and as a mixed bag of individuals,
with needs, disappointments and fears.

Silence

In all things, Father:
we pray your kingdom in.

We lean on your wisdom as we pray
for local, national and international leaders,
subject to pressures and conflicting values.

Silence

In all things, Father:
we pray your kingdom in.

We lean on your affectionate understanding
as we pray for our homes and all homes in this area,
with their expectations and misunderstandings,
their security and insecurity.

Silence

In all things, Father:
we pray your kingdom in.

We lean on your compassion as we pray
for all who are hurting in body, mind or spirit.

Silence

In all things, Father:
we pray your kingdom in.

We lean on your faithfulness as we pray
for those who have died, and those who mourn.

Silence

In all things, Father:
we pray your kingdom in.

We lean on your accepting love as we pray
in thankfulness for all you are doing in our lives,
and all you have in mind for us in the future.

Silence

Father, we bring you
not only our prayers
but our lives
to be used in the service of your kingdom:
through Jesus Christ, our Lord.
Amen.

ALL THINGS ARE POSSIBLE

Let us pour out to our loving heavenly Father
the areas of need and concern
in the Church and in our world.

We commend to our loving Father
all who persist in working
to spread the news
of Christ's saving love
in spite of poor conditions,
hostility or danger.

Silence

Lord of our strength:
with you all things are possible.

We commend to our loving Father
all who have been elected to govern
both locally and internationally;
that being guided by the light
of truth and goodness
they may be good stewards
of the resources in their care.

Silence

Lord of our strength:
with you all things are possible.

We commend to our loving Father
the chronically and critically ill,
and those who tend them;
the babies being born today,
and the people who will die today.

Silence

Lord of our strength:
with you all things are possible.

We commend to our loving Father
those we love who do not yet know Christ,
or have turned away from him;
that through circumstances
and relationships
they may be drawn to seek him.

Silence

Lord of our strength:
with you all things are possible.

In the knowledge
that God our Father hears us,
let us offer
our own particular prayers.

Silence

Father of mercy,
hear our prayers
which we offer through Jesus Christ.
Amen.

OUR GOD IS ABLE

We pray for everyone who has never yet
heard of Jesus,
and all those who don't yet know
how much God loves them.
Enable us to use each opportunity
we are given
to show God's love in our behaviour.

Silence

With the Lord our God:
nothing is impossible!

We pray for the Queen and those who
govern our country;
we ask God to be among them as they
make important decisions.
We bring to God the many problems
that are so difficult to solve lovingly.

Silence

With the Lord our God:
nothing is impossible!

We pray for all who spend their lives
feeling dissatisfied;
for those who are unhappy, lonely or overworked.
We ask God to lift their spirits
and give them peace and joy.

Silence

With the Lord our God:
nothing is impossible!

We pray for those in pain
and those whose peaceful lives
have suddenly been shattered.

May God help them gather the fragments to start again;
give courage and hope.

Silence

With the Lord our God:
nothing is impossible!

Lord, we thank you that your grace
is sufficient for us,
no matter what happens to us.
In a time of silence in God's company,
let us thank him for his many blessings.

Silence

God of great power and love,
we cast all our care on you:
in the name of Jesus,
Saviour, Lord and Friend.
Amen.

WE PUT OUR TRUST IN GOD

We call to mind all who are insulted
or persecuted for their faith;
all who speak out
and those who are afraid to.

Silence

Help us, O Lord:
we put our trust in you.

We call to mind those working for peace,
justice and hope in an aching world.

Silence

Help us, O Lord:
we put our trust in you.

We call to mind those whose lives
are bound up with ours;
we remember all the families and streets
represented here.

Silence

Help us, O Lord:
we put our trust in you.

We call to mind those whose bodies
battle against disease or pain;
those whose minds battle against confusion
and depression.

Silence

Help us, O Lord:
we put our trust in you.

We call to mind those who are dying
in fear or loneliness;
those who have recently passed into eternity.

Silence

Help us, O Lord:
we put our trust in you.

We call to mind the ways we have been helped
through difficult times,
and have grown to understand more
of your loving care.
And we commend the rest of our life to your keeping.

Silence

Father, trusting in your love,
we lay these prayers before you:
in the name of Jesus Christ.
Amen.

TAKE US BY THE HAND

In our need and human weakness,
let us come to Almighty God with our prayers.

Unchanging God, change us from the heart
until the whole Church awakens to your love
that reaches out, nurtures and celebrates,
neither holding back from what is difficult,
nor rushing where angels fear to tread.
We pray for sensitivity and courage.

Silence

Lord, take us by the hand:
and lead us.

Almighty God, give us such love for the world
that we may pray with longing and desire,
'Your kingdom come.'
Give our leaders the grace to see
their work as service and their role as stewards;
and sharpen both the recognition of needs
and the commitment to just provision.

Silence

Lord, take us by the hand:
and lead us.

Merciful God, break all habits
of destructive behaviour
in our homes and families and friendships.
Develop our ability to celebrate what is good
and face what is not with honesty.

Silence

Lord, take us by the hand:
and lead us.

Healing God, lay your hands on those who suffer,
so that they may know the support of your presence
and find wholeness and peace in your love.
We pray especially for those who are locked
into the conviction
that they are beyond your forgiveness.
May they quickly discover
the freedom of your acceptance.

Silence

Lord, take us by the hand:
and lead us.

Eternal God, in your unchanging love
receive all those who have died in faith,
that they may rejoice in you for ever.

Silence

Lord, take us by the hand:
and lead us.

Gracious God, we thank you for providing us
with a sure hope in which we can face the worst
and not be overwhelmed.

Merciful Father:
accept these prayers
for the sake of your Son,
our Saviour Jesus Christ.
Amen.

Draw us closer

Let us pray to God,
who knows us better than we know ourselves,
and understands our world.

Lord, we know we are called
to be the Body of Christ;
make us worthy of that calling,
fervent in all our prayer and worship,
loving, faithful and honest in our lives,
so that the whole Church displays
what God is like.

Silence

Draw us closer:
closer to your heart, O God.

We pray for the grace and wisdom
to care for this world we have been given as our home;
for perception in the difficult decisions,
and commitment to justice and peace.

Silence

Draw us closer:
closer to your heart, O God.

We pray for the homes of this community,
whose hopes and struggles, sorrows and fears
are already known to you.
May each household be blessed as we pray,
and may your love fill each life.

Silence

Draw us closer:
closer to your heart, O God.

We pray for all who do not yet know you,
and all whose hearts are poisoned with hate

or weighed down with despair.
May your light scatter their darkness
and bring them hope and healing.

Silence

Draw us closer:
closer to your heart, O God.

We pray for those who have died to this life
and are born into your heaven;
comfort those who miss their physical presence,
and bring us all to share in the fullness of your life.

Silence

Draw us closer:
closer to your heart, O God.

We give you thanks for all that points us
towards the beauty of your love,
and draws us closer to you.

Merciful Father:
**accept these prayers
for the sake of your Son,
our Saviour Jesus Christ.
Amen.**

WE SHALL BE IN SAFETY

When following you brings danger, Lord,
or weariness or discomfort,
we long for your help.

Silence

In the shadow of your wings:
we shall be in safety.

When we watch the violence and selfishness
of this world,
its bewilderment and fear,
we long for your peace.

Silence

In the shadow of your wings:
we shall be in safety.

When we work through our relationships
and feel for those we love,
we long for your guidance.

Silence

In the shadow of your wings:
we shall be in safety.

When our hearts touch those who suffer,
and know their pain and distress,
we long for your healing love.

Silence

In the shadow of your wings:
we shall be in safety.

When those we love meet death
and we must let them go,
we long for your mercy and welcome.

Silence

In the shadow of your wings:
we shall be in safety.

When we see the beauty and wonder
of your glorious creation and of your holiness,
we long for an eternity to praise you.

Silence

Lord, you have made us long for you.
Help us to find you in love and in prayer:
through Jesus Christ, your Son.
Amen.

GOD OUR REFUGE

Father, we pray for all whose Christian ministry
brings hardship and persecution.

Silence

Keep us safe, O God:
for in you we take refuge.

Father, we pray for all in positions of power
and responsibility,
and those negotiating for peace.

Silence

Keep us safe, O God:
for in you we take refuge.

Father, we pray for those amongst whom
we live and work,
for our friends and all whom we value.

Silence

Keep us safe, O God:
for in you we take refuge.

Father, we pray for all who feel
overwhelmed with troubles,
and all who are mentally or physically impaired.

Silence

Keep us safe, O God:
for in you we take refuge.

Father, we pray for those who are fearful
or superstitious,
and those who long to believe in your reality.

Silence

Keep us safe, O God:
for in you we take refuge.

Father, we thank you for all you have taught us
and all you are teaching us in our lives
at the moment.

Silence

Lord God, we put our trust in you,
who made us and redeemed us:
through Jesus Christ, our Lord.
Amen.

LEAD US NOT INTO TEMPTATION

As children of our heavenly Father,
who knows us so well and loves us completely,
let us pray.

Father, knowing our weakness in the face of temptation,
we ask for your strength and protection
so that, though we stumble,
we shall not fall headlong.

Silence

Lead us not into temptation:
but deliver us from evil.

Father, we pray for all those who are fighting temptation
and finding it difficult to resist.
We ask you to help them see clearly,
and equip them with all they need
to choose what is right.

Silence

Lead us not into temptation:
but deliver us from evil.

Father, we pray for the Church
as it struggles to steer a straight course
true to your calling.
We pray for wisdom and courage,
honesty and the willingness to be vulnerable.

Silence

Lead us not into temptation:
but deliver us from evil.

Father, we pray for those we love,
whose company we enjoy.

We pray too for those who irritate us
and those whom we annoy.

Silence

Lead us not into temptation:
but deliver us from evil.

Father, we stand alongside all those who suffer,
all whose lives are in chaos or despair,
and all who live in the dark prison of guilt.
We pray for your reassurance and peace,
your understanding and compassion.

Silence

Lead us not into temptation:
but deliver us from evil.

We pray for the dying,
especially the unnoticed and despised.
We pray for those who have gone through death
and now see you face to face,
that they may receive your merciful forgiveness
and know the joy of living with you for ever.

Silence

Lead us not into temptation:
but deliver us from evil.

Father, we thank you for the knowledge
that nothing is beyond your forgiveness,
and no one beyond the limits of your love.

Silence

Merciful Father:
accept these prayers
for the sake of your Son,
our Saviour Jesus Christ.
Amen.

DELIVER US FROM EVIL

Companions in Christ,
knowing that our heavenly Father
has sufficient grace for all our needs,
let us pray to him now.

Lord, we pray for the leaders and ministers
of your Church, especially those for whom
your work has brought danger and persecution;
may they never lose sight of your presence,
which comforts and protects.

Silence

Lord of power:
deliver us from evil.

We pray for clear light and guidance as our world faces
the problems and crises of another week;
for the willingness of leaders
to be wisely advised and courageous
in doing what is right.

Silence

Lord of power:
deliver us from evil.

We pray for a greater willingness in us
to live and work in your strength;
for a deepening trust in your power
to save, heal and overcome temptation.

Silence

Lord of power:
deliver us from evil.

We pray for all addicted to drugs,
alcohol, solvent abuse, violence,

or any other habit that enslaves;
for all victims of war, and abuse;
for the terrified and the suicidal.

Silence

Lord of power:
deliver us from evil.

We pray that all who have passed from this life
may live in the joy of your presence for ever.

Silence

Lord of all power:
deliver us from evil.

Thank you, Father, for all the evils
that have been conquered,
and all the good that is done through your power
every day throughout our world.
Help us to notice your goodness.

Silence

Father, we bring these prayers
trusting in the power of your love,
which you have shown to us
in Jesus Christ, our Lord.
Amen.

COURAGE IN SUFFERING

As children and heirs through adoption,
and knowing that Jesus shares in all our suffering and joy,
let us confide in our heavenly Father
who knows us so well.

Father, into your enlightenment and perception
we bring all whose faith is limited by fear or prejudice;
all whose living faith has been replaced
by the empty shell of habit.

Silence

Father, give us courage:
you are our only strength.

Father, into the depths of your wisdom
and understanding we bring those with responsibilities,
and all who have difficult decisions to make;
all those in charge of hospitals, schools,
industry and all community services.

Silence

Father, give us courage:
you are our only strength.

Into your tireless faithfulness we bring any
who rely on us for help, support or guidance;
any whom we are being asked to serve
or introduce to your love.

Silence

Father, give us courage:
you are our only strength.

Into the gentleness of your healing love
we bring all who are in pain;
all those recovering from surgery;

those involved in crippling accidents
or suffering from wasting diseases.

Silence

Father, give us courage:
you are our only strength.

Into your light and peace
we commend those who have died,
especially any dear to us
whom we name in the silence of our hearts.

Silence

Father, give us courage:
you are our only strength.

Father, we thank you for supporting us
and encouraging us when life is hard,
and for all the exuberant vitality
of the world you have created for us to live in.

Silence

Give us the faith to see that you are with us
in sorrow as well as in joy,
in darkness as well as light:
through Jesus Christ, our Lord.
Amen.

Our Lord
Jesus Christ

THE WORD MADE FLESH

Let us pray to the God
who loved us enough to come and save us in Jesus.

We pray for the areas of the Church
which are weak in faith,
despondent or complacent;
that we may be recharged
with the power of your love,
reawakened to the good news,
and revitalised with the breath of the Spirit.

Silence

Living Word of God:
be spoken in our lives.

We pray for all areas of misunderstanding
between peoples and nations,
between needs and offers of help;
make us more ready to listen than instruct,
more ready to encourage than crush.

Silence

Living Word of God:
be spoken in our lives.

We pray for family feuds and difficulties
to be resolved and learnt from;
for the words we speak
to express love and respect,
with true charity and forgiveness.

Silence

Living Word of God:
be spoken in our lives.

We pray for all who have difficulty
hearing and speaking,

reading and writing;
for the oppressed and persecuted
whose voices are silenced,
and for all who have yet to hear
the good news of your love.

Silence

Living Word of God:
be spoken in our lives.

We pray for those who have died
and those who are dying now;
may your Word of life
encourage them on their journey
and bring them safely to your eternal kingdom.

Silence

Living Word of God:
be spoken in our lives.

We pray in thankfulness
for the joy of human communication
and the privilege of communing with the living God.

Merciful Father:
accept these prayers
for the sake of your Son,
our Saviour Jesus Christ.
Amen.

LIVING WORD

Let us pray to God our Father
because he loves us so dearly.

We pray that the Word who became flesh
may be so manifest in our lives
that other people notice
and are attracted to Jesus
by the way we live and love.

Silence

Living Word:
speak to us today.

We pray that the world may stop
its noise, chatter and arguing
long enough to recognise
the Word of hope and peace.

Silence

Living Word:
speak to us today.

We pray that God will bless and support
all expectant mothers
and those in labour;
and that all new-born babies
and young children
may be cherished, loved
and protected
as they bear God's love
to us anew.

Silence

Living Word:
speak to us today.

We pray that there may be more
understanding and mercy
in our family relationships,
with Christ always among us –
not an occasional visitor.

Silence

Living Word:
speak to us today.

We name in this silence
any known to us
with particular needs and burdens.

Silence

Father,
we can never thank you enough
for coming to save us;
please hear our prayers which we offer
through Jesus, your Son.
Amen.

EMMANUEL

God is here with us now.
Let us pray.

Lord, we want to be ready to receive you.
Take us as we are and cultivate in us
a heart that longs for you and worships you
above and beyond everything else.

Silence

Come, O come:
Emmanuel, God with us.

We open to your love
the spiritual journeys of all who walk your way;
protect them from evil
and keep them steadfast in faith.

Silence

Come, O come:
Emmanuel, God with us.

We pray for those who give us support
and encourage us and listen to us
and make us laugh and share our sorrows.
Bless their lives and give them joy.

Silence

Come, O come:
Emmanuel, God with us.

We remember in your presence
those whose memories are painful,
and those whose bitter resentment
cramps and distorts present relationships.
We ask for the healing only you can give.

Silence

Come, O come:
Emmanuel, God with us.

We call to mind those we know who have died,
and any who are close to death at the moment.
As they meet you, the one true God,
open their hearts to receive your love,
mercy and forgiveness.

Silence

Come, O come:
Emmanuel, God with us.

We give you thanks, Lord,
for the way none of us is beyond your saving love
and the way you have promised
to keep us ultimately safe.

Merciful Lord:
accept these prayers
which we bring in your name,
our Saviour Jesus Christ.
Amen.

CHRIST'S HEALING POWER

Bound together in the Spirit of Christ,
let us pray together
for his healing power.

We pray that wherever there is blindness,
prejudice or lack of vision in the Church,
Christ will work his healing power
to refresh, enlighten and transform.

Silence

Fill us, Lord Jesus:
with your healing power.

We pray that wherever personality conflicts,
errors of judgement or insensitivity
threaten peace,
God's Spirit may be allowed access,
to work towards harmony and goodwill.

Silence

Fill us, Lord Jesus:
with your healing power.

We pray that all who are troubled and distressed
by pain, illness,
poverty, hunger
or any other suffering,
may experience the personal love
and loyalty
of the healing Christ.

Silence

Fill us, Lord Jesus:
with your healing power.

We pray that we may be more sensitive
to the needs of those with whom

we live and work,
less critical,
and better prepared
to encourage and forgive.

Silence

Fill us, Lord Jesus:
with your healing power.

To God our heavenly Father,
we pray for our own needs and concerns.

Silence

Father,
you pour out your blessings so richly on us;
with thankful hearts we praise you,
and ask you to hear our prayers,
through Jesus Christ our Lord.
Amen.

JESUS KING OF LOVE

As we welcome Jesus,
and hail him as our King,
let us offer to him in prayer
the deep concerns and needs
of the Church and the world.

We bring to his love all who are baptised,
and especially those who have lost their faith
or stopped praying;
that they may be brought back
through Christ's love,
and put into contact with those
who can guide and reassure them.

Silence

Jesus, King of Love:
we pledge ourselves to your service.

We bring to his love all gatherings of people:
all meetings, or political demonstrations,
social and sporting events,
that they may be peaceful and ordered,
offering enjoyment, or influencing for good,
rather than inciting to violence and evil.

Silence

Jesus, King of Love:
we pledge ourselves to your service.

We bring to his love those suffering
from incurable or life-threatening diseases;
those who are denied necessary medical care;
that we may be ready to use our time,
money and influence,
so that unnecessary suffering and death are avoided.

Silence

Jesus, King of Love:
we pledge ourselves to your service.

We bring to his love our own loved ones,
families and friends,
and especially those
from whom we are separated;
people who are missing from their homes
and those who wait for them;
that God's powerful love
may be a protection against all evil.

Silence

Jesus, King of Love:
we pledge ourselves to your service.

Knowing that God our Father
hears the cries of his children,
we pray in silence for our own needs and cares.

Silence

Merciful Father,
we know that you hold all life in your hand;
please hear our prayers,
through Jesus our Redeemer.
Amen.

CHRIST THE GOOD SHEPHERD

As followers of the Good Shepherd,
let us bring with us the needs
of all our brothers and sisters.
Let us pray together.

We pray for the Church,
that in its various ministries
it may never lead any astray,
but always follow faithfully
the way of Jesus Christ
the Good Shepherd.

Silence

Guide us, Good Shepherd:
along the right path.

We pray for the world,
that in striving to do God's will
we may not abuse or waste our talents
in thoughtless destruction,
but rather work with our Creator
to heal, conserve and fulfil.

Silence

Guide us, Good Shepherd:
along the right path.

We pray for those who are ill,
and those who look after them;
that even in pain and discomfort
they may recognise Christ,
who also suffered,
and who is full of caring
and compassion.

Silence

Guide us, Good Shepherd:
along the right path.

We pray for all of us here,
and the families we represent;
that in following Jesus, the Shepherd,
we may be liberated
to live selfless, generous lives.

Silence

Guide us, Good Shepherd:
along the right path.

In a time of silence
we share with God our Father
our personal burdens, joys and sorrows.

Silence

Father,
hear our prayer;
in joy may we follow the way of Christ,
who alone has the words of eternal life,
through the same Jesus Christ, our Lord.
Amen.

THE LORD IS MY SHEPHERD

The Lord is our shepherd,
and we are the sheep of his pasture.
Let us bring to him our cares and concerns
for the Church and for the world.

Good Shepherd of the sheep, we pray for the Church;
for all congregations, for pastors
and all who minister in word and sacrament.
We pray for clear guidance and direction
in those issues which disturb us,
asking not that you lead us the easy way
but the way that is right and good.

Silence

The Lord is my shepherd:
there is nothing I shall want.

Good Shepherd of the sheep,
we pray for the world we inhabit –
the world we have inherited
and will pass on to successive generations.
Teach us to look after it carefully and wisely,
to share its gifts more fairly,
and work together to ease its sufferings.
Turn the hearts of those who are excited by evil things
and encourage the timid to speak out
for what is wholesome and good.

Silence

The Lord is my shepherd:
there is nothing I shall want.

Good Shepherd of the sheep, we pray for our
places of work, our colleagues, friends and neighbours,
and the members of our families.
We ask not for popularity at all costs,

but the grace to do your will and be your witnesses
to what it means to live lovingly,
both when this is easy and also when it hurts.

Silence

The Lord is my shepherd:
there is nothing I shall want.

Good Shepherd of the sheep,
we pray for the weak and vulnerable,
for those who must live
depending on others for every need,
and for those who are bullied, or constantly despised.
We pray for a greater reverence, one for another,
for a greater willingness
to uphold and encourage one another;
we pray for healing and wholeness.

Silence

The Lord is my shepherd:
there is nothing I shall want.

Good Shepherd of the sheep,
we pray for those who have died;
we pray for those who ache with sorrow at their going;
we commend them all into your unfailing care
which lasts throughout this life and on into eternity.

Silence

The Lord is my shepherd:
there is nothing I shall want.

Good Shepherd of the sheep, we give you thanks
that in you we are able to live through good and ill
with abundance of life.

Merciful Father:
accept these prayers
for the sake of your Son,
our Saviour Jesus Christ.
Amen.

THE BREAKING OF BREAD

As we gather to hear the word of God
and to break bread in the presence of Jesus,
let us pray.

Walk with us, Lord, on our journey of faith,
both as individuals and as the Church of God;
open up to us the truths you long for us to understand,
and inspire all who teach and interpret the scriptures.
Equip us all to pass on the good news of your love.

Silence

Make yourself known to us, Lord:
in the breaking of bread.

Walk with us, Lord, down the streets
of our cities, towns and villages,
drive with us down the motorways
and fly with us down the air corridors.
Meet all those who are curious, searching,
or moving in the wrong direction.
Let your presence be sought
and recognised in all the world.

Silence

Make yourself known to us, Lord:
in the breaking of bread.

Walk with us, Lord, in our life journeys,
guiding, teaching and correcting us,
as we learn the lessons of loving
in our homes, our work and our communities.

Silence

Make yourself known to us, Lord:
in the breaking of bread.

Walk with us, Lord,
through the times of suffering and pain,
alerting us to one another's needs
and providing for us in whatever ways are best for us.
Help us to trust you through the dark times;
breathe new life and hope
into those who are close to despair.

Silence

Make yourself known to us, Lord:
in the breaking of bread.

Walk with us, Lord, through the valley of death;
may our love and prayers support those
who walk that journey today.
Draw close to them and welcome them
into the joy of heaven.

Silence

Make yourself known to us, Lord:
in the breaking of bread.

Lord, we thank you for walking with us
wherever we travel.
We thank you that you are indeed
real and alive every step of the way!

Merciful Father:
**accept these prayers
for the sake of your Son,
our Saviour Jesus Christ.
Amen.**

RISEN LORD

As sharers in Christ's risen life,
in trust and thankfulness
let us pray to the Lord.

We pray for the work of the Church
in every country,
especially where Christian witness
brings danger;
that the Spirit of Christ
may nurture life and hope
in the world's darkest areas.

Silence

Risen Lord:
instil in us your peace.

We pray for all who encourage others
to squander their time,
money or talents;
all who lead others into drug addiction;
that they may come to know Christ
as the only treasure worth worshipping.

Silence

Risen Lord:
instil in us your peace.

We pray for all whose characters
have become hardened and twisted
through jealousy, resentment or hatred;
that they may at last recognise
their need for repentance
and come to Christ to be restored
to the joy of new life in him.

Silence

Risen Lord:
instil in us your peace.

We pray for those who helped
to bring us to know Christ,
and those who turn us back to him
when we wander away;
that in humility we may always be glad to learn
and ready to accept criticism,
in order to grow as Christians.

Silence

Risen Lord:
instil in us your peace.

We name in silence now
any known to us
with particular needs and burdens.

Silence

Heavenly Father,
slow to anger and quick to forgive;
immerse us in your Spirit
and let your will be done in our lives,
through Jesus Christ our Lord.
Amen.

LIFE-GIVING LORD

In the presence of the risen Christ,
let us lift our hearts and pray.

We pray for all who are called
to particular ministries
within the Church;
all ordained ministers,
theological students and teachers,
that as they learn together
they may grow in wisdom and humility
and be increasingly filled
with the life of Christ.

Silence

Lord, stand among us:
and give us new life.

We pray for all areas of bureaucracy
which frustrate and delay
the course of useful action;
for all areas of instability
and political corruption;
that whatever is good may flourish and grow,
so that evil may be overcome
and rendered powerless.

Silence

Lord, stand among us:
and give us new life.

We pray for all who suffer from pain or disease,
and those who tend them;
that they may be comforted.

Silence

Lord, stand among us:
and give us new life.

We pray for all who are engaged
or newly married;
for those coping with family problems,
difficult circumstances or bereavement;
that they may lean on
the loving presence of Christ
who dispels all fear
and brings life and peace.

Silence

Lord, stand among us:
and give us new life.

Trustingly, we pray in silence
to our loving Lord
who considers each one of us special.

Silence

Lord,
we thank you for your constant
life-renewing love,
and offer these prayers
in your name.
Amen.

MY LORD AND MY GOD!

Knowing that the risen Christ is here among us,
let us pray in his name
for the Church and for the world.

Living Lord, we pray for your blessing
on every group of Christians worshipping today
all over the world;
and we pray for all who doubt your truth.
We pray that our hearts may be set ablaze
with love,
and that we may walk as children of light.

Silence

My Lord and my God!
My Lord and my God!

Living Lord, we pray for all the areas of your world
which are torn apart by hatred and violence,
famine, disease, or religious differences;
we pray for an end to war
and a deeper commitment to peace.

Silence

My Lord and my God!
My Lord and my God!

Living Lord, we pray for those who face family rejection
if they become Christians,
and for all families divided by beliefs
or persecuted for their faith.
We pray for the children of our church
that they may grow up strong in the faith
with good role models to guide them.

Silence

My Lord and my God!
My Lord and my God!

Living Lord, we pray for those who wake up
to the prospect of another day filled with pain;
for those who long for someone
to spend time with them, enjoying their company;
and we pray for sight that notices needs.

Silence

My Lord and my God!
My Lord and my God!

Living Lord, we pray for those who mourn,
and we pray for those they love and miss,
commending all who have died
to the everlasting arms of the God of love,
in whom there is life in all its fullness.

Silence

My Lord and my God!
My Lord and my God!

Jesus, our Redeemer, with joy in our hearts we thank you
for the new life you have opened up to us all.

Accept these prayers:
which we ask in your name.
Amen.

RISEN WITH CHRIST

Let us pray to our Lord Jesus Christ,
who is familiar with our world
and understands our humanity.
Lord of all, wherever Christians are ridiculed
or persecuted for their faith,
we ask your courage and inner strength;
wherever we are called to be your witnesses,
we ask for the grace to communicate your love.
Wherever love for you has grown cold
we ask to fan the flames again.

Silence

In Christ we can be dead to sin:
and alive to God.

Lord, wherever the human spirit
is ground down by oppression,
and wherever our silence allows injustice
and corruption to flourish,
we ask for deeper compassion and commitment;
we ask for our kingdoms to become your kingdoms,
and the desires of your heart to be ours.

Silence

In Christ we can be dead to sin:
and alive to God.

Lord of all, wherever families are struggling
to stay together,
and wherever there are ongoing arguments
and family feuds,
we ask your anointing for tranquillity and harmony.
Wherever children are unwanted and unloved,
neglected or in danger, we ask your protection and help.

Silence

In Christ we can be dead to sin:
and alive to God.

Lord, wherever bodies, minds or spirits
are wracked with pain,
or too weak or exhausted to pray,
we ask the bathing love of your presence,
and the practical caring of hands working in your name.
Wherever there are doubts and the battle is strong,
we ask your empowering and clear guidance.

Silence

In Christ we can be dead to sin:
and alive to God.

Lord of all,
wherever the dying are anxious and afraid,
we ask your peace;
wherever the faithful have passed
from this life into eternity,
we commend them to your unchanging
and everlasting love.

Silence

In Christ we can be dead to sin:
and alive to God.

Wherever nature's beauty or the daily miracles around us
alert us to see your face, we thank you for the grace
to live this resurrection life.

Merciful Lord:
accept these prayers
which we ask in your name,
our Saviour Jesus Christ.
Amen.

CHRIST THE WAY

My companions in Christ,
as we gather in the great hope
of our risen Lord who leads us,
let us pray for the needs of his Church and world.

We pray for unity among all who follow
the Way of Christ;
that in keeping our eyes fixed on him
we may be enabled to dissolve barriers,
to forgive and be reconciled,
through the healing power of accepting love.

Silence

Lord, guide us:
to do things your way.

We pray for all in positions of responsibility
and leadership,
both internationally and in our own community;
that they may themselves be led by Christ's Spirit
to make wise decisions
and help create a humane caring world.

Silence

Lord, guide us:
to do things your way.

We pray for our homes and families,
with their hopes and sorrows,
difficulties and celebrations;
that all our relationships may be bathed
in Christ's love and compassion.

Silence

Lord, guide us:
to do things your way.

We pray for those who incite others
to antisocial or criminal behaviour;
for all involved in drugs traffic;
that they may open their hearts
and allow Christ to transform and heal;
for the weak, lonely, young and depressed
who are so vulnerable to their temptations;
that they may have help and strength to resist
the pressures on and around them.

Silence

Lord, guide us:
to do things your way.

We pray that those who have died in faith
may be welcomed into the eternal joy of heaven,
to live with Christ for ever.

Silence

We thank you, Lord, for all the richness of this beautiful world;
for the gift of life and time to spend;
for your example and companionship,
who are the Way, the Truth and the Life.

Silence

Lord, hear our prayers:
and make us ready to accept your way.
Amen.

CHRIST THE KING OF GLORY

Let us pray in the name of Jesus Christ
in whom is our hope of redemption.

We pray for all those involved
in spreading God's word
of truth and joy;
that their lives may be instruments
by which God's love
is spread through the world.

Silence

Christ, King of Glory:
help us to do your will.

We remember in prayer
the many different cultures and races
which make up Creation;
that we may all learn
from one another,
until God's kingdom
is established on earth.

Silence

Christ, King of Glory:
help us to do your will.

We pray for the casualties of materialistic,
unjust or corrupt society;
that, in the light of Christ,
people may recognise needs
and have the courage to act.

Silence

Christ, King of Glory:
help us to do your will.

We hold in the light of Christ's love
each person here,
and the circle of lives
linked to each one
at home and at work;
that with these immediate contacts
we may open the way for God to act
by becoming channels of his peace
and his redemptive love.

Silence

Christ, King of Glory:
help us to do your will.

We pray in silence, now,
for our own particular needs and concerns.

Father,
accept our prayers;
fit us for heaven,
to live with you for ever,
through Jesus Christ our Lord.
Amen.

CHRIST OUR KING

Let us pray in the name of Christ,
who is here among us
and cares for us all.

We pray for the needs of his Church
as it works to reconcile humanity
with its Creator;
that Christians may speak
in words the world understands,
advising wisely, counselling lovingly
and welcoming wholeheartedly.

Silence

Christ, our King:
guide us in love.

We pray for the needs of each community
on this planet;
that wherever feelings have boiled over
and are out of control,
the calm reassurance of Christ
may restore harmony and goodwill.

Silence

Christ, our King:
guide us in love.

We pray for those attending hospitals and clinics,
those in residential homes;
for their relatives and friends,
and the staff who look after them;
that they may be sustained, strengthened,
and brought to wholeness
by the healing God of love.

Silence

Christ, our King:
guide us in love.

We pray for all who lead lonely, unhappy lives;
all whose marriages are crumbling;
all who cannot cope
with the demands of family life;
that as members of Christ
we may be shown where we can help,
and be given courage to act.

Silence

Christ, our King:
guide us in love.

We name in silence now
any known to us
with particular needs or burdens.

Silence

Loving Father,
we bring you these prayers
through Christ our Lord,
and through him we offer ourselves
to be used in your service.
Amen.

REIGN IN OUR HEARTS

Trusting in Christ's victory over all evil,
let us pray to him
for the world and the Church.

Lord, we pray for all who witness to you
in spite of danger and persecution;
all who work to bring others to know and love you;
that in your strength they may be blessed,
encouraged and bear much fruit.

Silence

King of glory:
reign in our hearts.

We pray for those who have never received
the good news of your saving love;
for those areas where violence and terrorism
make normal life impossible;
that your spirit, the spirit of Peace,
may filter through to increase love
and understanding, respect and goodwill.

Silence

King of glory:
reign in our hearts.

We pray for our families
and those with whom we live and work;
for particular needs known to us personally;
that in everything we do,
and every minute we live,
your name may be glorified
and your will be done.

Silence

King of glory:
reign in our hearts.

We pray for the sick and the dying;
that their trust in you may deepen
until their fears are calmed
and they can look forward with real hope
to meeting their Saviour face to face.

Silence

King of glory:
reign in our hearts.

We pray for those who have died;
may they wake to the joy of eternal life with you.

Silence

King of glory:
reign in our hearts.

We offer you thanks and praise
for your constant love and kindness,
and especially for the joy of your salvation.
Accept these prayers
for the sake of Jesus Christ, our Lord.
Amen.

RULE IN OUR LIVES

Through Jesus, our King, let us pray.

Lord Jesus, head of the Church, your body,
we pray for all the members
with their various gifts and ministries;
we pray that even our weaknesses
can be used to your glory
for the good of the world.

Silence

Jesus, our King:
rule in our lives.

May all governments and heads of state
be led in ways of truth and righteousness,
and recognise with humility
that they are called to serve.
We pray for all rescue teams and trouble-shooters;
for all who work to recover the lost.

Silence

Jesus, our King:
rule in our lives.

May we reach out to one another
with greater love and better understanding;
we pray for our homes, our relatives,
our neighbours and our friends,
particularly those who do not yet realise
the extent of your love for them.

Silence

Jesus, our King:
rule in our lives.

May those who have been scattered
far from their homes and loved ones

be enabled to live again in peace and happiness;
may the bitter and resentful find hope again
and the confused find new direction.

Silence

Jesus, our King:
rule in our lives.

May the dying know your closeness,
and those who mourn their loved ones
know for certain that your kingdom
stretches across both sides of death.

Silence

Jesus, our King:
rule in our lives.

Our hearts are filled with thanksgiving
as we realise again
the extraordinary extent of your love for us.

Merciful Father:
**accept these prayers
for the sake of your Son,
our Saviour Jesus Christ.
Amen.**

GIVE US YOUR STRENGTH

Fellow pilgrims, as we come to Jesus
and hail him as our King,
let us offer to him in prayer
the deep concerns and needs
of the Church and of the world.

We bring to your love all who are baptised,
and especially those who have lost their faith
or have stopped praying;
may they be brought back through your love,
and put into contact with those
who can guide and reassure them.

Silence

Christ, our King:
give us your strength.

We bring to your love every meeting, demonstration,
convention and all large crowds; may they be peaceful
and ordered, inspiring those present for good,
rather than inciting them to violence.

Silence

Christ, our King:
give us your strength.

We bring to your love our own loved ones,
the members of our families, our friends
and especially those from whom we are separated,
 either by distance or death;
and all who are missing from their homes;
may your powerful love protect us from all that is evil.

Silence

Christ, our King:
give us your strength.

We bring to your love those suffering
from incurable or life-threatening diseases;
those who need medical care, but are either too poor
or live too far away to receive it;
make us more ready to help
with our time, money and influence,
so that unnecessary suffering and death are avoided.

Silence

Christ, our King:
give us your strength.

We bring to your love those who have died;
may they rest in the light and joy
of your presence for ever.

Silence

Lord, may we praise you not only with our voices
but also in the lives we lead,
that the words of our prayers
may be always more than matched
by the value of our deeds.
Christ, our king:
give us your strength.
Amen.

CHRIST OUR HOPE

In the spirit of Christ,
who has promised he will return,
let us pray together
for the needs of the Church
and of the world.

Let us pray that the Church
and all its members
may never become static
but flow constantly forward
in the direction God wants us to go,
true to Christ's teaching,
in unswerving loyalty to him
and undistracted by worldly values.

Silence

Lord Jesus, give us wisdom:
to know and love you more.

Let us pray that we may tend
and care for the world
God has given us;
that its food and riches may be shared
and wisely used,
and its resources safely
and thoughtfully deployed
without waste or destruction.

Silence

Lord Jesus, give us wisdom:
to know and love you more.

Let us pray that all those
who are ill, injured or distressed
may be touched
by the healing hand of Jesus

and be made whole,
comforted by his presence.

Silence

Lord Jesus, give us wisdom:
to know and love you more.

Let us pray that we may be more watchful,
preparing ourselves more thoroughly
day by day
to meet our Lord
face to face.

Silence

Lord Jesus, give us wisdom:
to know and love you more.

In a time of silence,
we share with Jesus
our personal burdens, joys and sorrows.

Silence

Lord,
whose character is full
of mercy and compassion,
accept these prayers
for your name's sake.
Amen.

THE HOPE OF THE WORLD

Trusting in the promise of God
that he will never desert us,
let us approach him
with our cares and concerns.

Let us pray for all people
who are imprisoned or persecuted
because of their faith;
for the lapsed and the doubting;
that they may know
the sovereignty of God,
and his presence in Christ,
in all areas of life.

Silence

O Lord, you are our hope:
you are the hope of the world.

Let us pray for the world of commerce,
trade and the media;
that Christ's peaceful presence
at the heart of business
may make them channels
for enlightenment and discernment,
and instruments for good
in our society.

Silence

O Lord, you are our hope:
you are the hope of the world.

Let us pray for the malnourished,
those whose land no longer supports them;
that all people may be inspired
to care for one another,
to share the world's resources

in mutual trust,
and be living signs of hope
for us all.

Silence

O Lord, you are our hope:
you are the hope of the world.

Let us pray for ourselves and our families,
that our day-to-day concerns
may not blind us to God's love,
but rather be infused by it
so that he is central in our lives.

Silence

O Lord, you are our hope:
you are the hope of the world.

In the silence of our hearts
we pray to our heavenly Father
about our own particular concerns.

Silence

Lord, we pray in hope;
hear these prayers
for the sake of Jesus, our Saviour.
Amen.

THE LIGHT OF THE WORLD

Fellow travellers of Christ's way,
let us pray together
for the Church and for the world.

Lord, may our Christian witness,
in a confused and nervous world,
shine with a piercing integrity and warmth
that awakens people's hearts to the love of their Creator.

Silence

Light of the world:
shine in our lives.

Bless and protect all travellers and pilgrims;
teach us to cherish the beauty of your world
and share its riches.

Silence

Light of the world:
shine in our lives.

Help us to see you in the eyes of all those we meet,
and delight in giving you glory
by serving others without expecting rewards.

Silence

Light of the world:
shine in our lives.

Direct our vision to see
the best practical ways of providing
shelter for the homeless,
safe accommodation for those who live in fear of violence,
and food for the hungry.

Silence

Light of the world:
shine in our lives.

May all who have died in faith
be bathed in the everlasting light
of your loving presence,
and may those who mourn be comforted.

Silence

Light of the world:
shine in our lives.

In thankfulness, Lord,
we offer you our lives.

Silence

May the light which we see in you
shine through us
for your name's sake.
Amen.

WAITING EXPECTANTLY

Since we are promised
that Christ will return,
let us pray in hope and expectation.
Let us bring to his healing and love
the needs of the Church
and the world.

Silence

Come, Lord Jesus:
live in us now.

We pray for all Christian people;
for increased love and commitment,
working within the world
as yeast within the dough.

Silence

Come, Lord Jesus:
live in us now.

We pray for those in authority,
that they may base their priorities
and decisions
on the foundations of God's power:
justice and mercy.

Silence

Come, Lord Jesus:
live in us now.

We pray for those who suffer;
for God's strength and support
during pain, grief or distress,
so that their very suffering
may become a channel
for God's redeeming love.

Silence

Come, Lord Jesus:
live in us now.

We pray for the local community,
that God's presence may be known
in the varied, separate lives surrounding us;
that, alerted to their needs,
we may work in Christ to care and provide.

Silence

Come, Lord Jesus:
live in us now.

In the silence of God's stillness
we name any we know
who specially need our prayer.

Silence

Lord Jesus
you came to show us the true way to life.
Help us to progress along that way
in your strength,
and for your sake.
Amen.

WHERE ELSE CAN WE GO?

We have chosen to serve the Lord.
Let us pray to him now.

We pray for those whose faith
is being challenged or undermined
by inner doubts or outside influences.
We pray for those who build up our faith
and all who strive to proclaim the Gospel
in language that people understand.

Silence

Lord, where else can we go?:
only you have the words of eternal life.

We pray for our torn and fragmented world,
wrestling to equate the deep yearning for peace
with the instinctive urge for gratification and power;
that many may have the courage to walk God's way.

Silence

Lord, where else can we go?:
only you have the words of eternal life.

We pray for our loved ones;
for those who lift our hearts
and those who turn our hair grey.
We pray for those we instinctively warm to
and those with whom
there are frequent misunderstandings.
We thank God for our opportunities of forgiveness.

Silence

Lord, where else can we go?:
only you have the words of eternal life.

We pray for all who are marginalised,
scorned or rejected;

for those isolated through illness or imprisonment;
for those who feel that no one understands.
Surround them all with such love
that they may know they are precious to you.

Silence

Lord, where else can we go?:
only you have the words of eternal life.

We pray for those approaching death,
that through our prayers they may know themselves
accompanied with love on that journey.
We pray for those who have died,
that they may come to know the full joy of heaven.

Silence

Lord, where else can we go?:
only you have the words of eternal life.

We thank you, Lord,
for making yourself known to us,
both in daily living
and sacramentally in the breaking of bread.

Merciful Saviour:
accept these prayers
which we ask in your name.
Amen.

WELCOMING CHRIST

In stillness let us pray
to our Lord Jesus Christ.

We lay before him the misunderstandings,
mistakes and foolishness
in the members of his body, the Church;
that through teaching us humility
and forgiveness
even our weaknesses may become
a source of strength and renewal.

Silence

Lord of all:
we welcome you into our lives.

We lay before him all worldly distrust,
revenge and corruption,
all deceit and injustice;
that God's loving Spirit may inspire,
guide, repair and renew,
even where the darkness is deepest.

Silence

Lord of all:
we welcome you into our lives.

We lay before him all those whose busy lives
leave little time for stillness;
the overworked,
those suffering from stress and exhaustion;
that they may find God's inner peace
and constant strength and refreshment.

Silence

Lord of all:
we welcome you into our lives.

We lay before him all the relationships
in our everyday lives;
the ordering of our own timetable;
that living closely with him
we may learn how to make room
for the important things
of eternal significance.

Silence

Lord of all:
we welcome you into our lives.

In the silence
of God's attentive love,
we bring our private prayers.

Silence

Lord Jesus
hear our prayer;
we ask you to help us fix our lives on you,
who are Jesus Christ our Lord.
Amen.

COMMITMENT TO CHRIST

We have pledged to commit our lives to Christ;
let us pray, then,
in his Spirit.

We pray that all Christians may witness
to the value of caring,
regardless of race or colour;
that they may be maintained
in the strength and humility of Christ
to serve the world in love.

Silence

Lord, take us:
help us to live.

We pray for all monarchs, presidents,
and those in powerful positions;
for those whom they govern,
and for those with whom they negotiate;
that their great resources of power and wealth
may be so used
that peace and justice may prevail
over all our earth.

Silence

Lord, take us:
help us to live.

We pray for the very poor,
the weak and oppressed,
the abandoned, rejected and abused;
that all obstacles to their healing and wholeness
may be removed,
all blindness, prejudice and greed
transformed through Christ
into an outpouring of love and hope.

Silence

Lord, take us:
help us to live.

We pray for ourselves;
that we may see our own faults more clearly,
acknowledge our weaknesses
as well as our strengths,
and offer both to Christ
who can make us new.

Silence

Lord, take us:
help us to live.

In silence, now,
we pour out to God our Father
any needs and burdens known to us personally.

Silence

Lord God of all creation,
accept these prayers,
though Jesus Christ our Lord.
Amen.

TRANSFORM OUR LIVES

Filled with hope
by our risen Lord,
let us pray to him
to transform our lives.

We pray for the healing of divisions
among all who follow Christ;
that filled with hope by his resurrection
we may be inspired to break down barriers
to forgiveness and reconciliation.

Silence

Risen Lord Jesus:
transform our lives.

We pray for all who hold positions
of responsibility and leadership,
both internationally
and in our own community;
that they themselves may be led by God's Spirit
to make wise decisions
and help create a humane and caring world.

Silence

Risen Lord Jesus:
transform our lives.

We pray for all who incite others to antisocial,
addictive or criminal behaviour,
that they may be transformed and redirected;
for the weak, lonely, young and depressed,
who are so vulnerable to their temptations;
that they may be given help and strength
to resist the pressures around them.

Silence

Risen Lord Jesus:
transform our lives.

We pray for all families represented here;
their hopes and sorrows,
difficulties and celebrations;
that all our relationships
may be bathed in the love of Christ,
full of tenderness and compassion.

Silence

Risen Lord Jesus:
transform our lives.

In a time of silence,
we share with God our Father
our own personal burdens, joys and sorrows.

Silence

Father,
we bring you our cares and concerns,
and ask you to hear these prayers
through Jesus Christ our Lord.
Amen.

MAKE US MORE LIKE YOU

In faith, knowing that where two or three are gathered
in Christ's name he has promised to be among them,
let our minds and hearts be filled
with stillness as we pray.

We pray for the Church;
that all Christ's ministers may be given
perception and understanding,
to lead people into the light of his truth.

Silence

Lord of glory:
make us more like you.

We pray for all councils, committees and conferences;
that a spirit of integrity may underlie all discussion
and a desire for goodness inspire all decisions.

Silence

Lord of glory:
make us more like you.

We pray for all families,
especially those who have troubles;
that they may not be damaged through their suffering,
but rather grow in compassion and understanding.

Silence

Lord of glory:
make us more like you.

We pray for those in pain and distress;
for the mentally, physically and emotionally disabled;
that they may be comforted
and strengthened by Christ's presence,
trusting in his love which never fails.

Silence

Lord of glory:
make us more like you.

We pray for the dying and those who have
already moved on from this world into eternity;
may they rest for ever in Christ's peace.

Silence

Lord of glory:
make us more like you.

In thankfulness and praise
we remember all God's many blessings,
given to us each day,
and ask him to help us become
more generous-hearted and appreciative.

Silence

Father, we thank you
for showing yourself to us
in Jesus Christ.
Help us to follow him day by day.
Amen.

USE US FOR YOUR GLORY

Companions in Christ,
let us quieten our hearts before our Lord,
and pray together for the needs
of the Church and the world.

We bring to you, Lord,
all who preach and teach the Christian message of salvation,
and those who hear it;
through your Spirit, may its reality, truth and hope
take root and grow.

Silence

Lord Jesus Christ:
use us for your glory.

We bring to you, Lord,
our stewardship of the world's resources;
all discussions and councils
where far-reaching decisions are made
concerning government, conservation,
international relations, methods of harnessing power,
and fighting diseases;
may your generous will prevail
over human greed and prejudice.

Silence

Lord Jesus Christ:
use us for your glory.

We bring to you, Lord,
all who are apathetic, mentally exhausted
or aimlessly wandering through life;
all who are eaten up with jealousy,
poisoned by hate or weighed down by guilt;
may they feel and know the warmth and depth
of your love, and your yearning for their peace.

Silence

Lord Jesus Christ:
use us for your glory.

We bring to you, Lord,
ourselves, our friends
and all we shall meet during this week, however briefly;
fill us with your love
so that others may see it
and be drawn towards their Saviour.

Silence

Lord Jesus Christ:
use us for your glory.

We bring to you, Lord,
the dying and those who have already passed
into the next stage of life;
may they live for ever in your peace.

Silence

Lord Jesus Christ:
use us for your glory.

Lord, we rejoice in your uncompromising love for us,
and thank you for all the blessings
we receive from you each day.

Silence

Loving Lord,
**help us to see the divine glory
in your face,
and to follow you more closely
day by day.
Amen.**

LIVE THROUGH OUR LIVES

Fellow travellers of the Way of Christ,
we know that Jesus loves us;
let us therefore pray to him now
about all that concerns us
in his Church and in the world.

We pray for the many groups of Christians
worshipping alongside us,
but in other communities and in other countries;
for all who risk persecution for their faith;
that we may support and encourage one another
and serve the world as Christ's body,
whatever the personal cost.

Silence

Take us, Lord Jesus:
and live through our lives.

We pray for the leaders of the nations,
all members of governments
and their financial and social advisers;
that they may be led in the Spirit of Wisdom
to work in harmony with God's will
so his values are reflected in all policy making.

Silence

Take us, Lord Jesus:
and live through our lives.

We pray for a lessening of selfishness
and a broadening of our characters,
until we are prepared to welcome,
love and care for whoever is in need,
working hand in hand with God wherever we are sent.

Silence

Take us, Lord Jesus:
and live through our lives.

We pray for all in intensive care at the moment;
all undergoing emergency surgery;
all women in labour and their babies;
all who are approaching death;
that God's great healing love
may wash through their bodies and minds
in a surge of peace.

Silence

Take us, Lord Jesus:
and live through our lives.

Lord, we thank you for your constant,
loving provision for us throughout our lives,
and commend to your safe keeping for ever
all who have died, especially . . .

Silence

Father, turn the words of our prayers
into lives of loving service,
through Jesus Christ, our Lord.
Amen.

TRUST IN JESUS

In the Sprit of Jesus,
let us pray to our heavenly Father.

We bring to his love
all those who are being trained
for ministry in the Church;
that their studies may teach them
not only knowledge but perception,
not only skills but sensitivity.

Silence

Guide us, heavenly Father:
to trust in your Son.

We bring to his love
all whose positions of responsibility
cause pressure and stress;
that in their weakness and weariness
they may come to Christ for refreshment,
and rely upon him for their strength.

Silence

Guide us, heavenly Father:
to trust in your Son.

We bring to his love all who are dying;
that their trust in Jesus may deepen,
until their fears are calmed
and they can look forward with real hope
to meeting their Saviour face to face.

Silence

Guide us, heavenly Father:
to trust in your Son.

We bring to his love
our own friends and loved ones;

all who live with us and near us;
all who rely on us,
and all who are influenced
by our behaviour.

Silence

Guide us, heavenly Father:
to trust in your Son.

In silence, now,
we bring to our heavenly Father
our own particular concerns.

Silence

God of all mercy,
our hope and our joy,
we ask you to hear our prayers,
through Jesus Christ our Lord.
Amen.

GLORIFYING CHRIST

Gathered in the presence of Christ,
let us pray.

We pray that the Church may worship and adore
faithfully and courageously
in every age,
coming to know Christ
more and more.

Silence

Hear us, Father:
may Christ be glorified.

We pray that the world may recognise
and believe
that Jesus is truly
the Son of God.

Silence

Hear us, Father:
may Christ be glorified.

We pray that all those in physical,
mental, emotional or spiritual need,
by the presence of Christ
may find comfort in the care of others.

Silence

Hear us, Father:
may Christ be glorified.

We pray that in celebrating our faith in Christ
we may be sensitive
to one another's needs,
kind, helpful
and full of gratitude.

Silence

Hear us, Father:
may Christ be glorified.

We pray in silence, now,
for our own particular
needs and concerns.

Silence

Heavenly Father,
accept these prayers
and give us the strength and the will
to walk in love,
through Jesus Christ our Lord.
Amen.

The Holy Spirit

COME, HOLY SPIRIT

Let us pray to the God
who calls us each by name.

We pray for all baptised Christians
to live out their calling in loving and holy lives.
We pray for those preparing
for Baptism and Confirmation;
for parents and godparents
to be given the grace and perseverance
to keep faithfully the promises made.

Silence

Come, Holy Spirit:
guide our lives.

We pray for peace and integrity
in all our dealings as individuals,
and in local, national and international conflicts;
for openness to hear God's wisdom
and courage to follow his lead.

Silence

Come, Holy Spirit:
guide our lives.

We pray for harmony and understanding
in our relationships with family and neighbours;
for the willingness both to give and to receive,
for the generosity of forgiving love.

Silence

Come, Holy Spirit:
guide our lives.

We pray for those whose weariness or pain
makes it difficult for them to pray;

may they sense the support and love
of the Church of God.

Silence

Come, Holy Spirit:
guide our lives.

We pray for those whose souls
have left behind their frail and broken bodies
to live in God's eternal company.
May he bless and comfort their loved ones,
and bring us all in his good time,
to share the joy of heaven.

Silence

Come, Holy Spirit:
guide our lives.

We give thanks that God has called us by name
and kept us safe
through all the storms and difficulties of this life,
in the power of the Holy Spirit.

Merciful Father:
accept these prayers
for the sake of your Son,
our Saviour Jesus Christ.
Amen.

Waiting for the Spirit

Let us pray together to our heavenly Father,
knowing his love for us.

Father, we want to live your way
and do your will,
offer you true worship,
and serve one another in love.
Empower your Church to do this, we pray;
live in us; transform us.

Silence

Lord, we wait on you:
fill us, Holy Spirit of God.

Father, we want our states and kingdoms
to display your love and truth, justice and mercy.
We want to break down walls of prejudice
and build bridges of reconciliation and trust.
Empower your world, we pray;
live in us; transform us.

Silence

Lord, we wait on you:
fill us, Holy Spirit of God.

Father, we want our children
to be safely and lovingly nurtured,
our elderly valued,
our homes to be places of welcome and warmth;
empower your people, we pray:
live in us; transform us.

Silence

Lord, we wait on you:
fill us, Holy Spirit of God.

Father, we want your healing
for those whose lives are aching and weary;
your comfort and reassurance
for all who are imprisoned by fears and hate;
empower these lives, we pray;
live in us; transform us.

Silence

Lord, we wait on you:
fill us, Holy Spirit of God.

Father, we want to commit our loved ones,
who have died, into your safe keeping for ever.
Prepare us all, Father, to live with you in heaven.

Silence

Lord, we wait on you:
fill us, Holy Spirit of God.

Father, we want to worship and praise you
with our voices and our lives;
shape us to your purpose, and use us.

Merciful Father:
**accept these prayers
for the sake of your Son,
our Saviour Jesus Christ.
Amen.**

LIVING SPIRIT OF GOD

Divine Spirit, we ask for your encouragement and inspiration
in all areas of ministry in the Church;
pour out your blessing on all who work
for the spreading of the kingdom.

Silence

Living Spirit of God:
you give us life in abundance.

Divine Spirit, we ask for your guidance and protection
in all areas of conflict and confusion;
pour out your wisdom on all who lead.

Silence

Living Spirit of God:
you give us life in abundance.

Divine Spirit, we ask for your faithful presence
in our homes, and all the homes in this community;
pour out your patience and forgiveness
wherever the sparks fly.

Silence

Living Spirit of God:
you give us life in abundance.

Divine Spirit, we ask for your reassurance and comfort
wherever people are hurting
or crying inside the brave face;
pour out your welcoming love
and give them the peace they crave.

Silence

Living Spirit of God:
you give us life in abundance.

Divine Spirit, we ask for your firm holding
wherever our journey leads,
and at the time of death, your mercy.

Silence

Living Spirit of God:
you give us life in abundance.

Divine Spirit, we ask you to accept with joy
our thanks and praise for all you are,
and all you accomplish.

Silence

Divine Spirit, we bring these prayers
in the name of him who came
that we might have life
and have it abundantly,
Jesus Christ, our Lord.
Amen.

FALL AFRESH ON US

As we still our bodies and open ourselves to God
we think of the Church leaders, preachers
and all who minister to God's people.
With them and for them we pray . . .

Silence

Spirit of the living God:
fall afresh on us.

We think of all the world's nations,
the problems, quarrels, misunderstandings
and mistakes.
With them and for them we pray . . .

Silence

Spirit of the living God:
fall afresh on us.

We think of those in our family,
those we like and those we seem to annoy.
With them and for them we pray . . .

Silence

Spirit of the living God:
fall afresh on us.

We think of those in hospitals and hospices,
outpatients at the local accident centre
and those ill at home.
With them and for them we pray . . .

Silence

Spirit of the living God:
fall afresh on us.

We think of those who are close to death,
those who have recently died

and those who miss them.
With them and for them we pray . . .

Silence

Spirit of the living God:
fall afresh on us.

We think of all your amazing creation,
from the microscopic to the cosmic,
and remember with thankfulness that we are part
of this glory you have made.

Silence

Spirit of the living God:
fall afresh on us
and bring new life and hope to your world,
through Jesus Christ, our Lord.
Amen.

SET OUR HEARTS ON FIRE

Let us pray to the God who has drawn us here today,
who loves us, and loves our world.

We pray that there may be a revival of longing
for your kingdom to come,
and a renewed commitment to working for it;
for a desire to live out our faith and worship
in our daily lives this week.

Silence

Come, Holy Spirit:
set our hearts on fire.

We pray that all who have authority and power
in our nation and our world may use it for good,
upholding and instigating what is right and fair,
and listening to the needs of those they represent.
May we recognise our responsibility
to support and stand up for your values.

Silence

Come, Holy Spirit:
set our hearts on fire.

We pray that within our homes and communities
there may be a new awareness
of one another's gifts and needs,
more sensitivity and respect in our relationships;
may we reverence one another as fellow beings,
born of your creative love.

Silence

Come, Holy Spirit:
set our hearts on fire.

We pray for all who are oppressed,
downtrodden or despised;

we pray for those who will not eat today
and all who live in the degrading circumstances
of poverty and powerlessness;
we pray for a heart to put injustices right
and strive for a fair sharing of resources.

Silence

Come, Holy Spirit:
set our hearts on fire.

We pray for those whose life expectancy is short,
for the babies and children who have died
while we have been praying;
for all who have come to the end of their earthly life
and made that last journey through death;
thank you for your welcoming mercy
and the promise of eternal life.

Silence

Come, Holy Spirit:
set our hearts on fire.

We offer you our thanks and praise
for the scriptures that remind and inspire us,
and for your living Spirit which enables us.

Merciful Father:
accept these prayers
for the sake of your Son,
our Saviour Jesus Christ.
Amen.

THE LIFE OF THE SPIRIT

In wonder let us pray
to the almighty and everlasting God.

We pray for the Church,
that in constant prayerfulness
Christians may be attentive
and receptive
to the Holy Spirit.

Silence

Father almighty:
may your Spirit fill us with life.

We pray for the world,
with all its mistakes and tragedies,
that God's active Spirit
will bring order,
serenity and hope.

Silence

Father almighty:
may your Spirit fill us with life.

We pray for those whose lives
are darkened by guilt,
resentment and despair;
for those who live violent and cruel lives;
for drug dealers
and all who corrupt young minds;
that God's generous Spirit of love
will bring light to their hearts.

Silence

Father almighty:
may your Spirit fill us with life.

We pray for our loved ones
and for anyone we find difficult to love;
that God's Spirit living in us
will increase our love
for each other.

Silence

Father almighty:
may your Spirit fill us with life.

Alive to the Holy Spirit,
we name those we know
who are in any particular need.

Silence

Father,
accept these prayers,
through Jesus Christ our Lord.
Amen.

THE BLESSING OF THE SPIRIT

As brothers and sisters in Christ,
let us pray together
to our loving, merciful Father
for the blessing of the Holy Spirit.

We pray that the Church
may be guided
and strengthened by the Holy Spirit,
and that all Christians
may be attentive to their calling.

Silence

Give us new life:
and bless us with your Spirit.

We pray that all nations
may be led by the Spirit to understand
God's way of love,
and that all decisions
may reflect his will.

Silence

Give us new life:
and bless us with your Spirit.

We pray that the lonely and frightened
may experience the joy of the Spirit of peace;
and the despairing may be filled
with the Spirit of hope.

Silence

Give us new life:
and bless us with your Spirit.

We pray that in all our relationships
the Spirit may enable us

to proclaim the Good News
of God's saving love
by the way we respond to one another.

Silence

Give us new life:
and bless us with your Spirit.

In the silence
which God our Father fills
with love and hope,
we offer our own particular prayers.

Silence

Father,
in deepest joy for the love
you have shown us
we ask you to accept our prayer,
through Jesus Christ our Lord.
Amen.

THE GIFT OF THE SPIRIT

Let us pray together
to our heavenly Father
who, through Jesus Christ,
has given us his Holy Spirit.

We pray that the Spirit of God
who anointed Jesus
will strengthen and uphold us
so that we live Christian lives,
flooding the world
with God's saving love.

Silence

Loving Father:
may your Spirit empower us.

We pray that all leaders
and those in positions of power
may understand the fundamental need
for God's Spirit of truth,
peace and compassion
and commit themselves
to his way of justice.

Silence

Loving Father:
may your Spirit empower us.

We pray that any who are living under
a burden of guilt
may be led by the Spirit to complete repentance
and find freedom and joy
in God's forgiveness.

Silence

Loving Father:
may your Spirit empower us.

We pray that, being filled
with the Spirit of Christ,
the quality and brightness
of our lives
may draw others into his love
and peace.

Silence

Loving Father:
may your Spirit empower us.

In the silence of God's attentive love,
we name those we know
who are in any particular need.

Silence

Father,
confident in your love,
we ask these things,
in Jesus' name.
Amen.

GOD'S SPIRIT IN US

As members of the body of Christ,
let us pray together.

We pray for all those who form the Church,
in its variety and richness
throughout the world;
that we may be encouraged
and strengthened
and our weariness
constantly refreshed
by the living Spirit of Jesus.

Silence

Come to us as we are:
and renew us by your presence.

We pray for all councils, committees
and governing bodies,
for those serving on juries,
for air, sea and mountain rescue teams,
that in working together
and enabled by God's Spirit
they may strive for what is good,
just and honest.

Silence

Come to us as we are:
and renew us by your presence.

We pray for the poor and for the hungry,
for the blind, the downtrodden
and those imprisoned;
that God's Spirit,
alive in his people,
will work his healing love.

Silence

Come to us as we are:
and renew us by your presence.

We pray for ourselves,
that we may be given deeper insight,
more awareness and greater love,
so that we can more effectively
serve the world
as living members
of the body of Christ.

Silence

Come to us as we are:
and renew us by your presence.

We bring our own personal prayers
in silence, now,
to God our loving Father.

Silence

Father,
we ask you to hear our prayers,
through Jesus Christ our Lord.
Amen.

SPIRIT OF THE LIVING GOD

May God be glorified now,
as we commit ourselves to the work of prayer,
interceding for those in all kinds of need.

In our worship,
and our openness to the Spirit of life,
in the Church's longing and outreach,
in the pastors, the ministers, the people,
in all seekers and honest doubters,

may the Spirit of the living God:
be at work among us.

Silence

In the welfare programmes
and peace-making missions,
in the struggle to uphold justice,
in the aid given to the hungry and homeless,

may the Spirit of the living God:
be at work among us.

Silence

In the loving and costly commitment
of mothers and fathers, brothers and sisters,
daughters and sons,
in the determination to forgive and forgive,
in all the lives shared and cherished,

may the Spirit of the living God:
be at work among us.

Silence

In the work of nursing, comforting and healing,
in the daily patient struggle
with pain and weakness,
and in the practical, good-humoured caring,

may the Spirit of the living God:
be at work among us.

Silence

In the twilight years and the facing of death,
in lives well lived and now breaking into eternity,

may the Spirit of the living God:
be at work among us.

Silence

In the freedom offered through forgiveness,
in the joy of Resurrection life,
in the hope of eternity,

may the Spirit of the living God:
be at work among us.

Silence

Merciful Father:
accept these prayers
for the sake of your Son,
our Saviour Jesus Christ.
Amen.

BREATH OF GOD

As the people of the living God,
let us join together in our prayers
for the Church and for the world.

Holy God, breathe your life into the Church;
breathe holiness and deepening faith,
breathe energy, inspired teaching and fervent praise;
unblock the channels and make us more receptive
to your gentleness and your power.

Silence

Breathe into us:
so that we live in you.

Holy God, breathe your life into the universe;
breathe responsible caring, honesty and compassion;
breathe right values and good stewardship,
peace and reconciliation, vision and hope.

Silence

Breathe into us:
so that we live in you.

Holy God, breathe your life
into our homes and places of work;
breathe increased patience and understanding,
and the courage to live the Christian life
when to do so brings ridicule or demands sacrifice.

Silence

Breathe into us:
so that we live in you.

Holy God, breathe your life into those who suffer;
breathe comfort and wholeness,
forgiveness and new confidence,

breathe peace of mind
and the knowledge of your love.

Silence

Breathe into us:
so that we live in you.

Holy God, breathe your life into the dead and dying;
breathe courage for the journey
and the realisation that you can be trusted.
Breathe life that lasts for ever.

Silence

Breathe into us:
so that we live in you.

Holy God, breathe your life into us now
as we offer you here our thanks and praise
for your life laid down out of love for us.
May our words be worked out
in fresh commitment to you.

Merciful Father:
**accept these prayers
for the sake of your Son,
our Saviour Jesus Christ.
Amen.**

THE BREATH OF THE SPIRIT

Spirit of God, into every situation of doubt and despondency
among your followers,
breathe your faithfulness.

Silence

Prepare us, O Lord:
to walk in your ways.

Spirit of God, into our strongholds of ambition
and defensiveness,
breathe your humility.

Silence

Prepare us, O Lord:
to walk in your ways.

Spirit of God, into the prisons of guilt and revenge,
breathe the grace of forgiveness.

Silence

Prepare us, O Lord:
to walk in your ways.

Spirit of God, into the darkness of pain and fear,
breathe your reassurance.

Silence

Prepare us, O Lord:
to walk in your ways.

Spirit of God, into the flabbiness of complacency,
breathe your zeal.

Silence

Prepare us, O Lord:
to walk in your ways.

Spirit of God, into our homes and places of work,
breathe your fellowship and love.

Silence

Prepare us, O Lord:
to walk in your ways.

Father, into the whole of your creation,
breathe your joy and peace:
and may your Spirit guide us
as we walk in your ways
with Jesus Christ, our Lord.
Amen.

Breathe your Spirit

Father, breathe your spirit of life
into all the members of your Church;
keep us open to your word
and sensitive to your will.

Silence

Spirit of God:
teach us your ways.

Father, breathe your spirit of counsel
into every debate and international conference;
alert us to act with responsibility and integrity.

Silence

Spirit of God:
teach us your ways.

Father, breathe your spirit of love
into every home and neighbourhood;
make us slow to criticise and quick to forgive.

Silence

Spirit of God:
teach us your ways.

Father, breathe your spirit of healing
into all those who are weakened or damaged,
whether physically, mentally, emotionally or spiritually;
give them the reassurance of your presence.

Silence

Spirit of God:
teach us your ways.

Father, breathe your spirit of peace
into those who are approaching death

and those who have recently died.
Help us to trust in your infinite mercy.

Silence

Spirit of God:
teach us your ways.

Father, breathe your spirit of thankfulness
into our hearts as we receive,
our minds as we notice,
and our lives as we journey.

Silence

Lord God, receive our prayers,
which we offer
in the name of Jesus Christ.
Amen.

BREATH OF GOD,
BREATHE IN US

Spirit of God, breathe your life
into every worshipping community,
and heal all disunity in your Church.

Silence

God of glory,
we thank you for loving us.

Spirit of God, breathe your peace into our world
both in individuals and in nations.

Silence

God of glory,
we thank you for loving us.

Spirit of God, breathe your joy into our homes
and places of work and leisure.

Silence

God of glory,
we thank you for loving us.

Spirit of God, breathe your comfort into all who suffer,
whether mentally, physically,
emotionally or spiritually.

Silence

God of glory,
we thank you for loving us.

Spirit of God, breathe your hope into those
who feel they have little to live for.

Silence

God of glory,
we thank you for loving us.

Spirit of God, breathe your refreshment and delight
into our attitudes,
until we live in thankfulness.

Silence

Father, breathe your Spirit into our prayers
that your love may channel through them
to our hearts and the needs of the world:
for the sake of Jesus Christ, our Lord.
Amen.

LET YOUR SPIRIT
LIVE IN US NOW

In wonder let us come before the almighty
and everlasting God, to pray in the Spirit of Christ.

We pray for every Christian;
that each may be more receptive to the Holy Spirit,
until every worshipping community is charged
with the vitality and love of the living Christ.

Silence

Loving Father:
let your Spirit live in us now.

We pray for the world and its leaders;
for its mistakes and tragedies,
misunderstandings and confusion;
may your active Spirit bring
order, serenity and hope.

Silence

Loving Father:
let your Spirit live in us now.

We pray for a deepening of our own faith,
more understanding of your will,
a clearer awareness of others' needs
and a greater desire to give our lives away.

Silence

Loving Father:
let your Spirit live in us now.

We pray for those whose lives are darkened by guilt,
resentment or despair;

for those who live violent and cruel lives,
and for all who are ill, injured or abused.

Silence

Loving Father:
let your Spirit live in us now.

We pray for those who have died in the faith of Christ,
especially . . . ;
may they enjoy life with you for ever.

Silence

Father, in grateful thanks for all
your blessings in our lives,
we relinquish our wills to yours.

Silence

Father, it is your Spirit
who teaches us to pray.
May he also teach us how to live:
through Jesus Christ, our Lord.
Amen.

GUIDED BY THE SPIRIT

As brothers and sisters in Christ,
let us pray that his living Spirit
will enthuse and activate
all people.

We pray for the Church,
especially for missionaries
both abroad and in this country;
that with inner quietness
they may be ready to listen
to the voice of the Spirit.

Silence

Father of our risen Lord:
may your Spirit guide us.

We pray for world leaders and their advisers,
that nothing may tempt them from integrity,
and that they may boldly work
for what is good, honest and just.

Silence

Father of our risen Lord:
may your Spirit guide us.

We pray for those who doubt,
those who have lost their faith,
and those whose faith is being tested;
that they may know the assurance
of God's presence and his love.

Silence

Father of our risen Lord:
may your Spirit guide us.

We pray for our own community,
that we may serve Christ

in caring for one another
and encourage one another
in the faith of our loving Lord.

Silence

Father of our risen Lord:
may your Spirit guide us.

In the name of the risen Lord,
we name our own particular cares
and concerns.

Silence

Father,
we know that you are here present;
hear the prayers we make,
confident of your love,
through Jesus Christ our Lord.
Amen.

FILLED WITH THE SPIRIT

Let the Spirit of God in our hearts plead
for the Church and for the world.

Great God of all time and space,
fill the Church with such joy in believing
that all Christians overflow with love,
compassion, generosity and humility.
Let us walk your way and live your life.

Silence

May the Spirit of God:
fill us to overflowing.

Great God of power and justice,
fill the arenas of leadership and conflict
with sharpened consciences and with courage,
so that wise decisions are made,
needs met and wrongs righted.

Silence

May the Spirit of God:
fill us to overflowing.

Great God of gentleness and truth,
fill every home with new insight
and greater understanding.
Break down the divisive barriers
and build up our capacity to love.

Silence

May the Spirit of God:
fill us to overflowing.

Great God of attentive caring,
fill us with your practical compassion;
may all who suffer be heard,

comforted and cared for.
Heal both their situation and our hardness of heart.

Silence

May the Spirit of God:
fill us to overflowing.

Great God of unending being,
fill death with your life
and the dying with hope in you.
Prepare us all for life which lasts for ever.

Silence

May the Spirit of God:
fill us to overflowing.

Great God of all creation,
fill our mouths with praises
and our hearts with gratitude,
for all the glory that surrounds us.

Merciful Father:
**accept these prayers
for the sake of your Son,
our Saviour Jesus Christ.
Amen.**

The family of God

THE FAMILY OF GOD

As children together in the family of God,
let us pray now to our Father in heaven.

Lord, we pray that as Christians
we may listen more attentively
and with greater urgency than ever before
to the words of Jesus;
give us more awareness of your presence with us,
both in our worship and in our daily ministry,
giving us the courage to live out your truth with joy.

Silence

Heavenly Father:
hear your children's prayer.

We pray for those who do not know you
or dismiss you as irrelevant to their lives;
we pray for those who influence and encourage others
in what is evil, destructive or depraved,
and ask for your protection
of all who are vulnerable and in danger.

Silence

Heavenly Father:
hear your children's prayer.

We pray for all who are adjusting
to new relationships in the family,
new homes or new work and leisure patterns;
we pray for stronger root growth in you,
so that we are not thrown
by the changes and troubles of everyday life,
knowing the reality of your faithfulness.

Silence

Heavenly Father:
hear your children's prayer.

We pray for all who are too exhausted
or overwhelmed by circumstances and pressures
to be able to pray;
surround all those who are troubled
and heavily laden
with the revitalising assurance of your presence,
your understanding and your love.

Silence

Heavenly Father:
hear your children's prayer.

We pray that those who have gone through death
may know the brightness of everlasting life
in your company;
may we, with them, come to experience
the glory and joy of heaven.

Silence

Heavenly Father:
hear your children's prayer.

Father, we thank you for the glimpses of glory
you give us in this life, for your friendship
and your promise to be with us always.

Merciful Father:
accept these prayers
for the sake of your Son,
our Saviour Jesus Christ.
Amen.

PEOPLE OF GOD

We call to mind all Church leaders
and the problems they face;
all ministers, evangelists, teachers and healers;
all who come thirsting and searching for God.

Silence

We are your people, O Lord:
and you are our God.

We call to mind the nations and their leaders;
the temptations that accompany power
and the people's needs and hardships.

Silence

We are your people, O Lord:
and you are our God.

We call to mind each home in this area;
the squabbles and tears, the laughter and affection.

Silence

We are your people, O Lord:
and you are our God.

We call to mind those in hospital and at home
who are in pain;
those who are frightened by their illness;
and all who care for them.

Silence

We are your people, O Lord:
and you are our God.

We call to mind those who have recently died
and can meet God face to face;

those for whom death is terrifying
and all who are unprepared.

Silence

We are your people, O Lord:
and you are our God.

We call to mind the glimpses of glory God shows us;
the times when we have known his presence
close to us;
the times of unexpected joy.

Silence

We are your people, O Lord:
and you are our God;
receive the prayers of your Church
and send us out in service and love,
for Jesus' sake.
Amen.

ALL GOD'S CHILDREN

Father, we bring to you our longing for unity,
our desire for a closer walk with you,
and our concern for all our Christian
brothers and sisters.

Silence

Creator of the human family:
bind us together in love.

Father, we bring to you our longing
for a world of peace and integrity;
a world of mutual respect
and international understanding.

Silence

Creator of the human family:
bind us together in love.

Father, we bring to you our love and concern
for our families, friends and neighbours;
particularly those facing change or feeling isolated.

Silence

Creator of the human family:
bind us together in love.

Father, we bring to you our desire for healing
and wholeness in those who are distressed,
uncomfortable or in great pain;
we bring our willingness to help
wherever you want to use us.

Silence

Creator of the human family:
bind us together in love.

Father, we bring to you our loved ones who have died,
and those who are dying with no one near them.

Silence

Creator of the human family:
bind us together in love.

Father, we bring to you our thanks for life
and all its blessings;
for the experiences we learn from and grow through.

Silence

Loving Father, hear our prayers
offered in the name of Jesus.
Amen.

CHILDREN IN GOD'S FAMILY

My brothers and sisters in Christ,
as members of one family let us talk to God our Father
about our needs, cares and concerns.

We pray for the life, teaching and fellowship
of the Church, our Christian family;
help us to support and care for one another
as true family members,
regardless of physical, cultural
or intellectual differences.

Silence f

God our Father:
hear your children's prayer.

We pray for friendship and good will
between all the different nations in our world;
teach us to enjoy the variety as richness,
rather than fearing it as a threat.

Silence

God our Father:
hear your children's prayer.

We ask for your blessing and guidance
in all the homes of this community;
as each problem and difficulty arises
may your loving wisdom steer us in the right direction.

Silence

God our Father:
hear your children's prayer.

We pray for all who have been damaged
by a disturbed or violent upbringing;
for children who are growing up

amid hatred and cruelty;
may they be healed by love.

Silence

God our Father:
hear your children's prayer.

We pray for those who have recently died
and commend them into your
everlasting care and protection.

Silence

God our Father:
hear your children's prayer.

We thank you for all the joys and blessings in our lives;
especially we thank you for the relationships
which enrich our lives so much.

Silence

God our Father:
hear your children's prayer
for the sake of Jesus Christ,
our elder Brother.
Amen.

CHILDREN OF ONE FATHER

As members of God's family,
let us pray together to our heavenly Father.

That as family members of the Church of God
we may show his likeness by doing his will;
that those visiting our churches
may find there God's beauty and truth,
open-hearted loving and a unity of purpose.

Silence

Father:
make all people one.

That as members of the human race
we may work together, share resources,
respect and learn from one another.
That leaders may inspire collective good,
and those with vision be valued and heard.

Silence

Father:
make all people one.

That we may give both support and space
to those we love and nurture;
that those of our own families
who do not yet know God
may come to understand the depth
of his love for them.

Silence

Father:
make all people one.

That all who come to Jesus in need
may find in him forgiveness, healing

and wholeness of body, mind and spirit,
strength to cope with their difficulties
and a constant inner renewing.

Silence

Father:
make all people one.

That as those coming to death
roll up the tents of their earthly existence,
they may be welcomed into the eternal home
prepared for them by their loving God.

Silence

Father:
make all people one.

That as we marvel at the generosity
of God's love, and his acceptance of us,
we may grow closer to his likeness
each day we live.

Merciful Father:
**accept these prayers
for the sake of your Son,
our Saviour Jesus Christ.
Amen.**

WE BELONG TO GOD

Brothers and sisters in Christ,
in the knowledge of God's love for us,
let us pray for the Church and for the world.

We pray for all ministers serving
in deprived or violent areas of the world;
all who are in personal danger for teaching the faith;
may they be reassured and their service blessed
by the power of your love.

Silence

Abba, Father:
we belong to you.

We pray for all who serve
in positions of authority in this country
and throughout the world;
for all debates and international talks;
may the power of reason you have given us
lead us towards your truth and wisdom.

Silence

Abba, Father:
we belong to you.

We pray for those we serve each day,
and those who serve us;
for relationships we find difficult,
and for situations which tend to make us irritable;
increase our generosity of spirit,
and our delight in serving others.

Silence

Abba, Father:
we belong to you.

We pray for the resentful,
and all who suffer injustice or neglect;
for all in need because of natural disasters,
war, famine or disease;
may your love reach them through our care.

Silence

Abba, Father:
we belong to you.

We pray that all who have died in faith
may know the joy of heaven for ever.

Silence

Abba, Father:
we belong to you.

We rejoice in all the goodness and generosity
your love has inspired in so many people;
for the way you encourage and guide us.

Silence

Abba, Father:
we belong to you.
Hear the prayers of your children,
through Jesus Christ, your Son.
Amen.

THANK YOU, FATHER

Father, we thank you
for welcoming us into your family;
for treating us as special and forgiving us.
We pray for all our Christian brothers and sisters
worshipping today all over the world.

Silence

Thank you, Father:
for loving us so much.

Father, we think of our parents
and all who have helped and looked after us
through our life;
we pray that you will make your home
in our homes.

Silence

Thank you, Father:
for loving us so much.

Father, we pray for those damaged
through bad relationships;
those who are lonely, rejected or broken-hearted;
we pray for the newly born and their parents.

Silence

Thank you, Father:
for loving us so much.

Father, we remember those who have reached death
and ask that you will welcome them
into your kingdom.

Silence

Thank you, Father:
for loving us so much.

Father, we thank you for the opportunities
to practise forgiveness;
for the different times that have enabled us to grow;
for the light-hearted times that have made us happy.

Silence

Heavenly Father, hear the prayers
of your family, the Church,
that your love may be made known
in all the earth:
for the sake of Jesus, your Son.
Amen.

THE LIFE WE LIVE TOGETHER

Father, we call to mind all pastors and ministers
in your holy, world-wide Church;
we thank you for them
and want to support them with our love.

Silence

The life we live together:
is your life within us.

Father, we call to mind the responsibilities
we share in acting as stewards of your creation;
increase our love and respect for one another,
regardless of nationality or colour.

Silence

The life we live together:
is your life within us.

Father, we call to mind those whom we love
and those who love us;
those we tend to criticise and those we admire.

Silence

The life we live together:
is your life within us.

Father, we call to mind all those who are feeling weak
or vulnerable;
all those struggling to make sense of their suffering.

Silence

The life we live together:
is your life within us.

Father, we call to mind those who grieve
for their loved ones who have died;
we remember those entering heaven.

Silence

The life we live together:
is your life within us.

Father, we call to mind your faithful love,
your patience and your mercy.

Silence

Loving Father, present among your people:
receive our prayers,
live in our hearts and minds
and go with us to our homes and work,
through Jesus Christ, our Lord.
Amen.

BIND US TOGETHER

Our God is always ready to hear our prayers.
Let us be still, and pray to him now.

Heavenly Father,
we thank you for all those who remind us
to be kind and loving by their words and example.
We pray that as a church
we may break through the barriers which separate us,
and put right whatever blocks us from your love.

Silence

Bind us together, Lord:
we know our need of you.

We pray that the lines of communication
between people and nations
may be kept open, respected and honoured,
and that where communication has broken down
there may be a new desire for reconciliation.

Silence

Bind us together, Lord:
we know our need of you.

Heavenly Father,
we pray for all those making and repairing roads,
travelling on them and stuck in traffic jams;
we pray for the towns and villages linked by roads,
for a public transport system that protects the environment,
and serves the community.

Silence

Bind us together, Lord:
we know our need of you.

We pray for those we see and talk to
every day or every week;

for those we often argue with or misunderstand;
for those who brighten our lives and make us smile;
for a greater thankfulness and appreciation
of those we usually take for granted.

Silence

Bind us together, Lord:
we know our need of you.

We pray for those we have hurt or upset;
for those who feel isolated and alone;
for the ill, the frail, the stressed and the bitter.

Silence

Bind us together, Lord:
we know our need of you.

We pray for the dying
and those who have died to this earthly life.
May they know the eternal peace of your heaven,
and may those who miss them be comforted.

Silence

Bind us together, Lord:
we know our need of you.

Heavenly Father, we thank you for helping us
to get ourselves ready to receive you.

Merciful Father:
accept these prayers
for the sake of your Son,
our Saviour Jesus Christ.
Amen.

THE CHURCH IN THE WORLD

My brothers and sisters in Christ,
bound together in love and faith
let us pray for the Church and for the world.

O Lord our God, we trust in your promise to hear us
when we pray in faith.

Strengthen us in the certain knowledge
of your constant presence,
so that we witness to your love by the way
we speak and act each day.

Silence

Heavenly Father:
hear us as we pray.

Teach us and guide us to use the resources of the world
wisely and unselfishly,
sharing its riches and respecting its beauty.

Silence

Heavenly Father:
hear us as we pray.

Alert us to the needs of those around us
and increase our friendliness and understanding
in all our relationships.

Silence

Heavenly Father:
hear us as we pray.

Bring your health and wholeness
to those in physical pain and mental anguish,
and give your inner peace
to those overwhelmed with worries.

Silence

Heavenly Father:
hear us as we pray.

Into your hands, Father, we commend
those who have died,
for we know that in your care they are safe.

Silence

Heavenly Father:
hear us as we pray.

And now we want to thank you
for your constant love and kindness,
support and protection.

Silence

Heavenly Father:
hear us as we pray,
for the sake of your Son,
our Saviour, Jesus Christ.
Amen.

WE ARE YOUR PEOPLE

Our heavenly Father assures us that
wherever two or three meet in his name
he will be with them; in confidence, then,
let us bring him our needs and cares.

We pray that your love will spill out
through your Church to the world,
filling all teaching, all advice and counsel,
all authority and correction.

Silence

We are your people:
hear us, Lord, we pray.

May your spirit of forgiveness and justice
permeate the social and political fabric of our world,
till we are able to rule wisely, discuss differences calmly
and be prepared to negotiate rationally.

Silence

We are your people:
hear us, Lord, we pray.

May your light shine in our hearts
to show us our faults and enable us to admit them;
to shine through our lives
in the way we treat one another,
especially when we disagree or feel hurt.

Silence

We are your people:
hear us, Lord, we pray.

May your comfort and consolation
soothe those who are afraid or in great pain,
refresh those who are mentally or physically exhausted

and be a lifeline to those who are broken-hearted
or in despair.

Silence

We are your people:
hear us, Lord, we pray.

May those who have passed into eternity
be welcomed into your heavenly kingdom
to live with you for ever.

Silence

We are your people:
hear us, Lord, we pray.

We praise you, Lord,
for all the joy and gladness of our lives;
for the beauty of your world
and the affection of our loved ones.

Silence

We are your people:
hear us, Lord, we pray,
for the sake of Jesus Christ,
our elder Brother.
Amen.

YOU ARE OUR GOD

Let us pray to the God who gives us so much
and loves us so completely.

We pray for a fresh outpouring of your Spirit
in all areas of the Church,
till our lives are so changed for good
that people notice and are drawn
to seek you for themselves.

Silence

We are your people:
and you are our God.

We pray for godly leaders and advisers
all over the world,
and for the courage to speak out
against injustice and evil.

Silence

We are your people:
and you are our God.

We pray for those affected
by our behaviour and our conversation,
that we may in future
encourage one another by all we say and do.

Silence

We are your people:
and you are our God.

We pray for those as yet unborn,
that the good news will reach them too;
we pray for those who have rejected you
because of the behaviour of your followers;
we pray for all who have lost their way.

Silence

We are your people:
and you are our God.

We pray for the dying,
especially those who are unprepared or frightened.
Welcome into your kingdom
those who have died in faith;
may they live with you for ever.

Silence

We are your people:
and you are our God.

Thank you, Lord, for the new life
you have enabled us to live.

Merciful Father:
accept these prayers
for the sake of your Son,
our Saviour Jesus Christ.
Amen.

THE SHEEP OF HIS PASTURE

Let us humble ourselves in the presence of God
and pray to him for the Church and for the world.

Loving God, in all our ministry as the Church,
on Sundays and on weekdays,
may we give glory to you
and further your kingdom.
Direct us to those who are searching
and give us the wisdom to know
how best to draw them to your love.

Silence

We are your people:
the sheep of your pasture.

Loving God, may we actively seek to do good,
to stand up against injustice and work for peace;
Lord, rid the world of the terrible evils
that result from unvoiced objections,
and unspoken misgivings.
Give us the courage to act as true citizens of heaven.

Silence

We are your people:
the sheep of your pasture.

Loving God, may the ways we manage our homes,
decisions, time and money be in keeping with our calling
as inheritors of the kingdom.
May your love undergird all our loving.

Silence

We are your people:
the sheep of your pasture.

Loving God, search for the lost,
bring back those who have strayed,

bind up the injured, and strengthen the weak;
help us all to share in this work of loving care.

Silence

We are your people:
the sheep of your pasture.

Loving God, welcome into your kingdom
all whose lives show them to be your servants,
whether or not they have known you by name.
Prepare us all to meet you with the confidence
of sins confessed and forgiven.

Silence

We are your people:
the sheep of your pasture.

Loving God, you have shown us such love and humility;
we offer you our thanks and praise.

Merciful Father:
**accept these prayers
for the sake of your Son,
our Saviour Jesus Christ.
Amen.**

CHOSEN AND CALLED

As God's chosen people,
his adopted sons and daughters,
let us pray to him now
in the Spirit of Jesus Christ.

We pray for all who are called
to spread the news
of hope and joy for humanity;
that their teaching may be inspired
so as to draw many, through Christ,
to their loving creator.

Silence

Father of Wisdom:
open our eyes to your truth.

We remember all those who are called
to sit on committees;
all decision makers and policy planners,
that they may be guided to work
in accordance with God's will,
so that the world is governed
and ordered wisely.

Silence

Father of Wisdom:
open our eyes to your truth.

We hold before God,
all who work with the sick;
those who are chronically ill,
or suffering from a long-term disability;
that even through intense pain
there may be positive, spiritual growth,
and a deeper awareness of God's presence.

Silence

Father of Wisdom:
open our eyes to your truth.

We pray for those who are called
to care for children,
through fostering, adoption,
or in residential homes;
also for children separated from their families,
for those waiting to be placed
in loving homes,
for a greater sharing of love
and the growth of mutual trust.

Silence

Father of Wisdom:
open our eyes to your truth.

In a time of silence
we share with God our Father
any needs and burdens
known to us personally.

Silence

Almighty Father,
hear our prayers,
and make us alert to your response,
through Jesus Christ our Lord.
Amen.

AT GOD'S INVITATION

Invited by our God, we have gathered here.
Let us now voice our prayers
for the Church and for the world.

Father, when either the traditional or the progressive
blinds us to the truth of your will,
clear our vision and speak through our prejudices
until we are once again open to your changing.
May we be, before anything else, your people,
sharing your concerns and desires.

Silence

At your invitation:
Lord, we come.

Father, we recognise how powerful
the influences are in our world
which distract many and lead away from your truth.
We pray for the quiet whisper of your wisdom
to be noticed and acknowledged in many lives;
we pray for widespread discipline of the heart,
a new openness to generosity of spirit.

Silence

At your invitation:
Lord, we come.

Father, may our homes and daily schedules
be part of the territory of your kingdom,
where it is your will which guides
and your love which rules.

Silence

At your invitation:
Lord, we come.

Father, our hearts rail against the cruelty
and unfairness of suffering and disease,
and we kneel now alongside all in pain
and weep with them, crying out to you
for comfort and the healing of your love.
For you are no bringer of evil to our lives,
but share our sorrow and give us the grace to bear it.

Silence

At your invitation:
Lord, we come.

Father, as death takes from us those we love
and we find it hard to live without them,
take from us all bitterness of heart and
let us share with them the peace you give,
over which death has no power at all.

Silence

At your invitation:
Lord, we come.

Father, it is such an honour
to be invited to your banquet;
make us worthy of our calling.

Merciful Father:
**accept these prayers
for the sake of your Son,
our Saviour Jesus Christ.
Amen.**

CALLED AND SENT

As members of the family of God,
let us pray trustingly
to our heavenly Father
who cares for us.

We pray for those involved in missionary work
all over the world;
that their work may be blessed and fruitful,
and that they may be constantly
strengthened and encouraged
by the caring presence of Christ.

Silence

Call us, loving God:
and send us out in your name.

We pray for the leaders and advisers
of all nations;
for diplomats, envoys and negotiators
in all areas of difficulty,
where tact and delicacy are needed;
that people may learn to respect
and honour one another.

Silence

Call us, loving God:
and send us out in your name.

We pray for all who are harassed and dejected,
overworked, stressed or bewildered;
that they may come to know
the liberating calm of God's peace
beneath all the activity and clamour.

Silence

Call us, loving God:
and send us out in your name.

We pray for increased trust and faithfulness
in our own lives;
for clearer knowledge of God's will
in how our time and ability is used;
for a greater readiness
to listen to God's voice
and respond to his calling.

Silence

Call us, loving God:
and send us out in your name.

In a time of silence
we share with God our Father
our personal burdens, joys and sorrows.

Silence

Father,
we ask you to hear these prayers
through Jesus Christ
our Saviour and Brother.
Amen.

LORD, WE COME TO YOU

Our loving God is here, attentive to his children.
Let us pray to him now.

Father, we pray that your Church
may always be open to receive your love;
keep us swept clean of pomposity,
complacency or self-righteousness;
let us come humbly and simply into your presence
and wait on you, knowing our dependence on you,
and rejoicing in it.

Silence

As you have called us:
Lord, we come to you.

Father, we pray for all world leaders
and their governments;
for the strength of authority
comes not through force and domination
but through co-operation and mutual respect;
we pray for greater consideration
of the needs of one another and of our planet,
and a desire to right past wrongs and injustices.

Silence

As you have called us:
Lord, we come to you.

Father, we pray for a growing maturity
in our thinking and our loving
that enables us to be childlike;
we pray for healing from all the damage
that prevents us from growing up;
we pray that our children in this church
may be helped to grow strong,
and we thank you for all we learn from them.

Silence

As you have called us:
Lord, we come to you.

Father, we pray for all who cry out for rest and relief,
all who are carrying terrible burdens
that weigh them down,
all whose poverty denies them the chance of healing,
all whose wealth denies them
the chance of knowing their need of you.

Silence

As you have called us:
Lord, we come to you.

Father, we pray for those who die unprepared to meet you,
and for all who have died recently,
both those well-known to us
and those dying unknown and unnoticed
all over the world.

Silence

As you have called us:
Lord, we come to you.

Father, we thank you for your gentleness and humility,
which puts our pride and vanity to shame.
Teach us to trust more and more in your truth,
discarding what the world considers essential
and rejoicing in your freedom.

Merciful Father:
**accept these prayers
for the sake of your Son,
our Saviour Jesus Christ.
Amen.**

RESTORE AND REVIVE US

Let us quieten ourselves to notice our God,
here with us now,
and attentive to our deepest needs.

Lord, we long for our Church to be alive and active,
attentive to you,
and ready to go wherever you suggest.
Show us the work of the Church
from your point of view,
and develop our will to co-operate.

Silence

We call on your name, O God:
restore us and revive us.

Lord, we long for your kingdom
to come in our world,
and to flood with truth and love
the disillusion, hopelessness and terror
which trap the human spirit
and choke its potential joy.

Silence

We call on your name, O God:
restore us and revive us.

Lord, come into the daily relationships
we so easily take for granted,
and enable us to value one another,
delighting in one another's richness,
and responding to one another's needs with love.

Silence

We call on your name, O God:
restore us and revive us.

Lord, you know the need and pain
of those we love and worry about.
As you look after them,
give them the sense of your caring presence
to uphold and sustain them.

Silence

We call on your name, O God:
restore us and revive us.

Lord, for us death can seem so cruel;
give us a better understanding of eternity,
and gather into your kingdom all those
whose earthly journey has come to an end.

Silence

We call on your name, O God:
restore us and revive us.

Thank you, Lord of hope,
for the way you surprise us with joy,
and show us the extraordinary and the wonderful
in the ordinary things of life.

Merciful Father:
**accept these prayers
for the sake of your Son,
our Saviour Jesus Christ.
Amen.**

GOD'S WILL
IN GOD'S PEOPLE

We remember all the Christians worshipping
all over the world;
especially those who are feeling discouraged
or inadequate.

Silence

In all your people, Father:
let your will be done.

We remember the leaders of the nations,
all in charge of making important decisions
and all who have sidled into corruption.

Silence

In all your people, Father:
let your will be done.

We remember the members of our families
and those who make life easy or difficult for us.

Silence

In all your people, Father:
let your will be done.

We remember those dependent on drugs or alcohol;
all whose bodies don't work properly,
and all who have been damaged by violence.

Silence

In all your people, Father:
let your will be done.

We remember those who have died
and those who miss their company.

Silence

In all your people, Father:
let your will be done.

As we delight in the rich variety of your creation,
we offer our lives for you to use
in whatever way you want.

Silence

In all your people, Father:
let your will be done
on earth as it is in heaven,
through Jesus Christ, our Lord.
Amen.

Lord, Comfort Your People

Father, we remember
those whose faith is fresh and fragile,
those who labour faithfully in your service
through difficult times;
all who minister by word and sacrament
throughout the Church.

Silence

Come, Lord:
comfort your people.

Father, we remember the needs of the world
and the unbalanced spread of wealth;
we remember the leaders and advisers,
the peace makers and the law makers.

Silence

Come, Lord:
comfort your people.

Father, we remember our own relatives and friends,
our neighbours and those we meet week by week;
we remember the laughter and tears we have shared,
the hopes, dreams and fears.

Silence

Come, Lord:
comfort your people.

Father, we remember the weary and heavily burdened,
the anxious, and those who have lost their way;
all whose lives are filled with suffering;
all who do not yet know Jesus.

Silence

Come, Lord:
comfort your people.

Father, we remember those
who have come to the end of their earthly life
and those who have nursed and cared for them
and will miss their physical presence.

Silence

Come, Lord:
comfort your people.

Father, we remember your kindness and mercy
to us at every stage of our journey,
and offer you our thanks and praise.

Silence

Loving Father:
accept these prayers
for the sake of Jesus Christ,
your Son, our Lord.
Amen.

BLESS OUR HOMES

As brothers and sisters in Christ,
let us pray to our heavenly Father
for the Church
and for the world.

We ask for grace
that we may open the doors of our homes
to welcome Jesus;
that Christian families
may be an example
and a source of strength,
a ministry of warmth and generosity.

Silence

God our Father:
bless our homes.

We pray that our society may be based
on mutual respect and understanding,
on co-operation and care.

Silence

God our Father:
bless our homes.

We pray for all families who are suffering
through poverty, sickness,
separation or war;
that God's presence
may comfort and strengthen them,
and that we may work in Christ
to ease their burdens
and minister to their needs.

Silence

God our Father:
bless our homes.

We pray for our own families and loved ones,
both living and departed,
both those we feel close to
and those we find difficult
to understand.

Silence

God our Father:
bless our homes.

As members of Christ's family,
we name those we know
who are in any particular need.

Silence

Father,
we ask you to hear our prayers,
through Jesus Christ our Lord.
Amen.

The way of love

LORD OF LOVE

Through Jesus
we are shown God's compassion and mercy;
let us pray for that love in our lives,
in the Church and in the world.

Let compassion and mercy
be the hallmarks of our church life
and all its activities;
let us be noticeable by their shining
in our behaviour and our conversations;
disrupt any rules which block them out.

Silence

Lord of love:
may your love fill our lives.

Let compassion and mercy
take root in every institution, policy and structure;
let them challenge accepted wrongs
and disturb complacency.

Silence

Lord of love:
may your love fill our lives.

Let compassion and mercy
guard every doorway and fill every room;
let them colour each encounter
and drive every decision.

Silence

Lord of love:
may your love fill our lives.

Let compassion and mercy
transform our attitudes

to all whose illness or frailty
makes them marginalised, ignored or despised.
Let there be healing of all damaged self-perception,
and restoration of jarred human dignity.

Silence

Lord of love:
may your love fill our lives.

Let compassion and mercy
accompany the dying
and welcome them into eternity.

Silence

Lord of love:
may your love fill our lives.

Let compassion and mercy
blossom in all of us,
as we live out our thankfulness
to the God of love,
for all his goodness to us.

Merciful Father:
accept these prayers
for the sake of your Son,
our Saviour Jesus Christ.
Amen.

LOVE ONE ANOTHER

As members of the body of Christ,
and united in his love,
let us pray
to our heavenly Father.

We pray for the work of the Church
in spreading the Good News of Jesus
who has brought life and hope
to the world.

Silence

Lord God of love:
teach us your ways.

We pray for all those with authority
and responsibility
in governing the nations
of this world:
for peace, for compassion,
forgiveness and generosity.

Silence

Lord God of love:
teach us your ways.

We pray for those who shut love out;
those who have been hurt
by lack of love;
those whose love
has become distorted
and twisted into hate.

Silence

Lord God of love:
teach us your ways.

We pray for those who live and worship here;
for particular areas in our own lives
where the love of God is desperately needed
to transfigure, refresh
and enrich.

Silence

Lord God of love:
teach us your ways.

In silence,
we make our private petitions to God,
who knows all our needs.

Silence

Father,
confident in your boundless love,
we place these prayers before you,
through Jesus Christ our Lord.
Amen.

As you have loved us

God remembers our frailty;
let us pray to him now.

When conflicts threaten to disrupt our fellowship
in the church community,
deal with our frustrations and anger,
and give us the grace to forgive.

Silence

May we love one another:
as you have loved us.

When the luggage we carry from the past
interferes with our capacity to cope with the present,
heal the damage from our memories
and transform our experiences for good.

Silence

May we love one another:
as you have loved us.

When the differences in cultures
block our understanding of one another
and obstruct the peace process,
broaden our vision to discern the common ground.

Silence

May we love one another:
as you have loved us.

When the layers of resentment
have turned into rock,
dissolve them with the rain of your loving mercy.

Silence

May we love one another:
as you have loved us.

As those we have known and loved
pass through the gate of death,
have mercy on them,
and receive them into the joy
of your eternal kingdom.

Silence

May we love one another:
as you have loved us.

As we acknowledge the beauty
of loving even our enemies,
we thank you for the extraordinary love
you show us in Jesus.

Merciful Father:
accept these prayers
for the sake of your Son,
our Saviour Jesus Christ.
Amen.

THE LAW OF GOD

In love and obedience, let us pray to our God.

Holy God, teach us to love you
with all our heart, mind, soul and strength,
and to love our neighbours as ourselves.
Thank you for the support
and love of other Christians in your church
and the richness of our varied traditions.
May we focus our attention on you with such love
that all unnecessary divisions between us crumble.

Silence

Lord, write your law in our hearts:
that we may gladly obey.

Holy God, we pray for our law makers and keepers;
may our laws work to uphold what is just and true.
We pray that we may live
in godly peace and goodwill through choice,
rather than through fear of punishment;
through the desire to live well,
rather than avoiding detection.

Silence

Lord, write your law in our hearts:
that we may gladly obey.

Holy God, in all our day-to-day living
may we reject deceit and flattery,
so that our motives and behaviour are honest,
and our love for one another clear as the day.

Silence

Lord, write your law in our hearts:
that we may gladly obey.

Holy God, we pray for all law breakers and their families;
for those in prison
and those returning to the community.
We pray for those imprisoned by guilt or shame,
or trapped by physical frailty, illness or paralysis.
We pray for those whose lives are tragically disrupted
by war and famine, poverty and disease.

Silence

Lord, write your law in our hearts:
that we may gladly obey.

Holy God, we remember those who,
dying in faith, rejoice to see you as you are.
We thank you for their example
and commend them to your peace for ever.

Silence

Lord, write your law in our hearts:
that we may gladly obey.

Holy God, we give you thanks for the love
poured out to us each moment of each day,
and ask of you the grace to live our gratitude
and give freely of what we have freely received.

Merciful Father:
**accept these prayers
for the sake of your Son,
our Saviour Jesus Christ.
Amen.**

THE NEW COMMANDMENT

Knowing God's love and affection for us,
let us pray to him now.

Father, wherever there is friction and conflict
in the Church,
and communities are divided and weakened,
give us a greater longing for your healing
and a deeper commitment to forgiving love.

Silence

Help us, Lord:
to love one another.

Father, wherever tangled political situations
seem impossible to solve,
wherever conflicting interests threaten peace;
wherever the ears of the powerful
remain insulated against the cries of the oppressed;
give us ears to hear your guidance.

Silence

Help us, Lord:
to love one another.

Father, wherever families are dysfunctional
or children are in danger;
wherever the daily living conditions
are damaging to health and self-respect;
let your kingdom come.

Silence

Help us, Lord:
to love one another.

Father, wherever the ill and injured
need comfort and assistance;

wherever the elderly and housebound
sit each day for hours alone;
may we bring your love and help.

Silence

Help us, Lord:
to love one another.

Father, wherever people are travelling
that last journey of death,
may they be surrounded by your love
and welcomed into your heaven,
and may those who mourn be comforted.

Silence

Help us, Lord:
to love one another.

Father, wherever the beauty of creation
reflects your love,
may our hearts be lifted to you
in thanks and praise.

Merciful Father:
**accept these prayers
for the sake of your Son,
our Saviour Jesus Christ.
Amen.**

THE WAY OF LOVE

Let us bring to the God who loves us
our prayers and concerns for the Church and the world.

God of compassion,
take our hearts of stone
and give us feeling hearts,
so that we as the Church
may be more responsive
to the needs and sorrows around us.

Silence

God of love:
show us the Way.

God of wisdom,
teach all in authority,
inspire those who lead,
protect each nation from evil,
and further each right decision.

Silence

God of love:
show us the Way.

God of tenderness,
dwell in our homes
through all the times of joy
and all the heartaches and sadness,
teaching us to show one another
the love you show to us.

Silence

God of love:
show us the Way.

God of wholeness,
speak into the despair and loneliness

of all who struggle with life and its troubles;
reassure, affirm and encourage them,
and alert us to ways we can help.

Silence

God of love:
show us the Way.

God of peace,
be with the dying,
and as you welcome those who have died in faith
into the full life of your kingdom,
we, too, remember them with thanks and love.

Merciful Father:
**accept these prayers
for the sake of your Son,
our Saviour Jesus Christ.
Amen.**

IN NEED OF LOVE

Humbled by the wonder
of God's love for us all,
let us bring before him
our concerns.

We bring before him all Christians
who are troubled by doubt,
all who have lapsed from worshipping
or whose prayer time is threatened
by over-busy lives;
that they may know the nearness of Christ,
and be touched by his calm and stillness.

Silence

Father of all:
we come to you for love.

We bring before him the heated arguments,
industrial disputes,
blinkered vision and stubbornness
of our world;
that the power of God's love may soften,
ease and coax us all
to be more understanding,
wise and forgiving.

Silence

Father of all:
we come to you for love.

We bring before him widows,
widowers and orphans;
all broken families
and the socially rejected;
those who are disfigured or incapacitated;
that the warmth of God's love may radiate

all aspects of life, even the most painful,
to heal, comfort and transform.

Silence

Father of all:
we come to you for love.

We bring before him the areas of our own lives
which are in shadow and darkness;
that in the light of God's love
we may see our faults
and weaknesses more clearly
and notice the needs around us more readily,
so that in Christ's strength
we can show love in practical ways.

Silence

Father of all:
we come to you for love.

Trustingly we pray to our loving Lord
for our own needs and cares.

Silence

Father,
we ask you to work your love in our lives,
and accept these prayers
we have brought to you,
through Jesus Christ our Lord.
Amen.

THE GIFT OF LOVE

Let us pray
to our heavenly Father,
and ask him for
the priceless gift of love.

We pray for a constant renewal
in the Church;
for a ceaseless deepening of love
and thankfulness.

Silence

Loving Father:
teach us your ways.

We pray for the world in which we live;
for more tolerance
and forgiveness
among its people;
for more understanding
and less fear;
for more friendship
and less bitterness.

Silence

Loving Father:
teach us your ways.

We pray for all who hate,
for all who seek revenge,
for all who refuse to forgive;
that love may transform
their hearts and minds.

Silence

Loving Father:
teach us your ways.

We pray for the people next to us here;
that, being open to the grace of God,
our community may be more deeply filled
with his Spirit of outgoing love.

Silence

Loving Father:
teach us your ways.

In the silence of God's attentive love,
we name those we know
who are in particular need.

Silence

God our Father,
hear these prayers;
give us all those qualities of faith,
hope and love
which last for ever.
In Jesus' name we pray.
Amen.

LET LOVE INCREASE

As members together of the body of Christ,
let us pray to the true and living God.

We pray for the nurture
of each member of the Church;
for the newly baptised and for all
in ordained and lay ministry,
that our love for one another may show
as we work for the coming of the kingdom.

Silence

Direct our hearts, O Lord:
to love you more and more.

We pray for the gift of discernment,
so that we recognise God's presence,
and reverence his face
in the faces of those we meet.

Silence

Direct our hearts, O Lord:
to love you more and more.

We hold before God our monarchy
and all those who govern our country
and make its laws,
that we may act responsibly and with compassion,
attentive to real needs and good values.

Silence

Direct our hearts, O Lord:
to love you more and more.

We pray particularly for homes
filled with suspicion and envy,
and ask for the healing of old hurts,

together with hope and perseverance
as people set out on paths of reconciliation.

Silence

Direct our hearts, O Lord:
to love you more and more.

We pray for those whose capacity for trust and love
has been damaged by other people's sin.
We long for your healing
so that all who are imprisoned by their past
may walk freely into God's future.

Silence

Direct our hearts, O Lord:
to love you more and more.

We pray for those who have recently
passed through death,
that God will judge them with mercy,
so that, made whole in his love,
they may know the joy of his eternity.

Silence

Direct our hearts, O Lord:
to love you more and more.

We give you thanks and praise
for the salvation and restoration
that is now possible for us
through Christ's victory over death.

Merciful Father:
**accept these prayers
for the sake of your Son,
our Saviour Jesus Christ.
Amen.**

INCREASE OUR LOVE
FOR ONE ANOTHER

My companions in Christ,
humbled by the wonder of God's love for us all,
let us lay before him our needs and concerns.

We lay before you all Christians,
especially Church leaders and all in ordained ministry;
Christians who have lapsed from worshipping
or whose prayer life is dead;
may all be touched and strengthened
by your caring love.

Silence

Father of all:
increase our love for one another.

We lay before you the heated arguments,
industrial action, blinkered vision
and stubborn behaviour of our world;
may the power of your love soften, ease and coax us all
to be more understanding, wise and forgiving.

Silence

Father of all:
increase our love for one another.

We lay before you the areas of our own lives
which are in shadow and darkness;
that in the light of your love
we may see our faults and weaknesses more clearly,
notice the good in those we live with,
and recognise the needs around us.

Silence

Father of all:
increase our love for one another.

We lay before you widows, widowers and orphans,
all broken families and all the lonely;
the disfigured, incapacitated and neglected;
those who daily persevere in tending a physically
or mentally sick relative;
may the warmth and joy of your love
comfort and transform.

Silence

Father of all:
increase our love for one another.

We commend to your keeping all those who have died;
may they rest in your peace.

Silence

We thank you for all the blessings
that enrich our lives;
for the opportunities to show our praise
in loving service to one another.

Silence

Father, teach us to live
as brothers and sisters in your family:
loving one another
through Jesus Christ, your Son.
Amen.

DEEPEN OUR LOVE

God our Father loves us
and longs for us to respond.
Coming together in faith,
let us pray to him now
for the Church
and for the world.

We pray for a deeper trustfulness
among all Christian people,
so that they may become
more and more open
to God's will.

Silence

Lord, our Redeemer:
deepen our love.

We pray that Love may make his home
in the hearts of people
all over the world,
to guide, sustain
and renew.

Silence

Lord, our Redeemer:
deepen our love.

We pray that every family
may become filled
with the life of Christ
and know his joy
and his transforming love.

Silence

Lord, our Redeemer:
deepen our love.

We pray for all expectant mothers,
for the children growing within them,
for the babies being born today,
and for those children
who are neglected or abused.

Silence

Lord, our Redeemer:
deepen our love.

We pray to our loving Father
in silence,
for everything we need.

Silence

In thankfulness we ask you, Father,
to hear our prayers,
through Christ our Lord.
Amen.

MAKE LOVE REAL

Let us pray to our heavenly Father
in thankfulness for his constant
love and loyalty,
bringing him our needs and concerns.

We pray for those involved in the planning
and leading of worship;
that all our worship
may be an outward expression
of deep, personal commitment
and never become careless
or empty repetition.

Silence

Father, hear us:
make love real in our lives.

We pray for those involved in welfare services,
prison management,
and those working in industry and commerce;
all whose work helps maintain peace and order;
that justice may always be administered with mercy,
and policies followed
which are grounded in loving care.

Silence

Father, hear us:
make love real in our lives.

We pray for all who have become
prisoners of habits,
whether drugs, self indulgence
or constant criticism;
that God may give us the power and confidence
to break those habits,
and that there may be mutual support

and encouragement
as we recognise our mutual
needs and weaknesses.

Silence

Father, hear us:
make love real in our lives.

We pray for our families, friends and neighbours;
that we may serve God in serving one another
cheerfully and ungrudgingly,
so that his kingdom of love and joy
may be established throughout the world.

Silence

Father, hear us:
make love real in our lives.

Trusting in God's loving mercy,
we pray in silence
for our own cares and concerns.

Silence

Father of mercy,
we rejoice at your welcoming forgiveness,
and ask you to accept our prayers
through Jesus Christ our Lord.
Amen.

TEACH US ALL TO LOVE

We belong to the body of Christ.
In his name let us pray to the Father
for the Church and for the world.

We commend to your care and protection
all who are abused, imprisoned or insulted
because of their faith.

Silence

Lord, by your example:
teach us all to love.

We commend to your light and truth
all governments and committees,
every head of state, and all leaders.

Silence

Lord, by your example:
teach us all to love.

We commend to your longsuffering patience
and compassion, ourselves,
with our frequent misuse of your blessings
and failure to serve.

Silence

Lord, by your example:
teach us all to love.

We commend to your healing and wholeness
all who are ill or injured;
those undergoing surgery
and those nearing death.

Silence

Lord, by your example:
teach us all to love.

We commend to your light and lasting peace
all those who have died, especially . . .

Silence

We thank you, Lord,
for all your guidance and loving care;
fulfil our needs in the way which is best for us
in the context of eternity.

Silence

Father, we ask these prayers
in the name of Jesus,
who shows us how to love.
Amen.

AWAKE AND SHINING

In the power of the Spirit,
let us pray to the Lord.

Heavenly Father, anoint your Church all over the world
with the oil of your Spirit, so that we burn brightly,
lighting the dark world with your love and truth.
Keep our church communities from error and sin,
and supply us all, through word and sacrament,
with all our souls require.

Silence

Waken us, Lord:
to shine with your love.

Heavenly Father, take the false values of our world
and upend them;
take the oppressed and free them;
take the leaders and inspire them;
take the past and redeem it, the present and fill it,
the future and guide us in it.

Silence

Waken us, Lord:
to shine with your love.

Heavenly Father, it is in our homes and daily tasks
that you train us in loving obedience.
We pray for those who have to live and work with us
and are familiar with our habits, gifts and faults.
May we make the most of the opportunities
to love, to forgive, to stand back and to reach out.

Silence

Waken us, Lord:
to shine with your love.

Heavenly Father, as we pray for all who are ill
in body, mind or spirit,
surround them with your love and healing,
your reassurance and peace.
We pray for those
who are too weak or exhausted to pray,
but simply know they ache for your comfort.

Silence

Waken us, Lord:
to shine with your love.

Heavenly Father, as real and living for the dead
as for those of us walking through time,
we commend to your mercy and love
those who have died in your faith and friendship;
may we all share in the joy
of Christ's coming in glory.

Silence

Waken us, Lord:
to shine with your love.

Heavenly Father, all the resources for holiness
you lovingly provide,
and we thank you
for your ongoing and unlimited provision.

Merciful Father:
accept these prayers
for the sake of your Son,
our Saviour Jesus Christ.
Amen.

SHINING WITH THE LOVE OF GOD

We are all brothers and sisters in Christ;
as children of God, our heavenly Father,
let us draw near and tell him of our needs and cares,
asking for his help and blessing.

We ask you, Lord, to bless and guide all who serve you;
to inspire their teaching,
nudge their memories,
instruct them through their failures
and mature them through their experiences,
so that in all activity, your will may be done.

Silence

Merciful Lord:
work on us till we shine with love.

We ask you to direct the people of the world
towards harmony and peace,
mutual respect and appreciation
of one another's cultures and traditions:
make us prepared to learn from one another.

Silence

Merciful Lord:
work on us till we shine with love.

We ask you into our homes and places of work,
so that all our friendships, and business transactions,
shopping and leisure times may be opportunities
for rejoicing in your love and spreading your peace.

Silence

Merciful Lord:
work on us till we shine with love.

We ask you to ease the burdens
of those bowed down by grief,
depression, pain or guilt;
encourage the timid and frightened,
refresh all who are overworked
or who have not been able to sleep;
break down all barricades of hatred and revenge.

Silence

Merciful Lord:
work on us till we shine with love.

We ask you to welcome into your kingdom
all who have died in faith;
may they live for ever in your perfect peace.

Silence

Every day we are given so many blessings;
we offer you our thanks and life-long praise.

Silence

Lord, receive our prayers,
and dispel the dullness of our faith
with the shining of your love:
for Jesus Christ's sake.
Amen.

FILLED WITH THE LOVE OF GOD

My friends in Christ,
mindful of God's steadfast love for us,
let us pray to our heavenly Father.

We pray for faithfulness among all Christians,
particularly when conflicts arise
between Christian values and social expectations;
for a drawing together towards unity
and an increase of the kind of caring
that should make Christ's followers stand out.

Silence

Father, live in us:
fill us with love.

We pray for all factories, mines, quarries,
all processing and refining plants
and all who work in them or live close by;
may they be safely and responsibly managed
with industrial relations based on mutual respect,
courtesy and goodwill.

Silence

Father, live in us:
fill us with love.

We pray for everyone who has helped us
and forgiven us this week
at home, work or school;
for anyone in need whom we could help;
make us more prepared to take the initiative
in caring for others, and taking ourselves less seriously.

Silence

Father, live in us:
fill us with love.

We pray for the malnourished and starving,
the grief-stricken and the bereaved;
for the homeless, and those surviving in inadequate
accommodation;
open our eyes to see Christ among all who suffer,
so we are inspired to spend our lives
in helping those in need.

Silence

Father, live in us:
fill us with love.

We pray for those who have died;
that falling asleep to pain and suffering
they may wake to the joy and freedom of your heaven.

Silence

Lord, your glory is everywhere for us to see,
and we thank you for all the love
that brightens our world.

Silence

Father of love:
accept these prayers
for the sake of your Son,
our Saviour, Jesus Christ.
Amen.

MAY WE LOVE YOU MORE AND MORE

As children of our heavenly Father,
and knowing the extent of his love for us,
let us pray to him now.

We pray for all whom you have called to serve you,
in different ministries and in every country;
may they work in your strength
and show your love and compassion.

Silence

Lord, how you must love us:
may we love you more and more.

We pray for all in positions of authority,
particularly when faced with moral dilemmas
and the temptation to act expediently;
may they see what is right
and be encouraged to stand firm.

Silence

Lord, how you must love us:
may we love you more and more.

We pray for the members of our family
and all whom we love and care for;
may we always be ready to forgive,
respect and value them.

Silence

Lord, how you must love us:
may we love you more and more.

We pray for all who know the pain
of rejection, vulnerability or torture;

for all innocent sufferers
and prisoners of conscience;
may they know your love for them.

Silence

Lord, how you must love us:
may we love you more and more.

We pray for those who are nearing death
and those who have moved on into eternity;
may we one day be welcomed into your kingdom.

Silence

Lord, how you must love us:
may we love you more and more.

Lord, how can we ever thank you
for what you have done for us!
May our lives proclaim our thanks and praise.

Silence

Father, accept these prayers,
which we ask in the name of Jesus,
who, by his life, death and resurrection
has shown us how much you love us.
Amen.

TO KNOW AND
LOVE YOU MORE

We pray for all whose faith is shaky,
those who hesitate to trust you
and those who are just beginning to believe.

Silence

Open our eyes, Lord:
to know and love you more.

We pray for the areas of fighting and bitterness,
for the downtrodden and despised,
for those with authority to improve conditions.

Silence

Open our eyes, Lord:
to know and love you more.

We pray for the very young and the very old,
for mothers, fathers and children
and all the homes in this community.

Silence

Open our eyes, Lord:
to know and love you more.

We pray for the ill and injured,
those who live fearful, anxious lives
and those who are disillusioned with life.

Silence

Open our eyes, Lord:
to know and love you more.

We pray for those who are approaching death,
those who have died recently
and all who fear death.

Silence

Open our eyes, Lord:
to know and love you more.

We pray for a deeper sense of thankfulness
for all you have given us
and for all you are in us.

Silence

Open our eyes, Lord:
to know and love you more,
as we see your love in Jesus
our Saviour and Friend.
Amen.

GOODNESS AND LOVE

We pray that your Church will have courage
to speak up for what is right and loving;
we pray for those who are persecuted
or imprisoned because of their faith.

Silence

Father, fill us up:
with goodness and with love.

We pray for integrity and wisdom
in all who advise and lead in our world;
we pray for the areas where law and order
have broken down.

Silence

Father, fill us up:
with goodness and with love.

We pray that our homes may be places of welcome,
comfort and friendship;
we pray for all who will walk in and out
of our homes this week.

Silence

Father, fill us up:
with goodness and with love.

We pray for all who are victims of greed,
cruelty and revenge;
we pray for those who hate,
and all who are finding it difficult to forgive.

Silence

Father, fill us up:
with goodness and with love.

We pray for those who have come to the end
of their earthly life,
and those who mourn.

Silence

Father, fill us up:
with goodness and with love.

We praise and bless you
for every scrap of tenderness,
every spark of joy,
and every glimpse of your glory.

Silence

Good and loving Father:
**accept these prayers
for the sake of your Son,
our Saviour, Jesus Christ.
Amen.**

BUILDING ON THE LOVE OF GOD

There are places where the Church is weak
and complacent;
where we are deaf and blind to how you are leading us.
Open our hearts to hear and see you more clearly.

Silence

Father, let our lives:
be strongly built on your love.

There are places where brutal force and corruption
seem to have the upper hand.
Quieten our lives and give space to all leaders
to hear your wisdom.

Silence

Father, let our lives:
be strongly built on your love.

There are homes where arguments flare up
all the time, and people are sad and lonely.
Fill each home in this community with peace and love.

Silence

Father, let our lives:
be strongly built on your love.

There are people with raging temperatures
and bodies full of pain.
Keep them safe and bring them to wholeness.

Silence

Father, let our lives:
be strongly built on your love.

There are people from every country
who have recently died.
Welcome them into your kingdom
and comfort those who miss them.

Silence

Father, let our lives:
be strongly built on your love.

The world you have given us to live in
is full of beauty.
We thank you for all that fills us with joy.

Silence

Father of Jesus,
accept our prayers,
which we ask in his name.
Amen.

ROOTED IN LOVE

Let us pray trustfully to the God
who has loved us into being
and cherished us all our life.

Loving God, guide your Church
into ways of spiritual beauty and gracious wisdom.
May your word be spoken out with passion
and heard with humility and joy.
Sustain and feed us so that we bear fruit in abundance.

Silence

Lord, root your people:
firmly in your love.

Loving God, may justice and righteousness
flourish in this neighbourhood, this country, this world.
Bless those who work to right what is wrong
and mediate where there is conflict.
Raise up leaders who are happy to serve
and protect them from power's corruption.

Silence

Lord, root your people:
firmly in your love.

Loving God, we thank you
for the nurturing we have received,
and pray for our children and young people as they grow.
Protect them from evil and strengthen them in faith;
may they continue to be yours for ever.

Silence

Lord, root your people:
firmly in your love.

Loving God, give comfort and healing to all
who are in any kind of need, sorrow or pain.

May they sense your reassuring presence
and know that you are there with them,
wherever their journey takes them.

Silence

Lord, root your people:
firmly in your love.

Loving God, we pray for those
who have died to this earthly life,
and now see you face to face.
We remember your mercy
and commit our loved ones
to the safety of your keeping.

Silence

Lord, root your people:
firmly in your love.

Loving God, we thank you for all the care
and attention that you lavish on us;
make us worthy of our calling
and continue your ongoing work in us.

Merciful Father:
**accept these prayers
for the sake of your Son,
our Saviour Jesus Christ.
Amen.**

GROWING IN LOVE

As we gather together
in the presence of our parent God,
let us pray.

Loving Father, we pray
for all who are persecuted for their faith,
and for whom following you brings danger.
We pray for those who are new to faith
and those who no longer walk with you.
We thank you for the example of those
whose faith shines out in their lives.

Silence

We are all your children:
help us grow in love.

Loving Father, we pray
for those who are forced to leave their homes,
their families or their countries.
We pray for those who, through war and famine,
must watch their children die.
We pray for your peace and comfort.

Silence

We are all your children:
help us grow in love.

Loving Father, we pray
for all the loving care that goes on in this community
and for those who crave tenderness
and are weary of the struggle to be strong.

Silence

We are all your children:
help us grow in love.

Loving Father, we pray
for all new parents and their babies,
and all giving birth today.
We pray for all who are vulnerable,
that they may be protected from harm.

Silence

We are all your children:
help us grow in love.

Loving Father, there are those here
whose loved ones have died,
and are still remembered with great affection.
We remember them now,
rejoicing in all they gave,
and commending them to your protection for ever.

Silence

We are all your children:
help us grow in love.

Loving Father, we give you thanks
for the comfort you provide in all our troubles,
and for the richness of all our relationships.

Merciful Father:
**accept these prayers
for the sake of your Son,
our Saviour Jesus Christ.
Amen.**

The way of service

SERVANTS OF GOD

Summoned by Christ
to live his risen life,
let us pray
in the assurance of faith
to our heavenly Father.

We pray that many may be receptive
to God's calling
and, acknowledging his authority,
be prepared to relinquish
personal ambitions and plans
in submitting their lives
to his service.

Silence

Lord of creation:
may your will be done.

We pray that the leaders of the nations
may be sensitive to the needs
of their people,
just and merciful,
caring and constructive.

Silence

Lord of creation:
may your will be done.

We pray that all who seek to heal,
restore movement, hearing,
sight or speech,
may be blessed as they work
in harmony with God;
that those they tend
may be given courage,
patience and wholeness.

Silence

Lord of creation:
may your will be done.

We pray that in every person we meet this week
we may look for the good
and be alert to needs;
that we may be ready to serve cheerfully,
without grudging,
happy to be serving Christ.

Silence

Lord of creation:
may your will be done.

Now, in the space of silence,
we bring to God our Father
our own private prayers.

Silence

Most merciful Father,
we ask you to accept these prayers,
through Jesus Christ.
Amen.

PLEDGED TO GOD'S SERVICE

Dear friends in Christ,
as we gather here in the presence of the living God,
let us ask for his help and guidance
in the Church and in the world.

We join in prayer with all other worshipping Christians;
give us an increasing love and affection
between individuals and groups
in every church and denomination;
increasing open-heartedness,
outreach and generosity of spirit.

Silence

Unchanging Lord,
we pledge ourselves to your service.

We pray for the breaking down of suspicion,
double standards and hypocrisy in our world;
that the nations may work together
to conquer the problems of food and water distribution,
so that our planet's resources are shared and not wasted.

Silence

Unchanging Lord,
we pledge ourselves to your service.

We pray for the homes and families represented here,
with all their particular joys and sorrows,
needs and resources;
that our lives may be practical witnesses to our faith.

Silence

Unchanging Lord,
we pledge ourselves to your service.

We pray for those involved in medical research,
and all who suffer from diseases

which are as yet incurable;
for any who are too weak or exhausted to pray;
for any who are desperate or suicidal.

Silence

Unchanging Lord,
we pledge ourselves to your service.

We pray that all who have died in faith
may rise to new life in glory.

Silence

Father, we thank you for your immense compassion,
understanding and encouragement throughout our lives.

Silence

Loving, heavenly Father,
we know you hear our prayers,
because we ask them in the name
of Jesus Christ, our Lord.
Amen.

WILLING SERVANTS

Bound together in the life of Christ
let us pour out our needs and concerns
before our Lord and Father,
who knows and loves us so well.

Father, we commend to your love
all ministers of your word and sacrament;
keep them true to their calling
so that their life and work
bring many into contact with you.

Silence

Lord, here we are:
use us for your glory.

Father, we commend to your wisdom
all who wield power;
help them to encourage
reconciliation rather than revenge,
friendship rather than aggression,
and flexibility rather than stubborn intransigence.

Silence

Lord, here we are:
use us for your glory.

Father, we commend to your peace and joy
our homes and all the homes in this community,
especially any where there is conflict or distress;
dwell with us, so that our homes speak
to every visitor of your love.

Silence

Lord, here we are:
use us for your glory.

Father, we commend to your healing
all who are in pain or danger;
all who are recovering from surgery;
all who depend on others for life and movement;
and who long for a friend who would visit them
and care about them.

Silence

Lord, here we are:
use us for your glory.

Father, we commend to your keeping
those who have left this life through the gate of death;
may they live with you in the light of heaven for ever.

Silence

We thank you for calling us
and we offer you the rest of our lives.

Silence

Father, we bring these prayers
in the name of Jesus.
Amen.

USE US, LORD

As members of the body of Christ
bound together in his love,
let us pray together now,
confident in God's promise to be amongst us.

We pray for all who form the Church
in its variety and richness throughout the world;
may the weak be encouraged and strengthened,
the wanderers return,
those besieged by doubt be given the assurance of faith,
and the jaded refreshed by your living Spirit.

Silence

Take us as we are:
and use us, Lord.

We pray for all councils, committees
and governing bodies,
for those serving on juries,
for air, sea and mountain rescue teams;
that in working together in your strength
they may strive for what is good, just and honest,
so that your will is accomplished in them.

Silence

Take us as we are:
and use us, Lord.

We pray for our families and our friends,
that we may be transformed and renewed
through the richness of your presence;
give us deeper insight, more awareness
and greater love for one another.

Silence

Take us as we are:
and use us, Lord.

We pray for the poor and for the hungry,
for all frustrated by damaged or crippled bodies;
for those in prison, and those enslaved
by drugs, alcohol, hatred or fear.

Silence

Take us as we are:
and use us, Lord.

We pray for those who have died
and those who are at present on that last journey;
may they have peace in the joy
of your presence for ever.

Silence

Take us as we are:
and use us, Lord.

Father, we thank you for all your glory
in the world you have made,
for all you have accomplished in our lives
and in the lives of the saints.

Silence

Father, we offer you
both our prayers and our lives:
in the name of Jesus Christ, our Lord.
Amen.

TAKE US AND USE US

Father, set your Church on fire with your love
for everyone, without exception.

Silence

Take us, Lord:
and use us wherever you need us.

Father, let the greed and selfishness
which tear our world apart,
be overcome with generosity of spirit
and concern for one another's good.

Silence

Take us, Lord:
and use us wherever you need us.

Father, let every home become a place of comfort;
safe, happy and welcoming.

Silence

Take us, Lord:
and use us wherever you need us.

Father, let those who are distressed
and diseased find healing, refreshment
and meaning for their lives.

Silence

Take us, Lord:
and use us wherever you need us.

Father, let those who have died
spend their eternity with you,
at peace and in joy for ever;
and may their loved ones be comforted
in their sorrow.

Silence

Take us, Lord:
and use us wherever you need us.

Father, may we shine as lights
as you draw all people
to fulfilment in you.

Silence

Father, we bring both our prayers and our lives
to be used in your service:
through Jesus Christ, our Lord.
Amen.

HEAL US AND USE US

Let us focus our bodies, minds, hearts and wills
as we pray to the God of all creation.

Holy God, you are the focus of our love and worship,
because you alone are the Lord
who has made us and rescued us.
May we not return to the slavery of sin
but live in your freedom, serving you with joy,
in thankfulness for all you have done for us.

Silence

Heal us, Lord:
and use us to your glory.

Holy God, though the world may often reject you,
you never fail to believe in us all
and love us with tenderness.
We pray for all areas of conflict, deceit,
mismanagement and greed,
and for all who are drawn into the chaos of evil.

Silence

Heal us, Lord:
and use us to your glory.

Holy God, our daily lives provide such rich ground
for acts of loving kindness,
self-discipline and courage.
Remind us of the opportunities,
and strengthen us to use them.

Silence

Heal us, Lord:
and use us to your glory.

Holy God, we thank you for all
who lovingly look after those in nursing homes,

hospitals, nurseries and prisons,
and we pray for all who need such care
and rely on others' help.

Silence

Heal us, Lord:
and use us to your glory.

Holy God, we call to mind
those who have recently died
and thank you for each act of goodness in their lives.
Have mercy on them and forgive their failings,
so that they may share the joy of heaven for ever.

Silence

Heal us, Lord:
and use us to your glory.

Holy God, we thank you
for our human potential for good,
and for your gift of grace
that makes such goodness a real possibility.

Merciful Father:
**accept these prayers
for the sake of your Son,
our Saviour Jesus Christ.
Amen.**

WE OFFER YOU OURSELVES

Let us pray to the God who loves us
and knows the terrain we travel.

We thank God for all those who brought
the good news of Jesus to us,
and all who nourish our faith today.
We pray that the whole people of God
may work in unity and openness
for the coming of God's kingdom.

Silence

Lord God:
we offer you ourselves.

We thank God that salvation is for all people,
and pray for a just and accepting world
where none is rejected, despised
or treated with contempt.

Silence

Lord God:
we offer you ourselves.

We thank God for the privilege of parenting
and of living in communities;
we pray that our homes and churches
may be welcoming and generous-hearted.

Silence

Lord God:
we offer you ourselves.

We thank God for all who care
with such thoughtfulness and practical loving
for those who are vulnerable,
and especially for the very young.

We pray for healing and wholeness,
peace of mind, protection and hope.

Silence

Lord God:
we offer you ourselves.

We thank God for all who have reached
the end of their earthly journey in faith,
that they may be welcomed into his eternity.
May we use the time left to us here
as good stewards of God's gifts.

Silence

Lord God:
we offer you ourselves.

We thank God for including us
in the plan of salvation,
and pray that we may be made worthy
of our calling.

Merciful Father:
**accept these prayers
for the sake of your Son,
our Saviour Jesus Christ.
Amen.**

WALKING WHERE GOD IS

Father, in love we stand alongside
all those who lead and minister in your Church.
We ask you to bless their lives and their work.

Silence

God our Father:
we want to walk with you.

Father, in love we stand alongside
our Queen and all the leaders of the nations.
We ask you to guide them in your ways.

Silence

God our Father:
we want to walk with you.

Father, in love we stand alongside
all whose lives are bound up with ours.
Work with tenderness in the relationships
we bring before you now.

Silence

God our Father:
we want to walk with you.

Father, in love we stand alongside
all whose bodies, minds or spirits are hurting.
We ask you to minister to them now.

Silence

God our Father:
we want to walk with you.

Father, in love we stand alongside
all who are close to death,
and we pray now for your mercy.

Silence

God our Father:
we want to walk with you.

Father, with love in our hearts
we want to thank you
for all you are and all you do in our lives.

Silence

Loving Father:
be our companion on the way,
through Jesus Christ, our Lord.
Amen.

TEACH US TO CARE

As members of the body of Christ,
let us pray to the Father
for the Church and for the world.

Let us pray for all Christian leaders
of all denominations;
for the healing of old wounds,
for forgiveness and an openness
to the Holy Spirit
who alone can make us one.

Silence

Lord of love:
teach us to care.

Let us pray for the areas
where there are poverty,
overcrowding and neglect;
for areas of depression
and high unemployment;
that, working hand in hand with God,
we may bring to the world the freshness
and vitality of hope
and caring love.

Silence

Lord of love:
teach us to care.

Let us pray for all who are trapped
by disability, illness or addiction,
all who feel unwanted or rejected;
that they may experience as a living reality
the liberation of Christ's accepting love.

Silence

Lord of love:
teach us to care.

Let us pray for the areas of our own lives
which need to be remade in Christ;
for any trying or difficult relationships,
anyone we tend to criticise or despise;
that God's uncompromising love
may inspire us to give without limits
and without exceptions.

Silence

Lord of love:
teach us to care.

In silence filled with love,
we name our particular prayer burdens.

Silence

Father,
we ask you to accept these prayers
through Jesus Christ,
and use us for your glory.
Amen.

SERVING AND CARING

Gathered as the Church of God,
members of the Body of Christ,
let us pray together.

Fill your Church, O Lord,
with life and energy, spiritual health and vitality.
As we feed on you, may we grow more like you;
may we exercise your loving,
minister with your tenderness,
serve with your humility and co-operate with your vision.

Silence

O Lord of infinite love:
help us to serve and care.

Fill your world, O Lord, with wonder at creation,
recognition of our mutual human responsibility,
desire for reforming what is at fault,
and hope in the possibilities of living at peace
with you and with one another.

Silence

O Lord of infinite love:
help us to serve and care.

Fill our homes and neighbourhoods, O Lord,
with the generosity and trust that allows space
but is always ready to encourage and support.
May we cherish our bodies, minds and spirits
as temples containing your Spirit,
and honour one another as people of your making.

Silence

O Lord of infinite love:
help us to serve and care.

We pray for all who are ill at home or in hospital,
for all in emergency surgery or in casualty;
for those who have just discovered
that they have injuries or illnesses
that will change their lives.
We pray for the work of all who heal and comfort,
all who visit the sick and counsel the distressed.

Silence

O Lord of infinite love:
help us to serve and care.

We pray for the dying and those who love them;
we pray for those who have completed this life
and have made the journey through death.
We pray for the work of those who comfort the bereaved.

Silence

O Lord of infinite love:
help us to serve and care.

Fill our hearts, O Lord, with thankfulness and praise
as we recall your faithfulness and live in your love.

Merciful Father:
accept these prayers
for the sake of your Son,
our Saviour Jesus Christ.
Amen.

THE SERVICE OF GOD

God has chosen to call us here
and we have chosen to come.
Let us pray to him now.

Lord, we want to pray for stronger faith
and the courage to live up to our calling;
for the grace to act always
with the generosity of spirit you show to us,
until the whole Church models the wisdom
which the world counts as foolishness.

Silence

Holy God:
we commit ourselves to your service.

Lord, we want to pray
about all the unresolved conflicts in our world.
We ask you to give us your desire for peace,
your spirit of discernment,
your understanding of unspoken needs,
and your capacity for forgiveness.

Silence

Holy God:
we commit ourselves to your service.

Lord, we want to pray
for the homes and families we represent,
and for all with whom we live and work.
Help us to recognise the opportunities
for generous, loving service
and take away any destructive possessiveness
or self-interest.

Silence

Holy God:
we commit ourselves to your service.

Lord, we pray for peace of mind and spirit
in all those who are distressed or enveloped in pain.
May they know the reality of your inner healing,
and may even the worst situations
become places of growth and new life.

Silence

Holy God:
we commit ourselves to your service.

Lord, we pray for those approaching death
with fear, resentment and anger,
and for all who counsel the dying and the bereaved.
We pray that those who have died will know
the joy of everlasting life with you.

Silence

Holy God:
we commit ourselves to your service.

Lord, we thank you
for the extraordinary generosity of your love,
which takes us by surprise and refreshes us,
and which always appears
where we least think to look for it.

Merciful Father:
accept these prayers
for the sake of your Son,
our Saviour Jesus Christ.
Amen.

HEAR AND OBEY

As God has called us,
so we have come to pray.

We pray for the Church, the Body of Christ,
with all its collected gifts and weaknesses;
give us the grace to recognise
that in your Spirit we are one,
and curb in us all tendency to division.

Silence

May we hear you, Lord:
and want to obey.

We pray for the world
in all its beauty and richness;
give us the desire
to share our planet's food and resources,
to care for its people's well-being,
and to foster peace and justice for all.

Silence

May we hear you, Lord:
and want to obey.

We pray for those we love –
those we see each day and those we miss;
help us to cherish one another
as we live the loving way of your commands.

Silence

May we hear you, Lord:
and want to obey.

We pray for all victims of selfish or violent acts,
and for those whose lives are trapped in sin.
We pray for all whose bodies and minds

have difficulty functioning.
Make us more sensitive to their needs.

Silence

May we hear you, Lord:
and want to obey.

We pray for those who have died
and for those who miss their physical presence.
Have mercy on them;
may they, and we in our turn,
rest in the peace of your enfolding.

Silence

May we hear you, Lord:
and want to obey.

We give you thanks
for the loving example of Jesus,
who was obedient even to death
and strengthens us in all goodness.

Merciful Father:
accept these prayers
for the sake of your Son,
our Saviour Jesus Christ.
Amen.

FRUITFUL FOR GOD

Chosen by God to be members of his body,
let us gather our cares and concerns
and bring them before our heavenly Father
who loves us and knows us personally.

We pray for the many individuals
comprising the body of Christ,
with all their varied ministries;
for those unsure of your plan for them;
may your will be made clear to them
and may they be given courage to accept your call.

Silence

Lord, nourish us:
that we may bear fruit.

We pray for the world and its areas of conflict,
political unrest, decadence and deceit;
that Christ, the Lord of all truth and life,
may lead humanity to desire justice, peace and integrity.

Silence

Lord, nourish us:
that we may bear fruit.

We pray for a deeper trust in you among all of us here,
and the families we represent;
that we may spend our lives
in getting to know you better,
so we reflect your light more brightly
and can be of greater use to you in serving your world.

Silence

Lord, nourish us:
that we may bear fruit.

We pray for the bereaved and all who mourn;
for those who have miscarried
or given birth to a stillborn baby;
for those who feel uncared for and unloved;
for those who must watch their children
die from lack of food.

Silence

Lord, nourish us:
that we may bear fruit.

We pray for all the faithful who have died;
may they rest for ever in the peace and joy of heaven.

Silence

We offer you our thanks and praise
for the way you have guided us
and brought us to worship you now;
may we continue to praise you
in the way we live the rest of our lives.

Silence

Lord, hear our prayers,
which we ask in the name of Jesus,
our Saviour and our Friend.
Amen.

WORTHY OF OUR CALLING

Let us pray at the feet
of God our Father
who loves us so dearly
and has called us to serve him.

We pray for the spreading of the gospel
throughout all countries and cultures;
for all those working
to reconcile people
with their Creator;
for all involved in counselling
and spiritual teaching.

Silence

God, our loving Father:
make us worthy of our calling.

We pray for a deepening spirit
of fellowship and goodwill
among the people of this earth;
for a greater willingness to forgive,
negotiate, communicate and support.

Silence

God, our loving Father:
make us worthy of our calling.

We pray for all victims
of violence and aggression;
for those obsessed with hatred and retaliation;
for the injured, abused and the dying.

Silence

God, our loving Father:
make us worthy of our calling.

We pray for God's guidance and restoration
in our own lives;
for more awareness of our faults
and areas of blindness;
for a greater understanding
of God's love for us.

Silence

God, our loving Father:
make us worthy of our calling.

In silence, now,
we pour out to God our Father
any needs and burdens
known to us personally.

Silence

Heavenly Father,
trusting in your amazing love,
we ask you to accept these prayers,
through Jesus Christ our Lord.
Amen.

WORKING FOR GOD'S GLORY

We are God's children,
and he loves us;
let us pray to him now.

We bring to his love
those whose Christian ministry
is in prisons, hospitals,
schools or industry;
those who work among the homeless
and the very poor.

Silence

Father, you have called us:
let our lives show your glory.

We bring to his love
the areas of political tension
and unrest in our world;
the unresolved conflicts
and the deep seated grudges
that hinder peace.

Silence

Father, you have called us:
let our lives show your glory.

We bring to his love
the hurt and wounded,
the abused and the frightened;
women in labour and newly born babies;
those who are approaching death.

Silence

Father, you have called us:
let our lives show your glory.

We bring to his love the needs
of those who live or work in this area,
and any who have particularly
asked for our prayers.
(mention these by name)

Silence

Father, you have called us:
let our lives show your glory.

In silence, now,
we bring to God's love
the special needs and concerns
known to us individually.

Silence

With special joy, Father,
in the knowledge
that we can trust you unconditionally,
we offer you our prayers,
through Jesus Christ.
Amen.

SEND ME

Let us gather with our prayers
before the God who knows each of us by name.

Father, we thank you that your Church
is made up of real people,
that it is a school for sinners,
and that you can work with us and through us
straight away.

Silence

Here I am, Lord:
send me!

Father, we pray for the newly baptised
and those who have recently returned to you;
help us, as your Church, to support them well
and delight in them as members together
of the body of Christ.

Silence

Here I am, Lord:
send me!

Father, we pray for your strength and protection
against all hypocrisy and double standards
in our society.
We pray for a spirit of genuine service
among all who lead and in all areas
where we have authority.

Silence

Here I am, Lord:
send me!

Father, we pray that you will make
our homes and our relationships

places where people know,
by the way we look at them and treat them,
that they are valued, cherished
and respected for who they are.

Silence

Here I am, Lord:
send me!

Father, as we call to mind all who have learned
to regard themselves with contempt,
draw near to them and whisper their true name
so that they discern the truth
of your love and respect for them.
And use our lives to affirm one another.

Silence

Here I am, Lord:
send me!

We pray for the dying
and those who have recently died,
commending them to the joy
and safe-keeping of your love.
We give thanks for all those who know and love us
and help us grow in faith.

Merciful Father:
accept these prayers
for the sake of your Son,
our Saviour Jesus Christ.
Amen.

THE WAY OF LIFE

Gathered together in one spirit, let us pray to our God.

Father, wherever our attention
has wandered from your calling,
wherever we have fallen short of your will for us,
and failed to keep the spirit of your law of love,
forgive us and transform us,
so that we walk again the path that leads to life.

Silence

Show us the way of life:
and help us to walk in it.

Wherever the Church is asked
to give leadership on sensitive issues;
whenever the current world expectations of behaviour
need to be challenged in the light of your love,
give us the wisdom and guidance we need.

Silence

Show us the way of life:
and help us to walk in it.

Wherever our homes are lacking
in love and mutual respect,
wherever destructive relationships
cause distress and heartache,
and wherever people are made to feel they don't matter,
give a new realisation of your ways
and your hopes for us, so that your kingdom may come
and your will be done.

Silence

Show us the way of life:
and help us to walk in it.

Wherever there is illness, unhappiness, injustice or fear;
wherever people feel frustrated, imprisoned or trapped;
give us a greater sense of loving community,
a heart to put right whatever we can,
and the willingness to stand
alongside one another in our sorrows.

Silence

Show us the way of life:
and help us to walk in it.

Wherever earthly lives have come to an end,
and people are grieving the loss of their loved ones,
fill these places with the eternal peace of your presence
and prepare us all through our lives on this earth
for everlasting life with you in heaven.

Silence

Show us the way of life:
and help us to walk in it.

Father, we thank you
for the personal and affectionate way you care for us
and provide for all our needs;
may we spread the good news of your love
by the way we respond to you and to one another.

Merciful Father:
accept these prayers
for the sake of your Son,
our Saviour Jesus Christ.
Amen.

LEAD US, LORD

God is close to us as we pray.
He is attentive to us now.

Lord, whenever you weep over our harshness,
make your tears melt our hearts of stone.
Whenever you grieve over our double standards,
shock us into honesty again.
Make us receptive to your teaching,
willing to take your risks
and eager to run with our eyes fixed on Jesus.

Silence

Lead us, Lord:
to walk in your ways.

Whenever the news overwhelms us,
nudge us to fervent prayer.
Wherever leaders meet to negotiate peace,
be present at the conference table.
Breathe your values into our thinking,
tear down the divisive barriers
and renew us to lead the world into loving.

Silence

Lead us, Lord:
to walk in your ways.

Whenever tempers are frayed
and patience is wearing thin,
give us space to collect ourselves and try again.
Whenever the demands of family and friends
remind us of our limitations,
minister graciously through our weakness
and teach us the humility of apologising.

Silence

Lead us, Lord:
to walk in your ways.

Whenever people are enveloped by pain
or desolate grief or total exhaustion,
bring refreshment and peace, tranquillity and hope.
Wherever the grip of the past
prevents free movement into the future,
bring release and healing.

Silence

Lead us, Lord:
to walk in your ways.

Whenever the dying are fearful and distressed,
give comfort and reassurance on that last journey.
Bless those who care for them
and those who mourn their going.
In mercy receive the dead
into the life of your heaven,
and prepare us, through our lives now, for eternity.

Silence

Lead us, Lord:
to walk in your ways.

Holy God, we love the beauty and goodness
of your nature,
and thank you for the gift of your Spirit
to guide us to walk in your ways.

Merciful Father:
**accept these prayers
for the sake of your Son,
our Saviour Jesus Christ.
Amen.**

TEACH US YOUR WAYS

Followers of Christ,
let us call to mind now all those in need,
and pray for them to our heavenly Father.

Lord, we pray that all who teach the Christian faith
may speak with clarity and conviction
to get through to those who hear them,
so that they respond to the Gospel with joy.

Silence

Lord of life:
teach us your ways.

May all diplomats and negotiators seek
peace and friendship between the nations,
based on mutual respect and understanding.

Silence

Lord of life:
teach us your ways.

May we and our families, neighbours and friends
allow the Spirit of Christ to work among us,
making us more aware of the needs of others
and less concerned about ourselves.

Silence

Lord of life:
teach us your ways.

May those whose lives have been
shattered by crippling disease or injury
triumph over their adversity
by courage, faith and the encouragement of others.

Silence

Lord of life:
teach us your ways.

May those who have passed from this life
into eternity
rejoice for ever in the fullness of your glory.

Silence

Lord, we thank you for dealing with us so patiently
and with such compassion;
if we should close our hearts to your will
please keep knocking until we open the door!
Lord of life:
teach us your ways
and lead us in paths of justice and peace
through Jesus Christ, our Lord.
Amen.

SHOW US YOUR WAYS

As we gather in Christ's name,
let us bring to mind those
who particularly need our prayer support.

We remember those who teach the faith
throughout the Church and throughout the world.
Keep them close to your guiding,
and open the hearts of those they teach
to hear and receive your truth.

Silence

Show us your ways:
and help us to walk in them.

We remember those in positions
of authority and influence
in this country and in all societies,
that needs may be noticed and addressed,
good values upheld and all people respected.

Silence

Show us your ways:
and help us to walk in them.

We remember those who looked after us
when we were very young,
and those who have no one to love and care for them.
We remember all young families
and all the children in our community,
that they may be introduced to you, one true God
and live their lives in your company.

Silence

Show us your ways:
and help us to walk in them.

We remember the elderly faithful
and especially those who are housebound
and can no longer join us to worship in person.
We thank you for the example of their faith
and ask you to increase our love for one another
across the age groups.

Silence

Show us your ways:
and help us to walk in them.

We remember those who have finished their lives on earth
and commit them to your everlasting care and protection.
We ask you to keep us faithful to the end of our life.

Silence

Show us your ways:
and help us to walk in them.

We remember with thankfulness
our elderly friends and relatives
and celebrate the way their lives
enrich our community.

Merciful Father:
**accept these prayers
for the sake of your Son,
our Saviour Jesus Christ.
Amen.**

Living life God's way

Father, in our Christian ministry to one another
we need more discernment and less defensiveness,
more stillness and less rush.

Silence

Father, teach us:
to live life your way.

Father, in our national and international affairs
we need more listening and less bullying,
more giving and less taking,
more co-operation and less thirst for revenge.

Silence

Father, teach us:
to live life your way.

Father, in our relationships
we need more understanding and less intolerance,
more encouragement and less condemnation.

Silence

Father, teach us:
to live life your way.

Father, in our pain we need your comfort,
in our brokenness your forgiveness,
in our anguish the assurance of your love.

Silence

Father, teach us:
to live life your way.

Father, at the hour of our death
we need your presence and your mercy.

Silence

Father, teach us:
to live life your way.

Father, in you our every need is met and satisfied,
and we thank you for the personal love
you have for each one of us.

Silence

Father, you have given us life.
Help us to live it to the full
for the sake of Jesus Christ, our Lord,
in whose name we pray.
Amen.

WISE BUILDERS

As the community of God's people,
let us focus our attention and still our bodies to pray.

Father, we have heard your words and your challenge
to build our lives wisely on the bedrock of faith;
may all of us who profess to be Christians
act on what we have heard.
Bless and inspire all who preach and teach the faith
and make our worship pure and holy
and acceptable to you.

Silence

Lord God of wisdom:
we build our lives on you.

Father, we are conscious of the double standards
and inconsistencies in our world,
and ask for hearts to be opened to hear you
and recognise the wisdom of your law of love.
We ask you to strengthen and encourage each attempt
to govern with your principles,
and deal justly with your sense of mercy.

Silence

Lord God of wisdom:
we build our lives on you.

Father, we want to take more seriously
our community commitment to our children.
Show us what needs to be started,
developed or changed in our attitudes to one another,
and in the way we help one another's faith to grow.

Silence

Lord God of wisdom:
we build our lives on you.

Father, the needs and concerns of all who suffer
are our concern, through love.
May we strive to address
the imprisoning poverty and hunger
of much of our world,
and involve ourselves in the comfort, help and healing
we ask of you.

Silence

Lord God of wisdom:
we build our lives on you.

Father, we commend to your love and mercy
those who have died to this earthly life.
We thank you for lives well lived and love shared.
Bring them, and us in our turn, safely to heaven.

Silence

Lord God of wisdom:
we build our lives on you.

Father, we thank you that we can stand firm and strong
on the rock of Christ;
build us up in your love and wisdom.

Merciful Father:
**accept these prayers
for the sake of your Son,
our Saviour Jesus Christ.
Amen.**

The kingdom of God

GOD'S KINGDOM

As God has taught us, let us pray
for the coming of the kingdom in every situation.

We long for the Church to be pure and holy,
alight with God's love and compassion,
and free from behaviour which is unworthy
of God's chosen people.

Silence

God our Father:
let your kingdom come.

We long for the nations to be wisely governed,
with just laws and a sense of vision
which reflects the best of human nature.
We long for peace and mutual respect
in each community throughout the world.

Silence

God our Father:
let your kingdom come.

We long for our homes to be filled with God's love,
so we are happy to put ourselves out for others,
to listen with full attention, and to value one another.
We long to clear away anything in our life-style
which competes with God for our commitment.

Silence

God our Father:
let your kingdom come.

We long for those who feel neglected
or rejected by society
to know God's love and acceptance of them.

We long for all those in pain and distress
to be comforted and relieved.

Silence

God our Father:
let your kingdom come.

We long for the dying to recognise
their need of God and his power to save;
for those who have died to be judged with mercy
and rest in God's peace.

Silence

God our Father:
let your kingdom come.

We give you thanks, Lord God,
for your teaching and your example
which opens our eyes to your truth.

Merciful Father:
**accept these prayers
for the sake of your Son,
our Saviour Jesus Christ.
Amen.**

LORD OF HEAVEN AND EARTH

Lord of the earth we stand on,
the air we breathe, the food we grow,
keep us in touch with this planet we inhabit;
help us to tend it well and enjoy its beauty.

Silence

Lord of heaven and earth:
let your kingdom come.

Lord of our past and our future,
Lord of our longings and disappointments,
teach us to recognise you in every moment
and know you are there
through the good and the bad times.

Silence

Lord of heaven and earth:
let your kingdom come.

Lord of our fears and uncertainties,
of our laughter and our foolishness,
fill us with thankfulness
and remind us of how great it is
to be alive.

Silence

Lord of heaven and earth:
let your kingdom come.

Lord of our families and our friends,
of those we like and those we don't;
breathe into our loving
the loving you show to us.

Silence

Lord of heaven and earth:
let your kingdom come.

Loving Father,
hear the prayers we offer,
and use our bodies, minds and spirits
in establishing your kingdom:
through Jesus Christ, our Lord.
Amen.

LORD OF ALL THE EARTH

Full of thanks and praise,
we worship God our Father
for the earth is rich with his blessing;
let us pray to him now.

We pray that the will of God
may be accomplished
in every life and every situation;
that Christians may become
increasingly receptive
and ready to act as channels
of his redeeming grace.

Silence

Lord of all the earth:
rule in our hearts.

We pray that the world may be drawn
into a deep, abiding love:
the love of the Father and the Son.

Silence

Lord of all the earth:
rule in our hearts.

We hold in our prayers
all those who are physically
or mentally disadvantaged in any way,
and for all who minister to them.
For ourselves, we ask
for greater acceptance of others
who look, speak or behave
differently from ourselves.

Silence

Lord of all the earth:
rule in our hearts.

We pray that all of us here present
may become more aware
of the privileges
and responsibilities
of being the children of God.

Silence

Lord of all the earth:
rule in our hearts.

Now, in the space of silence,
we bring to God our Father
our own particular prayers.

Silence

Heavenly Father,
we ask this through Jesus Christ our Lord.
Amen.

OUR GOD REIGNS!

As brothers and sisters in Christ,
with our fellowship rooted
in the love God has for us all,
let us pray to him now.

We pray for the deepening of faith
among all Christians;
that our whole lives may rest
in the joy and security of knowing
that our God is alive and in charge.

Silence

Christ is alive for ever:
our God reigns!

We pray for the spreading of the Good News
throughout the world,
so that whatever important decisions are made
and policies planned,
people may work
in harmony with their creator,
for goodness, peace and reconciliation.

Silence

Christ is alive for ever:
our God reigns!

We pray for the healing
and repairing of broken lives,
for vision and enlightenment
among those darkened by fear and hatred;
that God's living Spirit, let loose,
may anoint and soothe,
pacify and recharge.

Silence

Christ is alive for ever:
our God reigns!

We pray for a more loving atmosphere
in our homes, our church and community;
more care and concern for each other,
more willingness to forgive,
understand and respect
those with whom we live.

Silence

Christ is alive for ever:
our God reigns!

Knowing that God loves us
personally and with full understanding,
we offer our private prayers
to him in silence.

Silence

Father,
coming together with thanks and praise
to worship you,
we ask you to accept these prayers,
for the sake of Jesus Christ.
Amen.

THE GROWTH
OF THE KINGDOM

Let us pray to the God of heaven and earth
for the growth of the kingdom.

May the kingdom grow
in clusters of Christians all over the world;
may it grow as hearts are warmed
by encounter with the living God;
nourished by word and sacrament,
private prayer and public worship.

Silence

Lord of heaven:
let the kingdom grow!

May the kingdom grow
in states, empires and monarchies,
in the crowded streets of cities
and in the scattered rural communities;
in all decision-making and all spending.

Silence

Lord of heaven:
let the kingdom grow!

May the kingdom grow
in every human shelter and home,
every place of work and education,
in each conversation and
in our mutual care of one another.

Silence

Lord of heaven:
let the kingdom grow!

May the kingdom grow
to bring peace and healing
wherever there is pain or sadness;
to bring reassurance, comfort, courage and hope.

Silence

Lord of heaven:
let the kingdom grow!

In the knowledge that we must all face judgement,
we pray for those who have died,
thanking God for his loving mercy,
and entrusting our loved ones
to God's safe keeping.

Silence

Lord of heaven:
let the kingdom grow!

As we thank God for all his blessings to us
we offer him the rest of our lives.

Merciful Father:
**accept these prayers
for the sake of your Son,
our Saviour Jesus Christ.
Amen.**

May your kingdom grow

Rooted in Christ,
let us call to mind now
all those in need, and pray for them
to our heavenly Father.

We pray that all who teach the Christian faith
may be given appropriate language
to get through to those who hear,
so that the word of God takes root
in many hearts.

Silence

Lord of life:
may your kingdom grow.

We pray that all diplomats and negotiators
may promote peace and friendship
between the nations,
fostering mutual respect
and understanding.

Silence

Lord of life:
may your kingdom grow.

We pray that those whose lifestyle
has been threatened or shattered
by crippling illness or injury
may find within their suffering
the seeds of hope,
bringing new meaning to their lives
and transforming their outlook.

Silence

Lord of life:
may your kingdom grow.

We pray that we and our families,
neighbours and friends
may become daily more Christlike
and less self-centred;
more responsive to the needs of those around us,
and less bothered by what we as individuals
get out of life.

Silence

Lord of life:
may your kingdom grow.

Knowing that God our Father is listening,
we pray in silence
for our own needs and cares.

Silence

Father,
we lay our needs and cares before you,
and ask you to hear us,
through Jesus Christ our Lord.
Amen.

PRAYING TO THE FATHER

As we have been invited to do,
we pray to our heavenly Father.

We pray for the continuous worship of the Church
in every different climate,
culture and season;
that the waves of constant praise
and thanksgiving
may never be broken;
that Christians may pray attentively,
joyfully and faithfully.

Silence

Our Father in heaven:
may your kingdom come.

We pray for those in positions of authority;
that they may neither abuse their power
nor ignore their responsibilities
but act with integrity, compassion
and generosity of spirit.

Silence

Our Father in heaven:
may your kingdom come.

We pray for all families split
by political boundaries,
war or natural disasters;
for all who have nowhere
to call their home,
and those for whom no one cares
or prays.

Silence

Our Father in heaven:
may your kingdom come.

We pray for our own parents,
for family life
throughout the whole world;
that all homes may be blessed
with love and security
and reflect God's love
for his children.

Silence

Our Father in heaven:
may your kingdom come.

In silence filled with love,
we name our particular prayer burdens.

Silence

God our Father,
rejoicing in your tenderness and compassion,
we bring these prayers before you
through Jesus Christ our Lord.
Amen.

KING OF LOVE

As children of our caring
heavenly Father,
let us pray for the coming
of his kingdom.

We pray for all Christians
throughout the world;
that they may wholeheartedly follow Christ,
so that their lives witness to the beauty
and peace of his kingdom.

Silence

King of love:
remake our lives.

We pray for all world leaders,
governments and their advisers;
that they may be inspired
to lead their people wisely and fairly,
with understanding and sensitivity.

Silence

King of love:
remake our lives.

We pray for all those who feel trapped
by the emotional, financial
or political circumstances
of their lives;
that in Christ they may find
freedom and vitality.

Silence

King of love:
remake our lives.

We pray for our own families and loved ones,
especially any from whom we are separated;
that we may learn to see Christ in each face,
and serve him in caring for each other.

Silence

King of love:
remake our lives.

Together in silence
we make our private prayers
and thanksgivings.

Silence

Father of all time and space,
accept these prayers
through Jesus Christ our Lord.
Amen.

YOUR KINGDOM COME

As sons and daughters of our heavenly King,
let us ask our Father's blessing
on the Church and on the world.

We pray for the work of your Church;
that all your people may be inspired
with a vision of your kingdom on earth.
Filled with your Spirit of peace and joy,
may we spread your love through all the world.

Silence

Lord, our heavenly Father:
may your kingdom come.

We pray for all who work for justice and peace.
May the nations learn to live in harmony,
and all peoples turn away from war and conflict,
in favour of sharing and co-operation.

Silence

Lord, our heavenly Father:
may your kingdom come.

We pray for our own part in the life of your kingdom;
that we may learn obedience
to your way of love
and serve you gladly
in the power of your Spirit.

Silence

Lord, our heavenly Father:
may your kingdom come.

We pray for those who care for the sick
in hospitals and nursing homes;
for doctors and nurses, paramedics and chaplains,

for all who work in medical laboratories
and those whose lives are in the hands
of surgeons and consultants.

Silence

Lord, our heavenly Father:
may your kingdom come.

We pray for all who have passed
through the gate of death to eternity;
may they live for ever in your heaven.

Silence

Lord, our heavenly Father:
may your kingdom come.

We rejoice for all the wonder
and beauty of your creation;
in the constant miracle of life and renewal;
in your amazing and undeserved love
and affection for us.

Silence

Father:
**accept these prayers which we ask
in the name of Jesus, our King.
Amen.**

LET YOUR KINGDOM COME (1)

As fellow disciples of Christ,
let us ask God's blessing
on the Church and on the world.

We pray for the work
of Christ's body, the Church,
that all may labour zealously
for the establishment
of God's kingdom on earth
until the world is drenched
in his peace, joy and love.

Silence

God, our heavenly Father:
let your kingdom come.

We pray for the work
of all peacemakers and reformers;
all who work for justice,
reconciliation and harmony;
that the God of peace and love
will bless, support
and encourage them.

Silence

God, our heavenly Father:
let your kingdom come.

We pray for the work of those who heal and tend
the injured, sick and dying,
and those in their care;
for all involved in medical research
and those whose lives depend
on drugs, dialysis or radiotherapy.

Silence

God, our heavenly Father:
let your kingdom come.

We pray for our own work in this life;
that we may dedicate our energies
and resources more fully
to establishing Christ's kingdom;
that we may undertake every task
and activity joyfully
in the strength of our King.

Silence

God, our heavenly Father:
let your kingdom come.

In the warmth of God's love,
we pray in silence now
for our own particular concerns.

Silence

God our Father,
we ask you to accept our prayers,
through Jesus Christ our Lord.
Amen.

LET YOUR KINGDOM COME (2)

Father, we ask for your will to be accomplished
in your Church.

Silence

God in heaven:
let your kingdom come.

Father, we plead for mercy
on behalf of a petulant, self-seeking world.

Silence

God in heaven:
let your kingdom come.

Father, we ask your blessing on all who strive
for peace and justice.

Silence

God in heaven:
let your kingdom come.

Father, we welcome your presence
in our families and friendships.

Silence

God in heaven:
let your kingdom come.

Father, we would stand in your name
against all that is evil.

Silence

God in heaven:
let your kingdom come.

Father, we ask you to prepare us for the day
when Jesus returns in glory.

Silence

God in heaven:
**let your kingdom come
and all the earth rejoice
that Jesus Christ is Lord.
Amen.**

LET YOUR WILL BE DONE

Bring to God's love
all who teach the faith to others;
pray for their work and their personal life.

Silence

Father:
let your will be done.

Bring to God's affection
all who feel worthless or inadequate.
Pray for their lives to be freed
and transformed.

Silence

Father:
let your will be done.

Bring to God's compassion
the areas of war and violence.
Pray for those caught up in the fighting
and for those trying to negotiate
a just settlement.

Silence

Father:
let your will be done.

Bring to God's peace
all the rush and busyness of our world.
Pray for a right balance in our lives
between doing and being;
between speaking out and holding our tongues.

Silence

Father:
let your will be done.

Bring your thankfulness to God
for his constant love and faithfulness.

Silence

Loving God, we bring you
all these concerns in prayer,
that you may overrule our sinful ways:
**and your kingdom come
and let your will be done
through Jesus Christ, our Lord.
Amen.**

YOUR WILL BE DONE

Let us pray to God,
knowing we can trust him.

We pray that as Christians we may take to heart
the need to walk the talk,
and live out what we profess.
We pray that nothing may get so important to us
that it pushes God's values aside.

Silence

Father:
let your will be done.

We pray that those in authority and power
do not lose touch with the needs of those they serve,
so that the poor and oppressed and vulnerable
are always given value and respect.

Silence

Father:
let your will be done.

We pray for those in our families
whom we love and have hurt or upset;
we pray too for those who have hurt or upset us,
and ask for God's reconciliation and healing.

Silence

Father:
let your will be done.

We pray for those who have lost hope
of being rescued, noticed or valued;
for the complacent who cannot see their poverty,
for the prejudiced who mistake blindness for sight.

Silence

Father:
let your will be done.

We pray for our loved ones
who have reached the moment of death,
and thank God for the example of their lives.
We commend them all to his safe keeping.

Silence

Father:
let your will be done.

We give you thanks, Lord God, for the hope
and encouragement you give us
on our journey of faith.

Merciful Father:
**accept these prayers
for the sake of your Son,
our Saviour Jesus Christ.
Amen.**

GOD'S WILL BE DONE
IN EVERY PLACE

In every church, in every Christian,
we long for God's love to blossom.

Silence

Amen:
let your glorious will be done.

In every country,
in everyone who has influence and authority,
we long for God's wisdom to prevail.

Silence

Amen:
let your glorious will be done.

In every home, in every neighbourhood,
we long for God's forgiveness to flourish.

Silence

Amen:
let your glorious will be done.

In every hospital, in every suffering person,
we long for God's healing to comfort and restore.

Silence

Amen:
let your glorious will be done.

In everyone who mourns, in all who are dying,
we long for God's peace to come.

Silence

Amen:
let your glorious will be done.

In all our joys, our sorrows and our choices,
we rejoice that God is indeed in control.
Amen:
let your glorious will be done.
We ask these prayers
in the name of Jesus,
who said, 'Not my will, but yours be done.'
Amen.

ON EARTH AS IN HEAVEN

Let us set aside our own agendas
and seek the face of God,
and his will for the Church and for the world.

We pray for all who are seeking God,
and for the nurturing process in this church
and community.
We pray for opportunities to share God's love
and draw others to meet him.

Silence

Your will be done:
on earth as in heaven.

We pray for all who are fighting against evil
for goodness, truth and justice,
both those who make the world news
and those whose battles are known only to God.
We pray for our country and its leaders,
that this nation may seek God.

Silence

Your will be done:
on earth as in heaven.

We pray that wealth and comfort may not divert us
from searching out the heart of God;
that we may hear God's challenging
and gladly respond to him;
that our homes and communities
may sparkle with God's glory.

Silence

Your will be done:
on earth as in heaven.

We pray for the disillusioned and depressed
and all who have lost their way in life;
we pray for those corrupted by evil,
trained in hatred and twisted by bitterness.
We pray for the transforming of these lives.

Silence

Your will be done:
on earth as in heaven.

We pray for those whose earthly life
has come to an end,
and for those who mourn their going.
May the dead rest in the peace and joy of heaven
through the mercy of God.

Silence

Your will be done:
on earth as in heaven.

With thankful hearts we recall the times
when God has rescued and forgiven us,
leading us deeper into his friendship.

Merciful Father:
**accept these prayers
for the sake of your Son,
our Saviour Jesus Christ.
Amen.**

HOLY GOD, TAKE CHARGE

Father, in all our preparation for worship,
in our committees and various groups and meetings,
be among us to work in us,
with us and through us.

Silence

Holy God:
take charge.

Father, in all our political debates and congresses,
in the hidden agendas and the gaps between words,
work your will and prepare our hearts
to work with you.

Silence

Holy God:
take charge.

Father, in all our times of shared laughter
and shared tears,
in our efforts to reconcile,
and our failures to please,
touch our lives with your compassion and affection.

Silence

Holy God:
take charge.

Father, in all the pain and suffering
of our brothers and sisters,
in the times which come close to despair,
lift us on your shoulders and carry us to safety.

Silence

Holy God:
take charge.

Father, as we release into your everlasting protection
those who have recently died,
renew and deepen our understanding
of what it means to have the gift of eternal life.

Silence

Holy God:
take charge.

Father, in all that we say and do during this week
may we know the freshness of your love
and the security of your hold on us.

Silence

Holy God:
take charge,
and answer these prayers
not according to our narrow vision
but according to your eternal wisdom,
through Jesus Christ, our Lord.
Amen.

FATHER, TAKE US OVER

We ask you to fill us with delight at doing
your will, and at bringing others to know you.
Refresh those whose faith is dry and stiff.

Silence

Father, take us over:
both inside and out.

We ask for integrity in our own community,
in local and world decisions.

Silence

Father, take us over:
both inside and out.

We ask for clear guidance in medical ethics,
and the courage to stand up for your values.

Silence

Father, take us over:
both inside and out.

We ask that you will welcome into your kingdom
all those who have recently died,
and we ask you to prepare us on earth
to live with you in heaven.

Silence

Father, take us over:
both inside and out.

We ask for the grace to live joyfully
as we travel with you through our lives,
and remember now all that you have done for us.

Silence

God, be around us;
God, be within us;
God, be at our side:
in the name of Jesus Christ.
Amen.

HELP US TO OBEY

Knowing that our Father loves us,
let us come to him,
as brothers and sisters in Christ,
with our prayers.

Let us pray for more courage
among all Christians;
that they may stand up
against evil and injustice,
wherever they find it,
trusting in God's power
and without thought for personal safety.

Silence

Lord, speak in our hearts:
and help us to obey.

Let us pray for those countries at war;
those between whom
there are distrust and suspicion;
that peace may never be dismissed
as impossible,
but acknowledged
as the only real victory.

Silence

Lord, speak in our hearts:
and help us to obey.

Let us pray for those who are living
through a personal crisis at the moment;
those who do not know which way
to turn for the best;
that God's will may be made clear to them,
so that they are guided and comforted.

Silence

Lord, speak in our hearts:
and help us to obey.

Let us pray for our own lives,
and those of our families,
that we may all know what work
God is calling us to do,
and trust him enough to do his will.

Silence

Lord, speak in our hearts:
and help us to obey.

We pray in silence
for those known to us
who have particular needs.

Silence

Father,
your glory fills and confronts the world,
and so we entrust our cares to you.
in the name of Jesus.
Amen.

WORK YOUR WILL
IN OUR LIVES

Let us pray together for the leaders
of the Churches
and for the spiritual growth
of all Christians.

Silence

Lord, establish your kingdom:
work your will in our lives.

Let us pray for the areas of our world
where there are oppression and violence,
pleading for peace and justice.

Silence

Lord, establish your kingdom:
work your will in our lives.

Let us pray for our home life,
for all the members of our families;
and for those who live
in our neighbourhood.

Silence

Lord, establish your kingdom:
work your will in our lives.

Let us pray for those who feel imprisoned
by bad health or some kind of disability.

Silence

Lord, establish your kingdom:
work your will in our lives.

Let us remember those who have died –
those known personally to us

and those we have heard about –
and pray for all who are torn apart by grief.

Silence

Lord, establish your kingdom:
work your will in our lives.

Let us give thanks for all that is good
and honest, loving and refreshing.

Silence

Lord, hear our prayers,
which we ask
in the name of Jesus.
Amen.

HELP US TO LIVE YOUR WAY

Father, you know our motives as well as our actions;
bless our decision-making,
so that we do not make wrong choices in our lives.

Silence

Teach us your ways:
and help us to live them.

Father, you know the strengths
and weaknesses of our Church;
we do not want to hide anything away,
but long for your advice and guidance.

Silence

Teach us your ways:
and help us to live them.

Father, you know us,
and those we live and work with;
you understand the real reasons
for our quarrels and upsets;
we long for you to work your healing
in those hidden areas.

Silence

Teach us your ways:
and help us to live them.

Father, you know the individual history
behind each person's revenge
and each country's difficulties;
we long for peace and tranquillity in our world.

Silence

Teach us your ways:
and help us to live them.

Father, you watch with the sick and the dying;
you feel their pain and know their fear;
we long for them to know
your loving presence with them.

Silence

Teach us your ways:
and help us to live them.

Father, your creation is indeed very good,
and we praise and thank you for all you provide.

Silence

Lead us, heavenly Father,
into the life of your kingdom,
as we follow Jesus Christ,
our Master and our Friend.
Amen.

TAKE ALL THAT
WE HAVE AND ARE

Father, take our faith and deepen it,
take our Church and renew it,
take our need and supply it.

Silence

My God and my All:
let your kingdom come.

Father, take our community and revitalise it,
take our government and guide it,
take our world and protect it.

Silence

My God and my All:
let your kingdom come.

Father, take the young and empower them,
take the old and refresh them,
take those who are damaged and restore them.

Silence

My God and my All:
let your kingdom come.

Father, take the suffering and comfort them,
take the frightened and reassure them,
take the lonely and befriend them.

Silence

My God and my All:
let your kingdom come.

Take the dying and whisper peace to them,
take the dead and welcome them,
take those who mourn and grieve with them.

Silence

My God and my All:
let your kingdom come.

Take our minds and think through them,
take our mouths and speak through them,
take our lives and live through them:
and accept these prayers
for the sake of Jesus Christ, your Son.
Amen.

TAKE US, REMAKE US

As friends in Christ,
and in the stillness of his peace,
let us pray together.

We pray for all those involved
with missionary work
both abroad and at home;
that they may be protected
from danger and disease,
and led in the way of God's will,
so that their caring, forgiving lives
witness to his love.

Silence

Take us, remake us:
and let your kingdom come.

We pray for all the peoples of this earth
who do not know God;
for those who see him only as a threat
or an excuse for violence;
that they may be brought into contact
with the living Christ
who longs to give them his peace.

Silence

Take us, remake us:
and let your kingdom come.

We pray for those in physical or mental pain;
those weakened and exhausted by illness,
those in intensive care
or undergoing emergency surgery;
that God's healing power
will sustain them
and make them whole.

Silence

Take us, remake us:
and let your kingdom come.

We pray for those with whom we live
and work and worship;
that we may use every opportunity
to care for each other
and grow in patience
and understanding.

Silence

Take us, remake us:
and let your kingdom come.

Confident in God's welcoming love,
we pray in silence now
for our own particular needs and concerns.

Silence

God our Father,
accept these prayers,
in Jesus' name we ask.
Amen.

LORD, CHANGE US
FROM THE INSIDE OUT

In all areas of weakness
and self-interest in your Church,
both as individuals and collectively,
Lord, change us:
from the inside out.

Silence

In all areas of hardened resentment
and desire for revenge among the nations,
Lord, change us:
from the inside out.

Silence

In all areas of discord and misunderstanding
in our relationships with one another,
Lord, change us:
from the inside out.

Silence

In all areas of guilt and regret
which haunt us from our past,
Lord, change us:
from the inside out.

Silence

In the time of our dying;
at the time of your coming in glory,
Lord, change us:
from the inside out.

Silence

Lord, enable us to praise you
not only with our lips

but in our lives.
Lord, change us:
from the inside out.

Silence

Lord, we ask in our prayers
not only that you will hear us,
but that we may hear you
and the challenge of your love,
through Jesus Christ, our Redeemer.
Amen.

YOUR COMMANDS ARE OUR DELIGHT

Father, we pray for all who are going through
a time of temptation at the moment.
Strengthen and protect them all.

Silence

Your commands, O Lord:
are our delight.

We pray that your Church may always
hold true to your truth
and love with your love.

Silence

Your commands, O Lord:
are our delight.

We pray for those in positions of power
that they may not give way to corruption
but work with integrity.

Silence

Your commands, O Lord:
are our delight.

We pray for those in our families
and those who live in our neighbourhood,
that we may live in harmony together.

Silence

Your commands, O Lord:
are our delight.

We pray for those in prison
and those imprisoned by guilt.

Silence

Your commands, O Lord:
are our delight.

We pray for those who have died through neglect,
mismanagement of resources,
violence and oppression.

Silence

Your commands, O Lord:
are our delight.

Father, we thank you
for the way you protect and enfold us
every moment of every day.

Silence

Father, we gladly bring our prayers:
may we as gladly do your will,
through Jesus Christ, our Lord.
Amen.

GIVE US YOUR PEACE

Let us bring our longing for peace
to the Creator and Lord of all the earth.

We pray for the Church throughout the world,
especially in areas of apathy,
and rejection of spiritual values;
that through Christian witness
many may come to find peace
and fulfilment
in Jesus, the Saviour.

Silence

Heavenly Father:
give us your peace.

We pray for all places of conflict;
for countries at war,
for all areas of violence
and bloodshed,
bitterness and hatred.

Silence

Heavenly Father:
give us your peace.

We pray for all who are distressed, bewildered,
lost or confused;
for those making painful decisions;
for those who have no one to turn to for help;
that they may be given guidance,
comfort and serenity.

Silence

Heavenly Father:
give us your peace.

We pray for ourselves,
the special needs and concerns known to us,
for our own spiritual growth;
that our ordered lives may proclaim
the beauty of God's peace.

Silence

Heavenly Father:
give us your peace.

God our Father loves us;
in silence we offer
our personal prayers to him now.

Silence

Father,
knowing that you alone
have the words of eternal life,
we lay our prayers before you.
Through Christ our Lord.
Amen.

JUSTICE AND MERCY

Let us draw near to the just and merciful God,
and pour out our concerns
for the Church and for the world.

Lord our God,
as we join the unending cycle of prayer on our planet,
turning through time and space,
we rejoice in your upholding, your mercy and forgiveness.
In all our small-mindedness we ask your inbreathing,
so that we learn to look with your vision
and act with your wideness of compassion.

Silence

God of justice and mercy:
hear us as we pray.

Lord our God,
be present at all meetings and negotiations,
where feelings run high,
and many lives are profoundly affected
by the decisions made.
We pray for real communication
which listens to needs and appreciates difficulties,
so that we may live on this earth together
in harmony and peace.

Silence

God of justice and mercy:
hear us as we pray.

Lord our God,
we pray for this neighbourhood
and the particular problems it has;
for communities split apart by conflict
or crushed by tragedy;
we pray for those involved with court proceedings;

may our judicial system uphold your principle
of justice with mercy.

Silence

God of justice and mercy:
hear us as we pray.

Lord our God,
we pray for those who have a raw deal in this life;
for those with ongoing health problems,
and all who are caught up in war and deprivation.
We pray for a just and realistic sharing of our resources,
and courage, support and healing for all who suffer.

Silence

God of justice and mercy:
hear us as we pray.

Lord our God, we pray for those who have died
and now see their lives as they really are;
we pray for your mercy on them,
and thank you for all their acts of goodness and love.

Silence

God of justice and mercy:
hear us as we pray.

Lord our God,
in all the events and phases of our life
we give you thanks
for your steadfast and unchanging love
which sustains and directs us.

Merciful Father:
accept these prayers
for the sake of your Son,
our Saviour Jesus Christ.
Amen.

THE LORD OUR HOPE

As sons and daughters of our heavenly Father,
let us pray together, trusting in his love.

We pray that the Church and all its members
may not be stagnant, but flow forward
in the direction you want it to go;
may the Christian hope burn brightly
in our lives and may your kingdom come.

Silence

Lord, you are our hope:
we believe and trust in you.

We pray that we may all tend and care
for the world you have given us to live in;
may we share its food and riches,
and use them wisely and safely
without waste or destruction.

Silence

Lord, you are our hope:
we believe and trust in you.

We pray for the sick, the injured and the distressed;
for the dying and for those who mourn;
may your healing presence
bring wholeness and comfort.

Silence

Lord, you are our hope:
we believe and trust in you.

We pray for our own circle of family and friends;
for personal spiritual growth;
may we be more watchful,

preparing ourselves more thoroughly
day by day to meet you face to face.

Silence

Lord, you are our hope:
we believe and trust in you.

We pray for those who have died in faith
and live with you in glory;
may we one day share with them
the joy of being in your presence for ever.

Silence

Lord, you are our hope:
we believe and trust in you.

We thank you, Father,
for all your goodness and kindness to us;
for the hope of heaven and the comfort of your love.

Silence

Lord of all hopefulness:
**accept these prayers
for the sake of Jesus Christ.
Amen.**

Faith and faithfulness

LIVING BY FAITH

Let us pray in faith
to our heavenly Father,
trusting in his infinite mercy.

We pray for all Christian people,
especially those whose faith
has been affected by
their experience of suffering;
that they may know
the support of God's living presence
which brings good out of evil.

Silence

Touch our lives, Lord:
that we may live by faith.

We pray for all administrative bodies
and political institutions;
that they may be always in touch with
the real needs of those they serve,
and be quick and effective
in meeting them.

Silence

Touch our lives, Lord:
that we may live by faith.

We pray for the dying
and those who love and care for them;
for the grieving and sorrowful;
that they may draw strength
from the reality of Christ's life
and his victory over death.

Silence

Touch our lives, Lord:
that we may live by faith.

We pray for our local community
with all its needs and cares;
that we may be ready to serve Christ
in our area
and spread his life-giving hope and joy.

Silence

Touch our lives, Lord:
that we may live by faith.

We know that our Father is listening;
in silence we bring to him
our own particular needs or concerns.

Silence

God our Father,
hear our prayer
and help us to do your will,
through Jesus Christ our Lord.
Amen.

FAITH IN GOD

Confident that God knows and loves each of us,
and understands our situation,
let us pray.

We pray for a deepening personal faith
in all Christians,
and renewed faith for all who are besieged by doubt.

Silence

You are our God:
in you we put our trust.

We pray that the Church
may be vigilant and courageous
in upholding the Christian faith,
and sensitive to the language and culture
of each person seeking for God in their lives.

Silence

You are our God:
in you we put our trust.

We long for a thirsting after God in our society;
for right living, justice and mercy
to be valued and worked for.

Silence

You are our God:
in you we put our trust.

We long for our homes and neighbourhoods
to reflect God's love
in our practical caring,
our hospitality and our parenting.

Silence

You are our God:
in you we put our trust.

We pray for those whose emotional pain
makes it difficult for them
to accept God's love and forgiveness;
and for all who feel that there is no hope.
We offer ourselves to be available
where God needs us.

Silence

You are our God:
in you we put our trust.

We commend into God's loving mercy the dying
and those who have made the journey through death.
With them we long to share the eternal joy
of God's presence in heaven.

Silence

You are our God:
in you we put our trust.

We give you thanks and praise
for the endless love and patience you show us;
whenever we turn away,
please turn us back to you.

Merciful Father:
**accept these prayers
for the sake of your Son,
our Saviour Jesus Christ.
Amen.**

TRUST IN GOD

Gathered together in faith
before our heavenly Father,
let us bring him
our burdens and cares.

We bring to him
all who teach the Christian faith
by word and example;
that Christ will work,
even through their weakness,
to reach the world.

Silence

Abba, Father:
we trust in you.

We bring to him
all who are striving
for peace and harmony
in local government,
national and international negotiations;
that nothing may deter or divert them,
so that the Father's will
may be done on earth.

Silence

Abba, Father:
we trust in you.

We bring to him all who trust
in worldly solutions or systems,
those whose ideals lead them
not to peace but to violence;
that they may see the great rewards
which come from living and trusting
in a God of selfless love.

Silence

Abba, Father:
we trust in you.

We bring to him our personal faith,
and our lack of faith;
our own efforts to reconcile,
and our sorrow for where these have failed;
we offer him ourselves
and ask him to increase our faith and trust.

Silence

Abba, Father:
we trust in you.

Together now in silence,
we pray our individual prayers
to our heavenly Father.

Silence

We commend all our cares
to the God who loves us as his children,
through Jesus Christ our Lord.
Amen.

ALL THINGS WORK TOGETHER

Let us attune our hearts to the God who loves us.

God of love,
we pray for all those who are newly baptised,
or who have recently found that you are real;
we pray for all in ordained and lay ministries,
and for those sensing a special calling.
Help us all to listen to your guiding.

Silence

In God:
all things work together for good.

God of power,
we pray for those who are in authority
and in positions of influence and responsibility;
may they be earthed in humility, courageous in integrity,
and mindful of the need to serve.

Silence

In God:
all things work together for good.

God of mercy,
we call to mind those with whom we share
the work and leisure of our life;
we pray for those we treasure and those we battle with,
and ask you to breathe into all our relationships
the forgiving love which cleanses and heals.

Silence

In God:
all things work together for good.

God of wholeness,
we remember those who are aching today

in body, mind or spirit;
knowing that nothing is unredeemable,
we ask that you will bring good
even out of these barren places.

Silence

In God:
all things work together for good.

God of life,
we pray for those whose earthly lives have ended;
we remember those who have died
violently and tragically, suddenly and unprepared.
We give you thanks for lives well lived
and for happy memories.
May they rest in the eternal peace of heaven.

Silence

In God:
all things work together for good.

God of faithfulness,
we thank you for the way
you always keep your promises
and never let us down.

Merciful Father:
**accept these prayers
for the sake of your Son,
our Saviour Jesus Christ.
Amen.**

WE SHALL NOT WANT

Let us pray to God our Father,
knowing that we are all precious to him.

Father, we thank you for all those
who give to support the work of the Church;
bless our giving, guide our spending,
and help us to value the true wealth
of your abundant love.

Silence

The Lord is our shepherd:
there is nothing we shall want.

We pray for the world's economy;
for fair management and distribution of resources;
for fair trade and just wages;
for greater awareness and concern about injustice;
for a commitment to our responsibilities
as planet-sharers and earth-dwellers.

Silence

The Lord is our shepherd:
there is nothing we shall want.

We pray for all parents with young children,
thanking you for them
and asking you to bless and guide their parenting;
we pray for families in debt;
for those whose homes have been repossessed,
and those whose financial security
makes them forgetful of your love.

Silence

The Lord is our shepherd:
there is nothing we shall want.

We pray for those who are burdened
with financial worries
and all who struggle to make ends meet,
all over the world;
we pray for the emotionally and spiritually bankrupt,
and those who do not yet know your love for them.

Silence

The Lord is our shepherd:
there is nothing we shall want.

We pray for those who have died,
and those on that last journey at this moment;
for a merciful judgement
and the everlasting joy of heaven.

Silence

The Lord is our shepherd:
there is nothing we shall want.

Father, we give you thanks
for the extraordinary generosity of your love for us,
which lasts beyond death into the whole of eternity.

Merciful Father:
**accept these prayers
for the sake of your Son,
our Saviour Jesus Christ.
Amen.**

HELP OUR FAITH TO GROW

As children and heirs through adoption,
let us confide in our heavenly Father
who knows us so well.

Father, into your enlightenment and perception
we bring all whose faith is limited by fear or prejudice;
all whose living faith has been replaced
by the empty shell of habit.

Silence

Lord, we believe:
please help our faith to grow.

Father, into the depths of your wisdom
and understanding
we bring those with responsibilities,
and all who have difficult decisions to make;
especially... ;
all in charge of hospitals, schools, factories
and all community services.

Silence

Lord, we believe:
please help our faith to grow.

Father, into your tireless faithfulness
we bring the members of our families;
any who rely on us for help, support or guidance;
any whom we are being asked to serve
or introduce to your saving love.

Silence

Lord, we believe:
please help our faith to grow.

Father, into the gentleness of your healing love
we bring all who are in pain;

all those recovering from surgery;
those involved in crippling accidents
or suffering from wasting diseases.

Silence

Lord, we believe:
please help our faith to grow.

Father, into your lasting peace
we bring all those who have died,
especially . . .

Silence

Lord, we believe:
please help our faith to grow.

Lord, we thank you that your character is always
full of mercy and faithfulness:
teach us to trust you more and more
through prayer, obedience and service,
for the sake of Jesus, our Brother.
Amen.

FATHER, INCREASE OUR FAITH

Father, increase our faith;
help us to grow closer and closer to you
as we live and pray and worship.

Silence

Lord, we believe:
help our unbelief.

Father, open the hearts and minds of all leaders
so that your will is done
and your kingdom spreads throughout
the whole world.

Silence

Lord, we believe:
help our unbelief.

Father, speak your love through our voices
and our actions, in our homes, our places of work,
and wherever we go.

Silence

Lord, we believe:
help our unbelief.

Father, let your comforting and healing presence
touch those who suffer
and those who are frightened,
to fill them with peace.

Silence

Lord, we believe:
help our unbelief.

Father, gather to yourself the souls of those
who have finished their earthly life,
and comfort those who mourn their going.

Silence

Lord, we believe:
help our unbelief.

Father, we offer you our thanks and praise
for all the signs of your glory we experience
and cherish.

Silence

Father, as we make the pilgrimage of life,
may we grow in faith
through sorrow and through joy:
following in the footsteps of Jesus, our Lord.
Amen.

RENEW OUR FAITH

Pray for all those
whose faith is worn or battered,
bringing to mind anyone known to you.

Silence

For with God:
everything is possible.

Pray for a deepening of faith in all church-goers,
particularly those in your own area.

Silence

For with God:
everything is possible.

Pray for our society to be changed
and renewed in God's way,
bringing to mind
the areas that particularly concern you.

Silence

For with God:
everything is possible.

Pray for those who are in pain or anguish
and those who are frightened,
that they may find strength in faith.

Silence

For with God:
everything is possible.

In a time of silence
we share with God our Father
our personal needs and concerns.

Silence

For with God:
everything is possible.

Thank God for what he is doing in your life,
and for his living presence with us
now and always.

Silence

Father, enlarge our faith
to see you at work in the world,
to feel you at work in our hearts:
**through Jesus Christ, our Lord.
Amen.**

FAITHFULNESS

Companions in Christ,
knowing the loyalty and faithfulness
of our Father in heaven, let us pray to him
for the Church and for our world.

Keep all Christians firm and steadfast in their faith,
with lives that witness clearly
to the power of your love.

Silence

Hear us, Father:
we come to do your will.

Guide our leaders, and all those in influential positions,
to uphold and promote Christian values.
all in charge of hospitals, schools, factories
and all community services.

Silence

Hear us, Father:
we come to do your will.

Be present in our homes and our relationships,
and increase our commitment to reconciliation,
encouragement and understanding of one another.

Silence

Hear us, Father:
we come to do your will.

Give reassurance and peace
to all who are anxious, depressed or confused;
and make us aware of the needs of others.

Silence

Hear us, Father:
we come to do your will.

Into your safe keeping
we commend all those who have died . . .
for with you there is eternal life, peace and joy.

Silence

We thank you for all the many blessings
we receive each day,
and in silence we pour out
our individual reasons for gratitude.

Silence

Father, in our prayers
may we not only ask for your aid
but listen for your word:
through Jesus Christ, our Lord.
Amen.

TEACH US HOW TO BE FAITHFUL

When we want to hide from serving you,
when we doubt your promise to be with us,
Lord, teach us:
how to be faithful.

Silence

When we find ourselves standing
against worldly values,
Lord, teach us:
how to be faithful.

Silence

When we meet with selfishness, laziness and criticism
in ourselves and others around us,
Lord, teach us:
how to be faithful.

Silence

When we hear of the ill and lonely
who would welcome some friendly contact,
Lord, teach us:
how to be faithful.

Silence

When we see others die
and remember that this life will pass,
Lord, teach us:
how to be faithful.

Silence

When we grumble and complain
instead of living thankfully,
Lord, teach us:
how to be faithful.

Silence

Lord, make us earnest in prayer,
bold in faith,
and loving in service:
**as we follow Jesus Christ,
our Companion and Friend.
Amen.**

KEEP US FAITHFUL

As children of our heavenly Father,
let us approach him
with our needs and cares.

We bring the problems of communication
in the Church, and in all church groups;
the difficulties of finding
enough church leaders, cleaners,
teachers, visitors
to work effectively for God
in our area.

Silence

Loving heavenly Father:
Keep us faithful to your will.

We bring the pressures
on those in business
to think only in terms
of what is profitable;
the problems of wealth distribution
which cause unnecessary suffering
in our world.

Silence

Loving heavenly Father:
Keep us faithful to your will.

We bring the shortage of staff
and resources in hospitals;
the distress of those
who have no hospital to go to;
the suffering of those
who are in physical pain,
mental anguish or spiritual darkness.

Silence

Loving heavenly Father:
Keep us faithful to your will.

We bring the things that irritate,
anger and frustrate us;
the jobs that we find difficult to do cheerfully;
the relationships we find demanding and tiring.

Silence

Loving heavenly Father:
Keep us faithful to your will.

Trustingly, we pray in silence
to our loving Lord,
who considers each one of us special.

Silence

Father,
you always give us far more
than we can ever deserve;
please fulfil our prayers
in the way that is best for us.
We ask in the name of Jesus Christ.
Amen.

FAITHFUL SERVICE

Together we walk the way of Christ;
let us now pray together in his name,
to our Lord and heavenly Father.

We pray that the spiritual life
of each church community
may be nurtured and grow,
so that Christians may have confidence
to reach out increasingly
to the particular needs
of their neighbourhood.

Silence

Lord, we trust you:
let us faithfully serve.

We pray that God's will may prevail
in the way we use our world's resources,
our intelligence,
our knowledge
and our power.

Silence

Lord, we trust you:
let us faithfully serve.

We pray that all those
who are living through some tempest,
whether physical, emotional,
mental or spiritual,
may know the peace and comfort
of God's absorbent love
which soaks up all hurt
and promotes healing and wholeness.

Silence

Lord, we trust you:
let us faithfully serve.

We pray that our homes may be havens
of caring and understanding,
where all who enter may find
the tangible and attractive peace
of the God we serve.

Silence

Lord, we trust you:
let us faithfully serve.

Trusting in God our Father,
we name our particular prayer burdens.

Silence

Father,
rejoicing that you are
in overall charge of all creation,
we offer these prayers
through Jesus Christ.
Amen.

LIVING OUR FAITH

Let us pray to God our Father,
bringing before him
our needs and concerns.

We pray for the Church,
its leaders and all the faithful;
that in setting our hearts steadfastly
on the eternal truth of God's love,
we may be nourished
and yield good fruit.

Silence

Lord, support us:
and help us live our faith.

We pray for those working in news coverage
in the media;
for all whose words influence our human society;
that integrity and honour may be valued
and responsibility never abused.

Silence

Lord, support us:
and help us live our faith.

We pray for those who delight
in scandal and gossip,
and for those whose reputations
are damaged by others,
that God's love will heal and renew,
challenge and convert.

Silence

Lord, support us:
and help us live our faith.

We pray for this church fellowship,
its worship, learning and social groups,
that our genuine love for one another,
and desire for one another's good,
may cleanse our hearts from all envy,
intolerance or spitefulness.

Silence

Lord, support us:
and help us live our faith.

In silence, now,
we name any known to us
with particular needs or burdens.

Silence

God our Father,
in our weakness may we rely
on your constant and almighty strength.
We ask you to hear our prayer,
through Jesus Christ our Lord.
Amen.

FAITH TEMPERED BY LOVE

United in his Spirit,
let us pray to our heavenly Father.

We pray that all Christian people
may proclaim the full truth
about Jesus Christ,
without dilution or distortion,
even though that truth
may sometimes be unpalatable.

Silence

Lord, give us faith:
faith tempered by love.

We pray that we may be
wise and careful stewards
of the resources of our world,
because we believe in the Creator.

Silence

Lord, give us faith:
faith tempered by love.

We pray that those who are physically hungry
may be fed;
and those who hunger and thirst
for real meaning in life
may be led to find lasting nourishment
in Jesus.

Silence

Lord, give us faith:
faith tempered by love.

We pray that having received Christ
into our hearts,

we may joyfully,
in words and actions,
spread the marvellous news of his saving love.

Silence

Lord, give us faith:
faith tempered by love.

Meeting our heavenly Father
in the stillness of silence,
let us bring to him
our own particular cares and concerns.

Silence

Father,
we can never thank you enough
for what you have done for us,
and for the way you are transforming our lives;
with grateful hearts we offer you these prayers
in the name of Jesus.
Amen.

FOLLOWING WHERE GOD LEADS

Let us pray, my brothers and sisters,
in the knowledge of our Father's infinite mercy.

We pray for all Christian people and Church leaders;
all whose faith is battered through disaster or suffering;
may we know the certainty of your abiding presence
which transforms and rebuilds.

Silence

Lord, give us faith to follow:
where you lead.

We pray for all world leaders,
all administrative bodies and political institutions;
may they be always aware
of the real needs of those they serve
and be effective in providing for them.

Silence

Lord, give us faith to follow:
where you lead.

We pray for our local community,
for our families and our friends,
with all the hopes, fears, problems and needs;
make us ready to serve you in our own area
and spread your life-giving joy.

Silence

Lord, give us faith to follow:
where you lead.

We pray for the dying
and those who love and tend them;
for the bereaved and desolate;
may all in trouble and sorrow

draw strength from your life
and your victory over death.

Silence

Lord, give us faith to follow:
where you lead.

We pray for those who have died
that, falling asleep to this life,
they may wake to eternal life
in the joy of heaven.

Silence

We thank you, heavenly Father,
for saving us from sin's destruction
and making it possible to live
in such abundant fullness.

Silence

Father, we offer these prayers
in the name of Jesus Christ, our Lord.
Amen.

WHEREVER YOU LEAD US WE WILL GO

In the muddle of our ecclesiastical arguments,
our narrow self-interest and our embarrassment,
teach us to fix our eyes on you.

Silence

Lord, wherever you lead us:
we will go.

In our defensiveness and nationalism,
and our fear of being considered weak,
teach us true courage to speak out
for what is right.

Silence

Lord, wherever you lead us:
we will go.

In the comfort of our homes and families,
give us the grace to be hospitable and welcoming.

Silence

Lord, wherever you lead us:
we will go.

In the needs of those who are ill and injured,
move us to see your face.

Silence

Lord, wherever you lead us:
we will go.

In the sorrow of dying,
inspire us to see also the gateway to heaven.

Silence

Lord, wherever you lead us:
we will go.

In all the beauty of your creation,
open our eyes to see the beauty of your holiness,
and sing your praise with joy.

Silence

Good Shepherd, be our guide.
When we are weary:
make us lie down in green pastures.
When we are anxious:
lead us beside still waters.
When we are under stress:
restore our souls.
When we are faced with temptation:
lead us in paths of righteousness.
When we come to the valley of shadows:
be with us, to bring us safely through.
In every circumstance of life and death:
be our sure and loving guide,
through Jesus Christ, our Lord.
Amen.

IN YOU WE TRUST

As God's people, gathered in his presence,
let us pray.

For all who preach and teach the Gospel
in word and sacrament
throughout the worldwide Church.
For those who lead prayer groups
and Bible studies,
and all who gossip their faith to others.

Silence

O Lord our God:
in you we trust.

For all who are tortured or persecuted
for what they believe;
for the voiceless and powerless,
for the powerful and coercive.

Silence

O Lord our God:
in you we trust.

For greater respect for one another
as children of God's making;
for God's presence in each conversation,
discussion and debate,
each concern and celebration.

Silence

O Lord our God:
in you we trust.

For healing and wholeness,
mending and comforting,

calming and refreshing,
wherever lives and bodies ache.

Silence

O Lord our God:
in you we trust.

For everlasting peace in the arms of God
for those who have come to the end
of their life on earth
and comfort for all who grieve.

Silence

O Lord our God:
in you we trust.

We give thanks for God's constant love
which upholds our being
and cradles our living in his hand.

Merciful Father:
accept these prayers
for the sake of your Son,
our Saviour Jesus Christ. Amen.

LEAD US TO YOURSELF

We pray for all who spend their lives
leading others to you,
supporting and encouraging them on your journey;
give them your ideas, your love for others,
your joy and your humility.

Silence

Father, today and every day:
lead us to yourself.

We pray for our leaders and advisers in politics,
business, education and health;
for good values, integrity and compassion,
for courage to stand up for what is right.

Silence

Father, today and every day:
lead us to yourself.

We pray for our relationships with our neighbours,
colleagues and those in our family;
for the grace to forgive readily,
listen attentively and to be available
whenever you need us.

Silence

Father, today and every day:
lead us to yourself.

We pray for the frail and the wounded,
the harassed and the despairing;
for hope in suffering, comfort in distress,
and healing of body, mind and spirit.

Silence

Father, today and every day:
lead us to yourself.

We pray for those who have died,
and for those who mourn and miss their company;
we pray for the grace to die a good death
and live with you for ever in the joy of heaven.

Silence

Father, today and every day:
lead us to yourself.

We thank you for all those who have helped
and inspired us on our Christian journey;
for the experiences that have led us
to know and love you more.

Silence

Father, today and every day:
lead us to yourself,
through Jesus Christ,
our Saviour, Companion and Friend.
Amen.

TRAVELLING WITH GOD

Through the adventures of Christian witness
and the dangers, insults, mocking and anger
we may meet,
keep us, and all your Church, loyal and strong.

Silence

Come with us, Lord:
and we will go with you.

Through the local, national and international tensions,
through rows in the community
and distortions of the truth,
keep us and all people honest,
just and compassionate.

Silence

Come with us, Lord:
and we will go with you.

Through the interrupted nights,
the quarrels and celebrations,
the unspoken needs and wounds,
keep us and our children safe and loving.

Silence

Come with us, Lord:
and we will go with you.

Through the dark hours of pain,
the struggle with guilt and the damage of hatred,
keep us trustful and open.

Silence

Come with us, Lord:
and we will go with you.

Through the last journey of death
and the ache of separation,
keep us both in and out of time,
held firmly by your love.

Silence

Come with us, Lord:
and we will go with you.

Through the sunlight and shadows of each day,
through storms and stillness,
keep us thankful and rejoicing.

Silence

Lord, teach us not only to ask
but to trust and obey:
through Jesus Christ, our Lord.
Amen.

WALKING HUMBLY WITH GOD

As children of our heavenly Father,
let us quieten ourselves and pray.

We pray for the Church,
that having led others,
Christians may not themselves
be found wanting;
that they may be open
to what Christ needs them to do.

Silence

Lord, give us faith:
to walk humbly with you.

We pray for our busy, rushed
and anxious world;
for those weighed down
with responsibilities,
and for the daily routine
of millions of individuals
on this earth;
that God's Good News
may bring to each separate person
life in all its abundance.

Silence

Lord, give us faith:
to walk humbly with you.

We pray for those who profess to believe,
but whose lives are dark and joyless;
that they may experience the
welcoming love of Christ
and be drawn more fully
into his resurrection life.

Silence

Lord, give us faith:
to walk humbly with you.

We pray for ourselves and our families;
that we may not waste our life on earth
pursuing futile goals,
but commit ourselves absolutely
to following Christ,
who has power to save us.

Silence

Lord, give us faith:
to walk humbly with you.

In silence,
we bring our individual prayers
to the Lord of all.

Silence

Heavenly Father,
we ask you to hear our prayers,
in the name of our Lord and Saviour,
Jesus Christ.
Amen.

EVERY STEP OF THE WAY

Drawn by the Holy Spirit,
let us pray together for the Church
and for the world.

Lord God, as members of your Church
in this generation,
we ask your guidance and blessing
for all our church leaders,
and all in training for lay and ordained ministry.
As the people of God, we ask for the gifts we need
for the work you need us to do.

Silence

Let us walk with you, Lord:
every step of the way.

Lord God, this fragile, vulnerable planet
is so beautiful, and in such need of your guidance;
we pray for a deeper valuing
of our universe and of one another;
for your kingdom to come on earth as in heaven.

Silence

Let us walk with you, Lord:
every step of the way.

Lord God, may our homes be centres of love,
acceptance and welcome;
we pray that you will make your home among us
in each room and each relationship.

Silence

Let us walk with you, Lord:
every step of the way.

Lord God, we pray for all who are weighed down
with doubts, fears and misgivings;

all who are haunted by the past
or scared by the future.
We ask for them awareness of your constant presence
and courage to place their hand in yours.

Silence

Let us walk with you, Lord:
every step of the way.

Lord God, as we remember those
whose earthly life has come to an end,
we pray that they, and we in our turn,
may recognise you in heaven
and live in your light for ever.

Silence

Let us walk with you, Lord:
every step of the way.

Lord God, we give you thanks
for all the blessings you shower on us
along the way of life,
and for the painstaking guidance you provide.

Merciful Father:
accept these prayers
for the sake of your Son,
our Saviour Jesus Christ.
Amen.

THE FUTURE IN GOD'S HANDS

Our God is the source of all holiness;
with the needs of the Church and the world
close to our hearts,
let us pray to the only one
who can renew and redeem.

Father, we are all too aware of our temptation
to place our trust in rules and traditions,
and we long for you to release in the Church
such a desire to serve the living God
that nothing is allowed to get in the way of that.

Silence

Into your hands, O Lord:
we commit the future.

Father, we recognise in ourselves
the universal dangerous wants and cravings
which are cultivated because they make money.
Give us universally such a loathing of evil
that there is international co-operation
and individual responsibility in fighting it
and building one another up in love.

Silence

Into your hands, O Lord:
we commit the future.

Father, may our homes, schools and churches
reflect and engender the Godly values
of mutual care, respect and responsibility,
of integrity and forgiveness.

Silence

Into your hands, O Lord:
we commit the future.

Father, we stand alongside all who are hurting
in body, mind or spirit;
all who need courage, support or practical help.
Make us willing to become
part of your answer to our prayers for them.

Silence

Into your hands, O Lord:
we commit the future.

Father, as Lord of both time and eternity,
we commit to your keeping
those who have died to this life;
that, freed from all pain, and forgiven,
they may live in the peace and joy of heaven.

Silence

Into your hands, O Lord:
we commit the future.

Father, write your Law of love on our hearts
and send us glowing with thankfulness
through the week ahead.

Merciful Father:
**accept these prayers
for the sake of your Son,
our Saviour Jesus Christ.
Amen.**

LORD, WE BELIEVE

In the Spirit of Christ and taught by his example,
let us pray trustingly to our heavenly Father.

We pray for Christian witnesses throughout the world, with all
their weaknesses, gifts,
victories and disappointments;
may all Christians reflect your brilliant light
to direct others to worship you
and experience the joy of your peace.

Silence

Lord, we believe:
help our unbelief.

We pray for all inhabitants of our planet
in the daily routines, the work and leisure;
for the silent majorities and all elected to govern;
may all leaders truly represent
the needs of their people,
and may we live in peace with one another.

Silence

Lord, we believe:
help our unbelief.

We pray for our loved ones;
for friends with whom we have lost touch;
for any we have let down; and for ourselves;
may the Spirit we have been so privileged to receive burn more
brightly in our lives.

Silence

Lord, we believe:
help our unbelief.

We pray for all who are undergoing
long-term or chronic illness,

slow recovery or mental anguish
with no end or hope in sight;
may they hold on to you,
receiving your strength and love
and knowing that in you they are safe.

Silence

Lord, we believe:
help our unbelief.

We pray that those who have died
may rise to eternal life in you,
and that, at our death,
we too may share your peace for ever.

Silence

We offer you all our thanks and praise
for your generous love and kindness
to all your people;
may we show our praise in our generosity to others.

Silence

Lord, receive our prayers
and answer them with your love,
through Jesus Christ, our Redeemer and Friend.
Amen.

HELP OUR UNBELIEF (1)

In faith,
knowing that where two or three
are gathered in Jesus' name,
he will grant their requests,
let us pray.

We pray for the Church,
that all Christian leaders
may be given insight and understanding
to guide their people
into the light of God's truth.

Silence

Lord, we believe:
help our unbelief.

We pray for all councils, committees
and conferences,
that a spirit of integrity
may underlie all discussion
and a desire for goodness
inspire all decisions.

Silence

Lord, we believe:
help our unbelief.

We pray for those in pain or distress,
physically, emotionally
or spiritually;
that they may hold to God
through all the bad times,
trusting in his love
which never fails.

Silence

Lord, we believe:
help our unbelief.

We pray for all families,
especially those who have troubles;
that they may not be damaged
through their suffering,
but rather grow
in compassion and understanding.

Silence

Lord, we believe:
help our unbelief.

Knowing that God our Father
hears the prayers of his children,
we pray in silence
our own individual prayers.

Silence

Father,
we ask all this
through Jesus Christ our Lord.
Amen.

HELP OUR UNBELIEF (2)

As God has called us by name
out into full, abundant life,
let us lay before him now our concerns
for the Church and for the world.

Father, chip away from your Church
all the built-up layers
of complacency or despondency,
of over-comfortable familiarity
or under-active expectation,
until we see again
with the freshness and wonder of deepened faith.

Silence

Lord, we believe:
help our unbelief.

Father, we call to mind
societies and systems of our world.
Question our assumptions
and challenge our destructive choices;
break away the unnoticed scales of prejudice
which blind us,
so that our world may become
increasingly under your reign of justice,
righteousness and love.

Silence

Lord, we believe:
help our unbelief.

Father, replace our pride with humility
until we learn from young children
the lessons of wonder and trust.
Keep the childlike as a living flame
in all of us, whatever our age,
and enable us to rediscover your glory all around us.

Silence

Lord, we believe:
help our unbelief.

Father, as the sick were brought to Jesus
by their loved ones,
so we bring to you now all those
whom we long to be healed.
May they hear your voice and sense your touch.

Silence

Lord, we believe:
help our unbelief.

Father, earth-bound we grieve
at the loss of loved ones through death;
yet we also rejoice in you calling them out
into the fullness of everlasting life.

Silence

Lord, we believe:
help our unbelief.

Father, we thank you for the amazing truth
that you always reach out to us in compassion,
and always have time for us.

Merciful Father:
**accept these prayers
for the sake of your Son,
our Saviour Jesus Christ.
Amen.**

KEEP US FAITHFUL

Let us pray now to the living God,
who always keeps his promises,
and who knows us so well.

Loving Father, keep the Church faithful
in telling the good news, comforting the desolate,
actively loving justice
and drawing many to freedom
through the joy of your forgiveness.

Silence

Keep us faithful:
to your calling.

As the Church, we pray for the world,
that there may be integrity in leadership;
mercy and justice for rich and poor,
strong and weak;
that there may be peace among nations
and respect for all.

Silence

Keep us faithful:
to your calling.

As the family of believers, we pray
for those around us now and their needs;
and for the families we represent, and their needs.
May the love of Christ be shown in what we do
and how we speak and how we spend.

Silence

Keep us faithful:
to your calling.

In compassion we call to mind
all who are locked in physical or emotional pain,

all who are weighed down with worry,
guilt or despair.
Restore and refresh them, comfort and free them.

Silence

Keep us faithful:
to your calling.

As resurrection people, we commend to your love
those who have died to this earthly life.
May they, and we in our turn, experience for ever
the joy of your eternity.

Silence

Keep us faithful:
to your calling.

As followers of the living Christ,
we praise you for the prophecies fulfilled,
the promises honoured and the victory over evil
gloriously accomplished in him
to fill our lives with hope.

Merciful Father:
accept these prayers
for the sake of your Son,
our Saviour Jesus Christ.
Amen.

FAITHFUL TO THE END

The Lord is always ready to listen;
let us pray to him now.

Lord, we pray particularly for those
whose faith is being battered
and those who no longer pray;
we pray for our training programmes
and our weekly worship;
for our faith to be deepened and strengthened.

Silence

Keep us faithful:
firm to the end.

We pray for those whose responsibility it is
to manage the world's economy,
and for those who have difficult
ethical decisions to make;
we pray for wisdom and courage to do what is right.

Silence

Keep us faithful:
firm to the end.

We pray for the world our children will inherit
and ask your blessing on all parents
and the responsibilities they face;
we ask for understanding, maturity,
and the gift of laughter.

Silence

Keep us faithful:
firm to the end.

We pray for the victims of disasters,
famines, earthquakes and plagues;

for all who are crying
and those who have no tears left.
We pray for comfort, renewed strength,
and available friends.

Silence

Keep us faithful:
firm to the end.

We pray for those who are nearing death
and those who have died;
especially we pray for those
who have died suddenly and unprepared.
We pray for mercy and forgiveness.

Silence

Keep us faithful:
firm to the end.

We give you thanks, Lord God,
that you always provide the grace we need
to accomplish what you ask of us.

Merciful Father:
**accept these prayers
for the sake of your Son,
our Saviour Jesus Christ.
Amen.**

Prayer

COME TO US, FATHER

As one family in Christ,
we come before our heavenly Father
and pray to him now.

We pray for all those Christians
who are persecuted for their faith;
that they may be strengthened
by the assurance of Christ's presence
for all time and in all places.

Silence

Come to us, Father:
our hope and our joy.

We pray for all politicians
and government ministers;
that they may discern Christ's truth
and be given the courage to walk faithfully in it.

Silence

Come to us, Father:
our hope and our joy.

We bring into the light of God's love
the malnourished and the starving,
all who have become diseased
from contaminated water supplies;
that as fellow human beings
we may be led by the love of Christ
to share the world's resources.

Silence

Come to us, Father:
our hope and our joy.

We remember in prayer our own community,
and especially the many groups of Christian people;

that Jesus' love and desire for our unity
may inspire us to break down barriers
and build bridges to the greater glory of God.

Silence

Come to us, Father:
our hope and our joy.

In silence,
we pray to the Lord
for our own intentions.

Silence

Father,
trusting in your love,
we lay these prayers before you
through Jesus Christ our Lord.
Amen.

Father, we ask you

Father, we ask you to strengthen
and purify your people;
teach us to be better listeners
to each other and to you.
Speak to our inmost being and show us your will.

Silence

When we call:
we know you answer us.

Father, we ask you to unravel the tangled problems
of our world;
help us to follow you, step by step,
towards harmony and peace.

Silence

When we call:
we know you answer us.

Father, we ask you to live in our homes
and in all hostels and orphanages.
Remind us to value the time we spend with our friends
and listen to one another with full attention.

Silence

When we call:
we know you answer us.

Father, we ask that the sick and injured
will be aware of your comforting presence;
that the very old and the very young
may know they are safe and loved.

Silence

When we call:
we know you answer us.

Father, we ask you to welcome into your kingdom
those who have recently travelled through death
from lifetimes all over the world.

Silence

When we call:
we know you answer us.

Father, we ask you to sharpen our awareness
of all that is beautiful, hopeful,
precious and eternal.

Silence

When we call:
we know you answer us,
because we ask in the name
of Jesus, our Lord.
Amen.

FATHER, WE PRAY

Father, we pray for the building up of your Church;
for each individual member
as we struggle with doubts, fears and weariness,
with scorn or persecution.

Silence

From eternity to eternity:
you are our God.

Father, we pray for the building of peace
between nations,
the building of honour and respect between people,
as we work through deep hurts from the past.

Silence

From eternity to eternity:
you are our God.

Father, we pray for the building up of communities
in areas where people feel lost and like strangers;
for a sense of trust and mutual support.

Silence

From eternity to eternity:
you are our God.

Father, we pray for those recovering
from surgery and illness;
for those who lack energy and vitality;
for those who cannot face the future.

Silence

From eternity to eternity:
you are our God.

Father, we pray for those who have finished
their earthly life and now enter eternity;

and we pray for those who badly miss
their physical presence.

Silence

From eternity to eternity:
you are our God.

Father, we pray that we may increasingly
notice your glory,
delight in your care of us
and rest in your peace.

Silence

Father, we acknowledge in our prayers
that you are our God,
and we dare to ask that you, in your answers,
will acknowledge that we are your people:
for the sake of Jesus Christ, our Saviour.
Amen.

HEAR OUR PRAYER

All our needs are God's concerns.
Let us pray to him now.

Father, make us a listening Church,
welcoming to the hesitant,
encouraging to the young,
sensitive to the differences and attentive to the needs.

Silence

God, in mercy:
hear us as we pray.

Father, make us a caring world,
wise in government,
honest in promises,
far-sighted in the management of resources,
and open-hearted in charitable giving.

Silence

God, in mercy:
hear us as we pray.

Father, make us a responsible community,
supporting our neighbours and friends,
sharing one another's sorrows and joys,
and opening our homes to your indwelling.

Silence

God, in mercy:
hear us as we pray.

Father, as we remember those
who have asked for our prayers,
take their needs and provide for them,
take their wounds and heal them,
take their suffering and comfort them.

Silence

God, in mercy:
hear us as we pray.

Father, as we call to mind those who have died,
may they know the welcoming of your love
into eternal joy.

Silence

God, in mercy:
hear us as we pray.

Thank you, Holy God,
for knowing our needs
even before we become aware of them ourselves.

Merciful Father:
accept these prayers
for the sake of your Son,
our Saviour Jesus Christ.
Amen.

ABBA, FATHER,
HEAR YOUR CHILDREN

Gathered together in the love and fellowship of God,
let us speak to our Father of our cares and needs.

We pray for the work of your Church
in suburbs, cities, slums and villages all over the world, especially
where there is violent opposition,
complacency or apathy;
that all who work in your name
may be blessed and encouraged,
so that many may find peace in your love.

Silence

Abba, Father:
hear your children.

We pray for the world;
for all areas in which there is a breakdown
of communication between individuals,
groups or nations;
may your unifying love draw people together,
helping them to find shared interests to build on,
rather than dwelling on hurtful divisions.

Silence

Abba, Father:
hear your children.

We pray for a greater love and fellowship
among us here in this community and in our families;
live in us, Father, and make us more ready
to respond and forgive, to help and to listen.

Silence

Abba, Father:
hear your children.

We pray for the homeless
and those living in crowded, inadequate accommodation;
those living alone and isolated;
for the hungry and malnourished;
may your love, working through us, your body,
reach those in desperate need and give them new hope.

Silence

Abba, Father:
hear your children.

We pray for those who have travelled through death to eternity;
may they live in your peace and joy for ever.

Silence

Abba, Father:
hear your children.

Rejoicing in your strength, love and fellowship
we offer you our thanks and praise.

Silence

Loving Father, we come to you
as children come to their parents,
asking and trusting.
**Hear our prayers, which we ask
in the name of Jesus, our elder Brother.
Amen.**

GOD HEARS OUR NEEDS

Father, the Church has its areas of weakness and pain;
we long to be truly and faithfully the body of Christ.

Silence

Father, we thank you:
for hearing our needs.

Father, the nations bicker and fight;
we long for a world where love and peace prevail.

Silence

Father, we thank you:
for hearing our needs.

Father, our homes and families have tensions
and misunderstandings;
we long for your wise parenting in every home.

Silence

Father, we thank you:
for hearing our needs.

Father, many are sad, stressed, in pain or in need;
we long for your healing presence to comfort and renew.

Silence

Father, we thank you:
for hearing our needs.

Father, some die destitute and unnoticed;
some die violently,
and many grieve for their loved ones;
we long for your reassuring love and hope.

Silence

Father, we thank you:
for hearing our needs.

Father, our lives are so rich with blessings;
we long to show our thanks in our lives.

Silence

Father, you know what is best for us;
help us to recognise it
and welcome it when it comes:
through Jesus Christ, our Lord.
Amen.

GOD LISTENS AND ANSWERS

Father, we call to mind all who teach the Christian faith,
all those in training for ministry,
and those preparing for baptism and confirmation;
we ask for the Spirit to guide us into all truth.

Silence

Our God listens to his children:
our God answers prayer.

Father, we call to mind all those involved in education,
those who report world events and comment on them;
we ask for your wisdom and integrity,
your discernment and values.

Silence

Our God listens to his children:
our God answers prayer.

Father, we call to mind those who have influenced
our thinking this week,
those we influence by our words and behaviour;
we ask you to realign our priorities
and give us courage to live your way.

Silence

Our God listens to his children:
our God answers prayer.

Father, we call to mind all who are suffering
in hospitals, bedsits, huts and houses
throughout the world.
We ask you to restore each person to wholeness and joy.

Silence

Our God listens to his children:
our God answers prayer.

Father, we call to mind those who have
reached the end of their earthly life
and are meeting you face to face;
we ask for your mercy on them,
and on those who miss them.

Silence

Our God listens to his children:
our God answers prayer.

Father, we call to mind the many blessings in our lives,
and the ways you reveal yourself to us;
we ask you to deepen our understanding of you,
so that we can love you more and more.

Silence

Father, you hear our prayers.
Teach us to listen to you:
through Jesus Christ, our Lord.
Amen.

THE LISTENING GOD

Our God is always ready to listen.
Let us pray to him now.

Father, continue to pour out your gifts on the Church,
so that many may be saved
and our faith may grow strong
and bear much fruit.

Silence

Listening God:
we put our trust in you.

Look with mercy on the conflicts of our world;
realign our values and goals
until they are in line with your will,
and our laws and expectations reflect your justice and love.

Silence

Listening God:
we put our trust in you.

Bless our homes and families
and all our neighbours and friends;
train us to listen to one another with full attention,
and recognise one another's gifts.

Silence

Listening God:
we put our trust in you.

Encourage the hesitant, curb the overpowering,
heal the sick, refresh the exhausted,
soften the hardened hearts,
open the eyes of the complacent,
and comfort all who are sad.

Silence

Listening God:
we put our trust in you.

Welcome into your eternity
all those who have died in faith;
may we in our turn share with them
the joy of living with you for ever.

Silence

Listening God:
we put our trust in you.

Thank you, Lord our God,
for the hope you have given us through Christ,
which enables us to enjoy living in eternity
even while we still journey here.

Merciful Father:
accept these prayers
for the sake of your Son,
our Saviour Jesus Christ.
Amen.

GOD MEETS OUR NEEDS

Let us gather together our concerns
and pray to our heavenly Father
who is always ready to listen
and eager to meet our needs.

We pray for the Church,
especially in its work of counselling
and welcoming those in great need or difficulty;
that our Christian witness
may vividly reflect
the generous love of Christ.

Silence

Hear us, heavenly Father:
and let your will be done.

We pray for the world's leaders
and all who hold positions of authority
and responsibility;
that the world's resources may be shared
and fairly distributed,
so that all its inhabitants
have enough for their needs.

Silence

Hear us, heavenly Father:
and let your will be done.

We pray for the starving and malnourished,
and for all who are weakened
by lack of sufficient food;
for all refugees and asylum seekers,
and those whose mental capacity
makes them vulnerable to inadequate provision
of food, clothing or housing.

Silence

Hear us, heavenly Father:
and let your will be done.

We pray for ourselves,
and for those we meet each day;
that we may be more prepared
to give our time,
energy, talents and money
in serving those in need
and working hand in hand with Christ.

Silence

Hear us, heavenly Father:
and let your will be done.

In the silence of our hearts,
we pray to our heavenly Father
about our own particular concerns.

Silence

Father of mercy,
you are always more ready to give
than we are to receive;
in thankfulness we welcome
your Spirit into our lives,
and ask you to accept our prayers,
through Jesus Christ, your Son.
Amen.

TRUSTING IN GOD WE PRAY

Trusting in your love we pray
for all arguments and conflicts in the Church;
for all who feel confused about their faith.

Silence

Father, you hold our lives:
safe in your hands.

Trusting in your authority we pray
for all international discussions and negotiations;
for all who give orders to others.

Silence

Father, you hold our lives:
safe in your hands.

Trusting in your gentleness we pray
for new-born children and their parents;
for all families in crisis.

Silence

Father, you hold our lives:
safe in your hands.

Trusting in your wisdom we pray
for those who labour to find cures
and protection from disease;
for all who suffer in body, mind or spirit.

Silence

Father, you hold our lives:
safe in your hands.

Trusting in your mercy we pray
for those who have reached physical death;
for those who miss them or feel guilty about them.

Silence

Father, you hold our lives:
safe in your hands.

Trusting in your goodness we pray
with thankfulness for all we have received
and been enabled to share.

Silence

Father, we trust you
with our prayers and with our lives.
**Use them according to your will,
and for the sake of Jesus Christ, our Lord.
Amen.**

GOD KNOWS EVERYTHING

Father, we pray that all Christians may grow
more loving, more active and more faithful,
starting now.

Silence

God is greater than our hearts:
and he knows everything.

Father, we pray for all world leaders
and those who advise them,
that they may make good decisions
and act wisely.

Silence

God is greater than our hearts:
and he knows everything.

Father, we pray for single parent families,
families under stress and all who are
separated from loved ones.

Silence

God is greater than our hearts:
and he knows everything.

Father, we pray for the mentally ill,
the physically damaged,
for the lonely and the fearful.

Silence

God is greater than our hearts:
and he knows everything.

Father, we pray for those who have come
to the end of their earthly life,
and for those who miss them,

or never had the opportunity
to put things right with them.

Silence

God is greater than our hearts:
and he knows everything.

Father, we bring to you our secret hopes
and longings and our gratitude.

Silence

Father, in your great wisdom
make up for what is lacking in our prayers:
**for the sake of Jesus Christ,
our Redeemer and Lord.
Amen.**

GOD KNOWS BEST

Father, we pray for the excited new Christians
and the mellow, experienced ones;
for the doubting, cynical ones
and the hesitant believers.

Silence

In every situation:
God knows best.

Father, we pray for the responsible
and the peacemakers in our world,
and for the defensive, arrogant and ambitious.

Silence

In every situation:
God knows best.

Father, we pray for the contented, thriving families
and for those struggling to survive each day.

Silence

In every situation:
God knows best.

Father, we pray for those recovering from surgery
and for all those in great pain.

Silence

In every situation:
God knows best.

Father, we pray for those who have recently died
and for those dying now.

Silence

In every situation:
God knows best.

Father, we thank you and praise you
for all the blessings you shower on our lives,
and ask you to keep us in closer touch
with you from now on.

Silence

Father, you know our needs
better than we do ourselves.
We trust that your answers to our prayers
will be for the greatest good:
through Jesus Christ, our Lord.
Amen.

JESUS, HEAR US

Jesus assures us that
wherever two or three
meet in his name
he will be with them;
in confidence, then,
let us bring to him
our needs and cares.

We pray that God's love
will spill out through his Church
to the world,
filling all teaching,
all advice and counsel,
all correction and guidance.

Silence

Jesus, hear us:
renew us in love.

We pray that God's Spirit
of forgiveness and acceptance
will permeate the social and political
fabric of our world
until we are able to criticise gently,
and accept criticism honestly;
discuss differences calmly,
and be prepared to negotiate rationally.

Silence

Jesus, hear us:
renew us in love.

We pray that God's comfort and consolation
will soothe those who are afraid
or in great pain,
refresh those who are mentally

or physically exhausted
and be a lifeline to those
who are broken-hearted or in despair.

Silence

Jesus, hear us:
renew us in love.

We pray that the light of God's goodness
may shine in our hearts
to show us our faults
and enable us to admit them;
to shine through our lives in
the way we treat each other,
especially when we disagree or feel hurt.

Silence

Jesus, hear us:
renew us in love.

In silence,
as Jesus listens with love,
we name our own particular cares and concerns.

Silence

Lord,
we ask you to gather up
these prayers of your people,
offered in your presence.
Amen.

Hear us as we pray

In the knowledge that God our Father
is here present,
let us pray.

We pray for the Church of Christ
and its mission to the world;
that it may be a sign of his presence,
call sinners to repentance
and bring many to the joy of living in your love.

Silence

Lord, our Father:
hear us as we pray.

We pray for the whole created world
and its people;
that no evil may thwart God's will,
but rather that his kingdom
may be established
and his will fulfilled.

Silence

Lord, our Father:
hear us as we pray.

We remember before God
all who suffer
mentally, physically and spiritually;
those who see no further
than immediate physical comforts,
and do not realise their spiritual poverty.

Silence

Lord, our Father:
hear us as we pray.

We hold before God this church
and the surrounding community,
with all who live and work within it;
that we may strive each day
to align ourselves
with the life of Christ,
who saves us from our sin.

Silence

Lord, our Father:
hear us as we pray.

In the silence of God's stillness,
we name any we know
who especially need our prayer.

Silence

Lord, our Father:
hear us as we pray.

Silence

Father,
trusting in your mercy,
we lay these prayers before you,
through Jesus Christ our Lord.
Amen.

LORD, HEAR AND ANSWER

We remember all the clusters of Christians in our area,
and pray that we may truly be one in Christ.

Silence

Hear, O Lord:
and answer our prayer.

We remember all the areas of violence
and hostility in our world,
and pray for peace between nations
and individual people.

Silence

Hear, O Lord:
and answer our prayer.

We remember all families struggling against poverty,
inadequate accommodation or illness,
and pray that you will show us
how best to help them.

Silence

Hear, O Lord:
and answer our prayer.

We remember the vulnerable and the ignored,
the outcasts and the oppressed,
and pray that we may open our hearts
to loving involvement.

Silence

Hear, O Lord:
and answer our prayer.

We remember those who have died
and their loved ones,
and pray that you will comfort all sorrow.

Silence

Hear, O Lord:
and answer our prayer.

We remember with joy
your constant loving and forgiveness,
and pray that we may show our praise
not only with our lips but in our lives.

Silence

O Lord, we trust you with our prayers;
may we trust you also with your answers:
through Jesus Christ, our Lord.
Amen.

LORD, IN MERCY HEAR OUR CRY

Sisters and brothers in Christ,
let us bring to the Lord of life
our concern and care for the Church
and for the world.

Lord, we bring before you all Christians,
especially Church leaders and pastors;
may they remain faithful in times of trial,
trusting in your everlasting love;
may all who take risks to witness
be given courage and inspiration.

Silence

Lord, in mercy:
hear our cry.

We bring before you all the diverse societies of our world;
may your living Spirit be spread
to purify the corrupt, inspire the apathetic
and unlock the hearts of the bigoted.

Silence

Lord, in mercy:
hear our cry.

We bring before you our own circle
of family and friends;
all our desires and attempts to follow you;
live within us to protect, guide,
and bring us to perfection in Christ.

Silence

Lord, in mercy:
hear our cry.

We bring before you the weak and the frightened;
all who are suffering in any way;
may they find you there with them,
and draw hope and courage from your presence.

Silence

Lord, in mercy:
hear our cry.

We bring before you those who have died in faith;
may they know the joy and peace
of your heaven for ever.

Silence

Lord, in mercy:
hear our cry.

We thank you and praise you
for all you were prepared to suffer for us;
bring the light of resurrection to all our suffering,
until we learn to praise you even through dark times.
We appeal to your mercy
as we bring these prayers
in the name of Jesus Christ, our Lord.
Amen.

HIS SPIRIT MOVES OUR PRAYERS

We pray for the Church, the body of Christ,
longing for its healing, strengthening
and openness to your will.

Silence

The Lord is among us:
his Spirit moves our prayers.

We pray for the world and all the nations,
longing for peace and tranquillity,
justice, mercy and forgiveness.

Silence

The Lord is among us:
his Spirit moves our prayers.

We pray for all our relatives
and the family life of our country,
longing for the grace to love and honour
one another,
to trust and to persevere.

Silence

The Lord is among us:
his Spirit moves our prayers.

We pray for those who are ill or in distress,
longing for your comfort, healing and refreshment.

Silence

The Lord is among us:
his Spirit moves our prayers.

We pray for those who are passing
through the gate of death,
longing for your merciful love.

Silence

The Lord is among us:
his Spirit moves our prayers.

We praise you and worship you
for all your blessings,
but especially for your generous saving love
and faithful presence with us.

Silence

Father, your Spirit has brought us
close to you in prayer;
may he keep us close to you in life:
through Jesus Christ, our Lord.
Amen.

WE REMEMBER IN PRAYER

Father, we remember in prayer all those who are
insulted or despised for their faith in you.

Silence

Lord, we take refuge:
in the shadow of your wings.

We remember in prayer those caught up in conflict,
and those who strive for peace.

Silence

Lord, we take refuge:
in the shadow of your wings.

We remember in prayer those who irritate and annoy us,
and those we irritate and annoy.

Silence

Lord, we take refuge:
in the shadow of your wings.

We remember those whose bodies are trapped in pain,
and those whose minds are trapped in confusion.

Silence

Lord, we take refuge:
in the shadow of your wings.

We remember those who have died
and those who ache with mourning.

Silence

Lord, we take refuge:
in the shadow of your wings.

We thank and praise you, O God,
for your parenting and special love for each of us.

Silence

Loving Father,
you know the needs of those for whom we pray.
Thank you for helping us remember them:
in the name of Jesus Christ, our Lord.
Amen.

IN YOUR PRESENCE

In your presence we bring to mind all Christians;
those recently baptised or recently returned to the faith,
all Church leaders and those whose faith is hesitant.

Silence

From eternity to eternity:
you are God.

In your presence we call to mind
the areas of conflict, righteous anger and
hardened attitudes,
and we pray for your lasting peace.

Silence

From eternity to eternity:
you are God.

In your presence we bring to mind
those who have influenced our faith development,
those we love, and those who love us.

Silence

From eternity to eternity:
you are God.

In your presence we call to mind
those who are enchained by guilt,
or bad and frightening memories
which need to be released.

Silence

From eternity to eternity:
you are God.

In your presence we call to mind
those who have died

and moved from time into eternity;
their families and all who miss them.

Silence

From eternity to eternity:
you are God.

In your presence we bring to mind
the beauty, love and peace which surround us
and bubble up even inside pain and grief.

Silence

Father, we ask that your presence in our prayers
may not only be with us
but with those for whom we pray,
today and every day:
through Jesus Christ, our Lord.
Amen.

GOD'S UNSEEN PRESENCE

We have met here
in the real presence of our God.
Let us pray to him now.

Silence

Though we cannot see you:
your love surrounds us.

We bring to mind the worldwide Christian Church,
both leaders and people.
We ask for a deeper awareness
of your presence among us.

Silence

Though we cannot see you:
your love surrounds us.

We bring to mind the troubled areas of our world
where corruption, injustice and violence
ruin lives and damage self worth.
We ask for your renewing and cleansing.

Silence

Though we cannot see you:
your love surrounds us.

We call to mind those we have spent time with
during the past week;
the good and the disturbing conversations,
the joys and the aches of those we love.

Silence

Though we cannot see you:
your love surrounds us.

We bring to mind all who live away from home,
all refugees and all children in care.

We ask for the security that only you can give.

Silence

Though we cannot see you:
your love surrounds us.

We bring to mind those who have died recently
and all who grieve for them.
We ask for comfort to be given to the dying
and the assurance of your presence.

Silence

Though we cannot see you:
your love surrounds us.

We bring to mind the risks you were prepared to take
in becoming one of us out of love for us,
and we offer you our thanks and praise.

Merciful Father:
**accept these prayers
for the sake of your Son,
our Saviour Jesus Christ.
Amen.**

INTO YOUR HANDS, O LORD

Father, we pray for all who follow Christ,
for those whose faith is being tested,
and for those who have drifted away.

Silence

Into your hands, O Lord:
we place our lives.

We pray for all leaders and advisers,
all meetings and councils,
that right decisions may be made.

Silence

Into your hands, O Lord:
we place our lives.

We pray for all those we love
and those we find it difficult to love;
for those whose loving is damaged
and those who have no one who cares about them.

Silence

Into your hands, O Lord:
we place our lives.

We pray for those who are persecuted or imprisoned,
for those locked in fear or hatred
and all who are in need of healing.

Silence

Into your hands, O Lord:
we place our lives.

We pray for those who have died alone or in fear,
for those who are finding it hard
to accept another's death.

Silence

Into your hands, O Lord:
we place our lives.

We give you thanks and praise
for bringing us safely to this moment,
and offer you the future,
with all that it holds.

Silence

Heavenly Father,
when we bring our human needs to you in prayer
help us to rest assured
that the whole world is in your hands:
through Jesus Christ, our Lord.
Amen.

WE LIFT OUR HEARTS

As we gather here in God's presence, let us pray.

We bring to you, Lord,
the Church in all its richness and all its need;
all its diversity and all its division.
Give us a fresh understanding
of what it means to live in you;
may all of us celebrate the reality
of your presence among us,
filling us with new life and new hope.

Silence

Lord, in your presence:
we lift our hearts to you.

We bring to you, Lord,
our nation, our world, our universe;
all the areas that are fastened shut to hold you out;
all the bewildered confusion
about who we are and why we are here;
all the doubts and insecurity,
and all the searching for inner peace.

Silence

Lord, in your presence:
we lift our hearts to you.

We bring to you, Lord, our homes and families,
and all the joys and sorrows of our relationships.
We bring the rooms in which we eat
and work and relax;
and invite you into them all.

Silence

Lord, in your presence:
we lift our hearts to you.

We bring to you, Lord,
those whom life has damaged,
and all who find it difficult to trust in you;
we bring you those who need refreshment and hope,
comfort, healing and inner serenity.

Silence

Lord, in your presence:
we lift our hearts to you.

We bring to you, Lord,
those who approach death with great fear
and those who die unprepared to meet you.
Have mercy on us all, forgive us all that is past
and gather us into your everlasting kingdom
of peace and joy.

Silence

Lord, in your presence:
we lift our hearts to you.

We bring to you, Lord, the love of our hearts
as we recall the extent of your love for us
which understands our frailty
and reaches out to us where we are.

Merciful Father:
accept these prayers
for the sake of your Son,
our Saviour Jesus Christ.
Amen.

LIFTED IN PRAYER

Father, you know us better than we know ourselves,
and are well aware of the needs and pains in your Church.
We lift them now to your healing love.

Silence

Father, we love you:
we love you and we trust you.

In our world there are decisions to be made,
countries to be governed and people to be honoured.
We lift them now to your grace and wisdom.

Silence

Father, we love you:
we love you and we trust you.

In our neighbourhood and in our homes
there are celebrations and tragedies,
times of hope, of weariness and tenderness.
We lift them now to your loving concern.

Silence

Father, we love you:
we love you and we trust you.

In our hospitals and clinics there are many in pain,
many who are fearful,
and many who have lost hope.
We lift them now to your comfort and protection.

Silence

Father, we love you:
we love you and we trust you.

As each day others die and enter your presence,
we ask for your mercy
and commend them to your safe keeping.

Silence

Father, we love you:
we love you and we trust you.

As we walk through our lives in your company,
we rejoice in your friendship
and delight in your love for us.

Silence

Father, we love you:
we love you and we trust you;
we trust you with our prayers
and we love you with our lives,
for the sake of Jesus.
Amen.

THROUGH OUR PRAYERS

Let us quieten our hearts
in the presence of the unchanging
and everlasting Father,
and pray.

We pray for all those involved
in the ceaseless praying
on our spinning earth;
for all contemplative orders,
and those whose lives
are rooted in prayer;
for those learning to pray
and those who feel they cannot pray.

Silence

Spirit of God:
reach out to the world through our prayers.

We pray for the world,
for victory of good over evil
in every situation
whether of international
or local significance;
for a deepening of trust
and a desire for truth and peace.

Silence

Spirit of God:
reach out to the world through our prayers.

We pray for the disheartened and uninspired;
for those whose lives are frustrating
and endlessly stressful;
for the homeless and the unemployed;
and for those addicted to drugs,
alcohol or gambling.

Silence

Spirit of God:
reach out to the world through our prayers.

We pray for the members of our own families,
with their particular needs,
for our local shopkeepers, teachers,
doctors, nurses,
and all who work in this area.

Silence

Spirit of God:
reach out to the world through our prayers.

In silence, we bring our own prayers
to God our Father,
who knows all our needs.

Silence

God, our heavenly Father,
bless our lives to your service,
and accept our prayers,
through Jesus Christ our Lord.
Amen.

HELP US TO HEAR YOU

Rejoicing in the amazing love of God our Father,
let us pour out to him our needs, cares and concerns.

Good Shepherd, as we see, with sorrow,
the divisions between Christian groups,
we ask you to enable us to become one flock.

Silence

Father, hear us:
and help us to hear you.

As we see the glaring injustices of wealth
and food distribution in our world,
we ask you to give us courage to work in your strength
towards building a safer and more caring society.

Silence

Father, hear us:
and help us to hear you.

As we watch our children growing up
and our parents growing older,
and feel anxious for their future,
we ask you for the assurance of your steadfast love,
and we entrust their lives to your perfect care.

Silence

Father, hear us:
and help us to hear you.

As we see and read in the news
of all those afflicted by natural disasters,
by terrible accidents and by war,
we ask you, O Lord of life,
to bring good out of every evil
and growth out of every suffering.

Silence

Father, hear us:
and help us to hear you.

As we remember our loved ones
who have passed through death into eternity,
we ask you to welcome them
into your light and joy for ever.

Silence

Father, hear us:
and help us to hear you.

Loving Lord, we thank you
for the many joys and blessings you give us each day,
and for this opportunity to worship you.

Silence

And now, Father, we ask
that the time we spend in prayer
may make us more kind to others,
more honest with ourselves
and more dedicated to you:
through Jesus Christ, our Lord.
Amen.

Hearing God's answer

Holy God, you have called us
to meet and pray together,
and here we are.

We pray for those called
to lay and ordained ministry in your Church,
and for those at present testing their vocation.
We lay before you the work that needs doing here
and ask you to provide people to do it.

Silence

We ask in Jesus' name:
give us grace to discern your answer.

We pray for those called to serve you
in positions of authority and influence;
for all leaders to see true greatness as service
and true strength as humility.

Silence

We ask in Jesus' name:
give us grace to discern your answer.

We pray for those called to marriage,
and those called to the single life,
for parents and grandparents,
sons and daughters,
for acceptance of what we cannot change
and strength to live the Christian life
in our present situation.

Silence

We ask in Jesus' name:
give us grace to discern your answer.

We pray for those whose lives
are full of disappointment, disillusion and discontent;

for all who struggle with great perseverance
in difficult circumstances.
We pray for your strength, encouragement and direction.

Silence

We ask in Jesus' name:
give us grace to discern your answer.

We pray for those called, through death, into eternal life
and freedom from all their pain and suffering.
Receive them with mercy
and welcome them into your kingdom.

Silence

We ask in Jesus' name:
give us grace to discern your answer.

We thank you, Holy God, for your promise
that where two or three are gathered in your name
you will grant their requests.

Merciful Father:
accept these prayers
for the sake of your Son,
our Saviour Jesus Christ.
Amen.

Thirsting for God

Thirsty for God, let us pray to him now,
in the knowledge that he will provide for us
in the way that is best.

Father, wherever the Church is dry and parched
may the water of your Spirit well up to refresh and renew,
to bring life and strong new growth.
Lord, make us more aware of our thirst for you,
so that we come to you ready and eager
to receive your living water.

Silence

Living God:
satisfy our thirst.

Father, from the conflicting needs
and agendas of the world we cry for mercy,
for a deeper understanding of one another
and a greater desire for co-operation and peace.
We pray for sensitivity in handling delicate negotiations
and the wisdom which respects and listens.

Silence

Living God:
satisfy our thirst.

We pray that in all our relationships
you will make us effective channels
of your love and forgiveness.
Make us awash with your living water
so that our homes and places of work,
our shopping and leisure centres,
our conversations and actions,
are always in touch with your renewing power.

Silence

Living God:
satisfy our thirst.

We stand alongside all those who are suffering,
whether in body, mind or spirit,
and long for your healing and comfort,
your strength for perseverance
and your patience in the dark times;
we long for your living Spirit to envelop and sustain them.

Silence

Living God:
satisfy our thirst.

We pray for those who have come
to the end of earthly life; have mercy on them.
May they, placing their faith in you, the God of life,
share in the light and joy of heaven for ever.

Silence

Living God:
satisfy our thirst.

O God, how we need you!
We thank you for supplying us and coaxing us forward
with such tenderness and affection.

Merciful Father:
accept these prayers
for the sake of your Son,
our Saviour Jesus Christ.
Amen.

My soul is
thirsty for God

Father, we pray for all Church leaders,
and all who minister to others
through their teaching of the faith.
Keep us available to encourage them
and help them wherever we can.

Silence

My soul is thirsty for God:
thirsty for the living God.

We pray for those who influence the thinking
and general behaviour of people all over the world;
for clear guidance in what is right and true.

Silence

My soul is thirsty for God:
thirsty for the living God.

We pray for all those entrusted
with the responsibility of bringing up children;
and for all those who are finding adolescence difficult.

Silence

My soul is thirsty for God:
thirsty for the living God.

We pray for all whose lives are restricted
through illness, disability or frailty;
we pray for all imprisoned by addiction.

Silence

My soul is thirsty for God:
thirsty for the living God.

We pray for those who have died
and for those who are finding life bleak
without them.

Silence

My soul is thirsty for God:
thirsty for the living God.

We pray with thankfulness for every reconciliation,
every flame of love and tenderness,
every word of forgiveness
and every act of loving care.

Silence

Father, we thank you that, through prayer,
you satisfy our deepest needs.
Refresh our souls
and send us on our way rejoicing
in the service of Jesus Christ, our Lord.
Amen.

BREAD OF HEAVEN

We have gathered here
to meet with our God in worship.
Let us pray to him now.

Lord, awaken in us our need of you
and make us hungry and thirsty for you,
both as individuals and as the Church of God.
Let no other issues side-track us from seeking you,
and increase our love and compassion
so that we long to serve out your love
to the world around us.

Silence

Bread of heaven:
on you we feed.

Lord, allow our world to see the true value of things,
so that the worthless and dangerous is unmasked
and real needs acknowledged.
Guide our leaders in wisdom and integrity,
and enable us all to co-operate in proper care
and stewardship of the world's resources.

Silence

Bread of heaven:
on you we feed.

Lord, as we eat our food this week,
remind us of your spiritual feeding.
May the meals we prepare and eat together
be opportunities for drawing closer
to one another and to you.

Silence

Bread of heaven:
on you we feed.

Lord, we pray for all who need medical treatment
or are waiting in pain for surgery.
We pray for those who have become addicted
and long to be set free.
We pray for all whose wrong choices
have ended in heartache, disillusion and despair.

Silence

Bread of heaven:
on you we feed.

Lord, welcome into your eternity
all who have spent their lives coming to you
and now come to be with you for ever.
Have mercy on all those approaching death
who do not know you
but reject what they imagine you to be.
May they respond to the true and living God
and know your love for ever.

Silence

Bread of heaven:
on you we feed.

Lord, thank you for feeding us
with spiritual food that satisfies our souls.

Merciful Father:
accept these prayers
for the sake of your Son,
our Saviour Jesus Christ.
Amen.

KNOWING GOD

We know that God is here with us,
and hears what is in our thoughts and in our hearts.

So we pray for all who claim to be Christians
all over the world.
We ask for a real longing for God in our lives;
a longing that is not satisfied by anything else.

Silence

Holy God:
we want to know you better.

We pray for the different countries
and those with power and influence.
We pray for honesty, justice and integrity.

Silence

Holy God:
we want to know you better.

We pray for those we love
and those we find it hard to relate to.
We pray for more love and forgiveness.

Silence

Holy God:
we want to know you better.

We pray for those in pain
and those imprisoned by addiction.
We pray for healing, wholeness and freedom.

Silence

Holy God:
we want to know you better.

We pray for those who have died
and now see you face to face.
We pray for those who miss them here.

Silence

Holy God:
we want to know you better.

We thank you for showing us
what needs putting right,
and for forgiving us all that is past.

Silence

Merciful Father:
accept these prayers
for the sake of your Son,
our Saviour Jesus Christ.
Amen.

Special days and seasons

ADVENT (1)

As we gather expectantly in God's presence,
at the beginning of Advent, let us pray.

God of cleansing and liberating power,
give us the courage and perception
to see ourselves as we really are,
and repent of our sin;
may the whole Church be cleansed and renewed.

Silence

Come, O come, Emmanuel:
come and live in us.

God of wisdom and truth,
we pray for the world's leaders and all in authority,
that they may lead and govern wisely and honestly,
without corruption and for the common good.

Silence

Come, O come, Emmanuel:
come and live in us.

God of love and faithfulness,
may every family be surrounded and upheld
by your presence,
the conflicts healed and needs provided for,
and every act of kindness blessed.

Silence

Come, O come, Emmanuel:
come and live in us.

God of wholeness,
bring your reassurance and healing,
your hope and patience
to all who are suffering in any way;

bring freedom to all imprisoned by hate or guilt,
and a change of heart to all who need to forgive.

Silence

Come, O come, Emmanuel:
come and live in us.

God of unending life,
bring life in its fullness to us here,
and to those who have completed their time on earth.
May they know the freedom and joy of your heaven.

Silence

Come, O come, Emmanuel:
come and live in us.

God of warmth and brightness,
we praise you for all our many blessings,
and above all for coming to save us and set us free.

Merciful Father:
**accept these prayers
for the sake of your Son,
our Saviour Jesus Christ.
Amen.**

ADVENT (2)

Let us pray to the God of all time and space,
in whose love we exist
and by whose love we are saved.

As we prepare ourselves
for the time when Christ comes again in glory,
we pray for the grace and honesty
to see what needs transforming in our lives as individuals
and as members of the Church of God.

Silence

O come:
let us walk in the light of the Lord.

May all church leaders, pastors and teachers be directed,
inspired and upheld by the living Spirit of God,
and may there be a deepening
of love and commitment in all Christians the world over.

Silence

O come:
let us walk in the light of the Lord.

May the leaders of this nation and of all the nations
be drawn increasingly to understand
God's ways of justice and righteousness,
and be filled with the longing
to do what is right and honest and good.

Silence

O come:
let us walk in the light of the Lord.

May all the families on earth be blessed with mutual love
and caring consideration one of another;
may arguments and misunderstandings

be properly resolved,
and difficult relationships refreshed and healed.

Silence

O come:
let us walk in the light of the Lord.

May those for whom the days and nights
creep past in pain or sorrow be given comfort and hope;
may the frightened find reassurance
and the anxious find peace of mind.

Silence

O come:
let us walk in the light of the Lord.

May those who have reached the point of death
be given the knowledge of God's closeness
on that last journey;
and may those who have died
know the eternal peace and joy of heaven.

Silence

O come:
let us walk in the light of the Lord.

May we all be given a new enthusiasm
for walking God's way, clothed in the armour of light.

Merciful Father,
**accept these prayers
for the sake of your Son,
our Saviour Jesus Christ.
Amen.**

CHRISTMAS DAY (1)

As we gather to worship the Christchild,
born today,
let us pray trustfully
to our heavenly Father.

Father, we pray for all Christians
celebrating with us all over the world,
in all climates, times and seasons
as our planet turns.

Silence

Light of ages:
be born in our hearts.

Father, we pray for all areas of darkness
where your light is desperately needed to bring peace,
understanding, sensitivity and compassion.

Silence

Light of ages:
be born in our hearts.

Father, we commend to you our homes,
families, neighbours and friends;
all children and babies, all those being born today.

Silence

Light of ages:
be born in our hearts.

We pray for those who are hungry, cold or homeless;
for all who are separated from their loved ones;
all who find the festivities of Christmas
emphasising their isolation and misery.

Silence

Light of ages:
be born in our hearts.

We thank you for all who have worshipped you
throughout the ages;
for the lives and examples of all
who shone with your light
and now rest in your peace.

Silence

Light of ages:
be born in our hearts.

Father in thankfulness we praise and worship you.
May Christ be born into the world
in every generation
through those who love and serve him.
Amen.

CHRISTMAS DAY (2)

As we celebrate the birth of Jesus, the Word of God,
let us pray with thankful hearts.

The bells and lights and presents and decorations
in church and in our homes
express our thanks to you, Lord,
for coming into the world in person.

Silence

On this Christmas Day we want to say:
Thank you, holy Father!

The world Jesus was born into was the world we know.
Thank you for being prepared to face the dangers and risks
of human mistakes and sin in order to save us.

Silence

On this Christmas Day we want to say:
Thank you, holy Father!

Many of us will be celebrating
with our families and friends.
We invite you to join us in all the festivities,
and ask you to teach us true loving.

Silence

On this Christmas Day we want to say:
Thank you, holy Father!

We remember those who find Christmas
a sad or lonely season;
we remember those for whom it brings to the surface
memories, anxieties or sorrows.
Through good and difficult times
you are always with us.

Silence

On this Christmas Day we want to say:
Thank you, holy Father!

We remember those
whose loved ones have died,
and all those who have finished
with earthly celebrations.
May they celebrate with you
and all the angels of heaven.

Silence

On this Christmas Day we want to say:
Thank you, holy Father!

For all the many blessings of this past year
and for all the good that you have enabled us to do;
for the experiences that have taught us
humility and patience,
we thank you.

Silence

On this Christmas Day we want to say:
Thank you, holy Father!

Merciful Father:
**accept these prayers
for the sake of your Son,
our Saviour Jesus Christ.
Amen.**

CHRISTMAS DAY (3)

As we gather to celebrate Christmas,
let us pray to the living God.

Lord God, thank you for our Church
and its people, ministers and leaders,
and all who pray.
Bless us all and strengthen us for your service
so we can touch the world with your love.

Silence

Holy God:
be born in us today.

Lord God, we thank you for our world
and all its beauty and blessing.
Teach us your ways, your love and your truth,
and let your kingdom grow and flourish.

Silence

Holy God:
be born in us today.

Lord God, we thank you for our families,
our neighbours and our friends,
for the happiness of human loving and sharing.
We pray for your blessing on all those we love,
whether present with us today or far away.

Silence

Holy God:
be born in us today.

Lord God, we thank you for health and strength,
and pray now for your help and healing
wherever people ache with pain and sorrow,
loneliness or fear.

Bless them in their need
and surround them with love.

Silence

Holy God:
be born in us today.

Lord God, we thank you for lives well lived,
and all who have guided us to you.
We pray for those who have died
and all for whom Christmas
sharpens the loss of loved ones.

Silence

Holy God:
be born in us today.

Lord God, we thank you for Christmas joy
and all the opportunities
to show our love for one another.
May our love, rooted in yours,
continue throughout the year.

Merciful Father:
**accept these prayers
for the sake of your Son,
our Saviour Jesus Christ.
Amen.**

EPIPHANY

We are all companions on a spiritual journey.
As we travel together, let us pray.

Silence

Light of the world:
shine in our darkness.

We pray that the worldwide Church
may always be ready
to travel in your way
and in your direction.

Silence

Light of the world:
shine in our darkness.

We pray for the nations
as they live through conflicts
and struggle with identity.
We long for all peoples
to acknowledge you, the true and living God.

Silence

Light of the world:
shine in our darkness.

We pray for the families and the streets we represent,
asking for a spirit of generous love,
understanding and mutual respect.

Silence

Light of the world:
shine in our darkness.

We pray for all who are finding their way
tedious, lonely or frightening at the moment;

for those who have lost their way
and do not know what to do for the best.

Silence

Light of the world:
shine in our darkness.

We pray for those who have come
to the end of their earthly journey,
and for those who have died unprepared.

Silence

Light of the world:
shine in our darkness.

We offer our thanks and praise
for the way you see us when we are still far off
and welcome us home.

Merciful Father:
**accept these prayers
for the sake of your Son,
our Saviour Jesus Christ.
Amen.**

LENT

Followers of the Way of Christ,
let us bring to our heavenly Father the needs of our times.

Father, we pray for your blessing
on all who confess belief in you;
that they may witness powerfully
to your unselfish love and humility
by the way they act and the lives they lead.

Silence

Father, lead us:
free us from all that is evil.

Father, we pray for your blessing
on all who administer justice;
those working in Law Courts and serving on juries,
and those who make laws;
that they may be given insight and integrity.

Silence

Father, lead us:
free us from all that is evil.

Father, we pray for your blessing on us during this Lent
as we examine our lives and draw closer to you;
that through our self-discipline and prayer
we may enter your stillness and know your will for us.

Silence

Father, lead us:
free us from all that is evil.

Father, we pray for your blessing on all in prison
or on probation;
on those living in acute poverty or in refugee camps;
on all who work among them
to heal, redirect, support and encourage.

Silence

Father, lead us:
free us from all that is evil.

Father, we pray for your blessing
on those who have passed through death, especially . . .;
may we one day share with them
eternal life in your presence.

Silence

Father, lead us:
free us from all that is evil.

In silence, Father, we bring to you
our individual concerns and joys.

Silence

Father, lead us:
free us from all that is evil.
both without and within,
through Jesus Christ, our Lord.
Amen.

MOTHERING SUNDAY

Let us pray to our loving parent God,
as children in one family.

We thank you, loving God,
for giving us one another to enjoy,
to laugh and cry with, to learn to live with.
May even our conflicts and arguments be used
in helping us to grow up in your love.

Silence

Loving God:
we give you thanks.

Thank you, loving God, for showing us the way to love
and giving us opportunities to give,
to take second place, to accept people as they are,
to forgive them when they annoy us,
and look for their needs before our own.

Silence

Loving God:
we give you thanks.

Thank you, loving God, for the world we live in,
for the colours and shapes, the sounds and textures in it.
Thank you for giving us minds and emotions
and help us to reverence the whole of creation.

Silence

Loving God:
we give you thanks.

Thank you, loving God, for comfort and sympathy,
reassurance and practical caring when we are ill or sad.
Make us all more aware of the needs of those around us
and let our loving show in action.

Silence

Loving God:
we give you thanks.

Thank you, loving God,
for your promise to be with us always,
and not just until we die.
We remember with affection
those of our parents who loved us into existence
and now live in eternity.
Gather up into your loving arms
those who have recently died
and comfort all whose memories
make them aware of loss today.

Silence

Loving God:
we give you thanks.

Thank you, loving God, for giving us space and support,
guidance and forgiveness, challenge and reassurance.

Merciful Father:
**accept these prayers
for the sake of your Son,
our Saviour Jesus Christ.
Amen.**

PALM SUNDAY

As we recall Jesus entering Jerusalem,
let us gather our thoughts to pray.

Father, as the crowds welcomed Jesus
and sang your praises,
we pray that many more will welcome you
into their hearts and lives over the coming year.
We pray for opportunities to spread your good news
and courage to take them.

Silence

You are our King:
we welcome you!

Father, we recall the donkey Jesus rode on,
and we pray for that real humility in our hearts
which treats status and image casually,
and truth and loving service seriously.

Silence

You are our King:
we welcome you!

Father, the children sang and shouted your praise,
and we pray for the children in homes,
throughout the land.
May we not fail them
in the support and teaching they need.

Silence

You are our King:
we welcome you!

Father, the crowds were responding
to the healing love they had seen in action in Jesus.
We bring to you in our love and imaginations now

all those we would have brought to Jesus
for healing and help.
Give them comfort and reassurance,
wholeness and hope.

Silence

You are our King:
we welcome you!

Father, Jesus knew he was riding to his death.
We pray for all on that last journey,
especially those burdened with fear and guilt.
We commend to your eternal love all who have died,
thanking you for the blessings we have received,
and even for the grief
which is part of the love we share.

Silence

You are our King:
we welcome you!

Father, we, too, spread our coats on the road
as we express our thankfulness
for all you have done for us
and the amazing extent of your love.

Merciful Father:
**accept these prayers
for the sake of your Son,
our Saviour Jesus Christ.
Amen.**

GOOD FRIDAY (1)

In gratitude for Christ's
saving death,
let us pray together
to our loving Father.

We pray for all who, in following Christ,
have encountered suffering,
danger or persecution;
that they may be supported and sustained
by the presence of the suffering Christ.

Silence

Heavenly Father:
Your love sets us free.

We pray for the innocent who suffer
as a result of the world's mistakes,
ineptitudes, misplaced priorities or greed;
that love may breach
the walls of prejudice
and bring fresh life
to the deserts of hopelessness.

Silence

Heavenly Father:
Your love sets us free.

We remember the aimless and bewildered;
those who grieve
and those who try to repress their grief;
all who are finding a burden
desperately hard to bear.

Silence

Heavenly Father:
Your love sets us free.

We offer to God
our own friends and loved ones
as well as ourselves;
that we may trust Jesus
to bring good out of every situation,
however hopeless it seems.

Silence

Heavenly Father:
Your love sets us free.

God our Father loves us.
In silence now
we bring our individual prayers to him.

Silence

Father,
in your unfailing mercy,
we ask you to accept these prayers,
through Jesus Christ.
Amen.

GOOD FRIDAY (2)

As we recall the extent of God's love for us,
let us pray.

Loving God, if we as the Church
are truly to be the body of Christ,
then let us stand at the foot of the cross
and learn what it means to love and keep on loving;
to serve and keep on serving.

Silence

Lord, in the light of the cross:
show us how to live.

If the world is ever to see real hope,
then purify and transform our lives
and stretch out our arms in loving forgiveness,
with no exceptions and no small print,
so that we shine as lights in the darkness.

Silence

Lord, in the light of the cross:
show us how to live.

If our work places and neighbourhoods and homes
are to display and respond to your values,
then make us more fervent in prayer,
more courageous in self-discipline
and, above all, more loving in outreach.

Silence

Lord, in the light of the cross:
show us how to live.

If the terrible suffering of extreme poverty,
injustice and oppression is to be addressed realistically,
then take away our greed and complacency

and our assumptions about appropriate living standards,
and teach us sacrificial self-giving
of time, energy and resources.

Silence

Lord, in the light of the cross:
show us how to live.

Father, through the life-giving death of Jesus,
may the dying turn to you
and know your merciful love;
may the grieving be comforted,
and may we all one day share
with those who have died
the eternal joy of your heaven.

Silence

Lord, in the light of the cross:
show us how to live.

Father, such amazing love is hard to grasp
and impossible to repay.
In thankfulness for lives set free to live
we offer you ourselves.

Merciful Father:
**accept these prayers
for the sake of your Son,
our Saviour Jesus Christ.
Amen.**

EASTER SUNDAY (1)

In the hope and joy of resurrection,
let us pray to the risen Lord
who loves us so completely.

We pray for all who have been called by Christ
to serve the world as his followers;
that initial enthusiasm
may not die but deepen
to set us all on fire
with his love.

Silence

Lord of life:
transform us all.

We pray for a fairer distribution
of the world's resources,
so that life and hope
are brought to the starving
and homeless;
for places where fear and violence rule;
that peace and justice may be restored.

Silence

Lord of life:
transform us all.

We pray for those who feel they are wasting their lives;
for those under pressure
at home or at work;
for all who feel lost,
uncertain or worthless;
that God's living power
may stabilise, heal and recreate them.

Silence

Lord of life:
transform us all.

We pray for ourselves,
our friends and relatives,
and any difficulties or problems
that may be known to us,
that in all our troubles
we may open ourselves
to the healing and renewing
life of Christ,
which has power to bring hope.

Silence

Lord of life:
transform us all.

In the silence of God's accepting love,
we pray our individual prayers.

Silence

In silence we praise you, Father,
for your abundant blessings,
and ask you to hear these prayers,
for the sake of Jesus Christ.
Amen.

EASTER SUNDAY (2)

As we celebrate the new life of Resurrection,
let us pray to the one true God, who brings us all to life.

Lord God, we pray that the Church
may proclaim with joy your message of hope for the world;
may our lives, as well as our worship,
testify to the truth of the Resurrection;
broaden our vision of what is possible
through new life in you.

Silence

Life-giving God:
transform our lives.

Lord God, we pray for the world we inhabit;
for those who lead, and take important decisions,
and for those who follow or are coerced,
or who have no voice.
We pray for mercy and justice, compassion and integrity.
We pray for protection against evil and strengthening of goodness.

Silence

Life-giving God:
transform our lives.

Lord God, we pray for all babies, and those as yet unborn,
that they may be born into a world of love and acceptance.
We pray, too, for those who provide foster care,
and for all children at risk.
We pray for all parents and those who support them.
We pray for the newly baptised and recently confirmed;
for a deeper commitment to supporting one another
as we grow in faith.

Silence

Life-giving God:
transform our lives.

Lord God, we pray for those who cannot think,
for the pain or anguish which engulfs them;
for all whose lives are troubled and insecure;
for those who have little energy left to rejoice.
Bring healing, and the resources to cope with suffering,
and give us the grace to carry one another's burdens in love.

Silence

Life-giving God:
transform our lives.

Lord God, we thank you for lives well lived,
and commend to your keeping those who have died.
Through the resurrection hope,
may they know the joy of heaven.

Silence

Life-giving God:
transform our lives.

Lord God, we thank you for the precious gift of new life;
may we never again take it for granted,
but live each moment in the fullness of life
that Jesus has gained for us.

Merciful Father:
accept these prayers
for the sake of your Son,
our Saviour Jesus Christ.
Amen.

EASTER SUNDAY (3)

As we celebrate the risen Christ,
let us pray to the God of life,
in whom we live.

That the Church of God
may be bursting with new life,
filled with the love
that takes even death in its stride;
that new and mature Christians together,
all in their various ministries,
may work in God's strength
for the coming kingdom.

Silence

Christ is risen:
Lord, raise us also to new life.

That the inhabitants of our planet
may recognise God's glory all around,
co-operate in the sharing of his gifts,
and cultivate the habit of caring love.

Silence

Christ is risen:
Lord, raise us also to new life.

That God will bless our homes and families,
our places of work and leisure,
with new life and the hope of new possibilities
touching the ordinary with beauty and joy.

Silence

Christ is risen:
Lord, raise us also to new life.

That all who feel trapped or imprisoned –
physically, mentally or spiritually –

may feel the stones rolled away
and new light pouring into their lives.

Silence

Christ is risen:
Lord, raise us also to new life.

That those who have died to this earthly life
may find the fullness of God's eternity,
flooded with the light of his love.

Silence

Christ is risen:
Lord, raise us also to new life.

That we may live each moment thankfully,
assured of God's company and mercy.

Merciful Father:
**accept these prayers
for the sake of your Son,
our Saviour Jesus Christ.
Amen.**

Ascension Day (1)

As we celebrate together, let us pray together.

God of love, as we celebrate this festival
of Jesus' entry into heaven as Saviour and Lord,
we pray for unity in the Church
and reconciliation and renewed vision.

Silence

Both heaven and earth:
are full of God's glory.

As we recall the shout of praise in heaven
as the Lamb of God appears,
we pray for all who are hailed as heroes
and given great honour on earth;
for all who worship anyone or anything
other than the true God.

Silence

Both heaven and earth:
are full of God's glory.

We pray for all farewells and homecomings
among our families and in our community,
and for all who have lost touch with loved ones
and long for reunion.

Silence

Both heaven and earth:
are full of God's glory.

We pray for those who are full of tears,
and cannot imagine being happy again;
we pray for the hardened and callous,
whose inner hurts have never yet been healed.
We pray for wholeness and comfort and new life.

Silence

Both heaven and earth:
are full of God's glory.

We commend to your eternal love
those we remember who have died,
and we pray too for those
who miss their physical presence.

Silence

Both heaven and earth:
are full of God's glory.

We praise and bless you, God our maker,
for the way you draw us deeper
into the meaning of life.

Merciful Father:
accept these prayers
for the sake of your Son,
our Saviour Jesus Christ.
Amen.

Ascension Day (2)

Rejoicing that Jesus has ascended into the heavens,
let us pray in confidence to God our Father.

We pray in thankfulness
for those who introduced us to Jesus
and who help us along our spiritual journey.
We pray for one another in this church
and for all Christians, young and old,
throughout the world.

Silence

Let your kingdom come:
the kingdom of your love.

We pray with longing
for the world to be governed
in accordance with your law of love;
that all your creation may be reverenced
and treated with respect.

Silence

Let your kingdom come:
the kingdom of your love.

We pray with concern
for all the homes, schools and places of work
in this community;
rejoicing in all that is of you,
and asking your healing forgiveness
wherever there is discord or bitterness.

Silence

Let your kingdom come:
the kingdom of your love.

We pray with hope
for the healing and restoration to wholeness
of all who are ill or troubled,
damaged or depressed.

Silence

Let your kingdom come:
the kingdom of your love.

We pray with confidence
for those who have come to the end
of their earthly lives,
that they may be given merciful judgement
and welcomed into the glory of heaven.

Silence

Let your kingdom come:
the kingdom of your love.

We pray with joy
as we celebrate Jesus entering the glory
he so richly deserves, and look expectantly
towards his second coming.

Merciful Father:
**accept these prayers
for the sake of your Son,
our Saviour Jesus Christ.
Amen.**

PENTECOST (1)

As the body of Christ,
in the power of the Spirit,
let us pray.

For a fresh outpouring of the Holy Spirit
on the people of God all over the world,
and in all worship traditions.
For a readiness to be changed and made new;
for a softening of the ground of our hearts
to receive without fear.

Silence

With our whole selves we pray:
come, Holy Spirit of God.

For all the peoples of the earth
to know God and honour his name.
For the healing of the nations
and a new thirst for righteousness and purity
at every level and in every aspect of society.
For a dissatisfaction with the pursuit of pleasure
and all that distracts us from our true calling.

Silence

With our whole selves we pray:
come, Holy Spirit of God.

For the grace and power to live out our faith
in the real and challenging world,
among those we meet and eat with,
whose lives we share,
without compromising that calling
to be the body of Christ,
living God's integrity and purity,
forgiveness and love.

Silence

With our whole selves we pray:
come, Holy Spirit of God.

For those whose lives feel empty or cheated,
or filled with pain, or worry or guilt.
For all whose hopes and dreams are in tatters;
all who are in any way imprisoned.

Silence

With our whole selves we pray:
come, Holy Spirit of God.

For those who walk the dark journey of death
and all who have come through it
into your presence;
for mourners distressed by regrets
or angry with God at their loss.

Silence

With our whole selves we pray:
come, Holy Spirit of God.

For all you have in store for us, we thank you;
we look forward to walking into the future
of your promise, alive with your life.

Merciful Father:
accept these prayers
for the sake of your Son,
our Saviour Jesus Christ.
Amen.

PENTECOST (2)

In the power of the Holy Spirit,
let us pray.

For a fresh in-breathing of life and power
in each church community,
which breaks down our barriers
and sets us on fire with God's love.

Silence

Come, Holy Spirit:
Holy Spirit, come!

For the grace to see this world
and its needs and problems
through the eyes of love, hope,
justice and mercy;
for the grace to abandon prejudice
and build bridges of reconciliation.

Silence

Come, Holy Spirit:
Holy Spirit, come!

For the Spirit of loving kindness
to fill our homes, schools and places of work;
for family rifts to be healed
and long-standing conflicts resolved.

Silence

Come, Holy Spirit:
Holy Spirit, come!

For the restoration of those who are sick
to wholeness and well-being;
for courage and patience in all suffering,
and for good to be distilled
from every painful, destructive experience.

Silence

Come, Holy Spirit:
Holy Spirit, come!

For God's merciful judgement
on those who have died,
and the opportunity for us all
to prepare carefully for meeting God
face to face.

Silence

Come, Holy Spirit:
Holy Spirit, come!

For a deeper knowledge and love
of the God who knows and loves us completely.

Merciful Father:
accept these prayers
for the sake of your Son,
our Saviour Jesus Christ.
Amen.

TRINITY SUNDAY (1)

Gathered together
in the love and fellowship
of God the Three in One,
let us speak to God of our needs and cares.

We pray for the work of the Church
in suburbs, cities, slums and villages,
especially where there is
violent opposition, complacency or apathy,
that people of all traditions and outlooks
who work with Christ
may be blessed and encouraged
so that many may find peace in God's love.

Silence

Father, Son and Holy Spirit:
keep us in your love.

We pray for the world,
with its mistakes and misunderstandings,
all the breakdowns in communication
between individuals, groups or nations,
that the unifying love of God
may draw people together,
helping them to find common ground
on which they can build.

Silence

Father, Son and Holy Spirit:
keep us in your love.

We pray for those who are without homes
or live in crowded, inadequate accommodation;
those living alone and isolated;
for the hungry and malnourished;
that God's love, working through us, his body,

may reach those in desperate need
and give them new hope.

Silence

Father, Son and Holy Spirit:
keep us in your love.

We pray for a greater love and fellowship
among ourselves in this church
and this community, and in our families;
that God's life living in us
may make us more ready to listen,
to respond and to forgive,
to put ourselves out and seek to understand.

Silence

Father, Son and Holy Spirit:
keep us in your love.

Together in silence
we name those known to us
who need our prayers.

Silence

Father almighty, in the Spirit we pray,
and ask you to hear our prayers,
through Jesus Christ our Lord.
Amen.

TRINITY SUNDAY (2)

Let us pray to the Father,
in the power of the Holy Spirit,
through Jesus, the Son.

We pray for all theologians
and those who teach the faith
in colleges and Bible study groups
throughout the Church.
We pray for godly wisdom and human insight.

Silence

Holy God:
help us to know you more.

We pray for peace and co-operation,
harmony and mutual respect
in all our dealings with one another
locally, nationally and internationally.

Silence

Holy God:
help us to know you more.

We pray for those who depend on us,
and those on whom we depend,
for our physical and spiritual needs.
Enable us to honour one another
as children of one Father.

Silence

Holy God:
help us to know you more.

We pray for those who feel fragmented;
and for those forced to live apart from loved ones
through war, political unrest,

natural disasters or poverty.
We commend their pain to your comforting.

Silence

Holy God:
help us to know you more.

We remember those who told us of you
through their words and lives;
we think of those who have died in faith
and ask that we may share with them
in the joy of your presence for ever.

Silence

Holy God:
help us to know you more.

We give you thanks for meeting us where we are,
and travelling with us in person.

Merciful Father:
**accept these prayers
for the sake of your Son,
our Saviour Jesus Christ.
Amen.**

ALL SAINTS' DAY

Let us pray to the God
who can love sinners into saints.

Thank you, Father, for the faithful prayers
of so many over the generations;
for the lifetimes of quiet godliness;
for the struggles bravely borne
and the witness of strong faith.

Silence

Lord, make us all:
worthy of our calling.

Thank you, Father, for all peace-makers
and those who strive for justice and reconciliation;
thank you for those who work to relieve suffering
and manage the world's resources more fairly.

Silence

Lord, make us all:
worthy of our calling.

Thank you for the blessing and hope
of each new generation;
for the richness of good friendships,
the happiness of those in love,
and the comfort of prayer support.

Silence

Lord, make us all:
worthy of our calling.

Thank you for the care and attention
given to those in pain and ill health;
for the example of those
whom it is always a pleasure to visit,

in spite of their suffering;
for those who allow their suffering
to be used for some good.

Silence

Lord, make us all:
worthy of our calling.

Thank you for the love and encouragement
we have received through the years
from those who have died in faith
and are remembered with great affection.

Silence

Lord, make us all:
worthy of our calling.

Thank you for all the saints of heaven
who join us as we praise God
in all his holiness.

Merciful Father:
**accept these prayers
for the sake of your Son,
our Saviour Jesus Christ.
Amen.**

INDEX

The following topics are not included in this index because they occur so frequently throughout the book: The Church, ministers and church leaders; the Kingdom of God; secular leaders and authorities; the dying, those who have died, bereavement, grief and comfort; families, homes, friends and neighbours; sickness and suffering; love, healing, forgiveness, compassion, joy, hope and life.

THE CHURCH